the
END
of
ACTING

THE APPLAUSE ACTING SERIES

the END of ACTING

A RADICAL VIEW

richard HORNBY

APPLAUSE
THEATRE BOOKS
211 WEST 71 STREET • NEW YORK NY • 10023

An Applause Original
THE END OF ACTING:
A Radical View

Copyright © 1992 by Richard Hornby

Library of Congress Cataloging-in-Publication Data

Hornby, Richard, 1938-
      The end of acting : aradical view / Richard Hornby
          p. cm. --(The Applause acting series)
      "An applause original"--T.p. verso
      Includes bibliographical references and index.
      ISBN 1-55783-100-9 : $21.95
      1. Acting. I. Title. II. Series
PN2061.H645   1992
792'.028--dc20

                            92-2502
                               CIP

British Library Cataloging-in-Publication Data

A catalogue record for this book is available from the British Library

                               Applause Books
211 West 71st Street   406 Vale Road
New York, NY   10023   Tonbridge, Kent TN9 1XR

Phone: 212-595-4735   Phone: 0732 357755
Fax: 212-721-2856   Fax: 0732 770219

First Applause Paperback: 1995

CONTENTS

PREFACE

This book is written for those who act, those who teach acting, and those who are interested in seeing it. It is both a theoretical work and a call for action.

The book is an unashamed attack on the American acting establishment. This establishment may be far less monolithic than I sometimes make it seem. More important, many of the concepts I try to develop need not be related to its current domination. The concepts derive from my graduate seminars in acting theory and history in the School of Theatre at Florida State University. Those seminars were lively affairs; most of the students were actors themselves, had taught acting, and held passionate opinions about it. Much of the feistiness of those classes carries over into this book. The aggressive tone will probably stimulate some readers and offend others. I hope that both types will look beyond the tone of the writing, however, to its substance. There has not been any serious theoretical discussion of acting in the United States for a long time. If my arguments serve only to stimulate new dialogue, they will have been valuable.

1

Sections of Chapters 2 and 3 have evolved from my previous book, *Drama, Metadrama, and Perception*. In researching that book, which was supposedly devoted to a "literary" topic, I became interested in acting theory, which led in turn to the seminars. I have long believed that separating dramatic literature from performance study is a mistake, as is the reverse.

A version of Chapter 8 appeared in *The Canadian Journal of Drama and Theatre*. An early version of Chapter 11 appeared in the Fall 1983 issue of the *Journal of Aesthetic Education*, published by the University of Illinois Press. Several chapters were delivered as lectures or conference papers. I wish to express my gratitude to the audiences, whose comments in every case were helpful. Dr. Helen Chinoy, co-editor of the famous *Actors on Acting* anthology, read several chapters and made helpful comments, particularly in regard to Chapter 5; I am grateful for those comments, and for her wonderful anthology, without which I could never have written my book. I also wish to express my gratitude to Dr. Alan Kagan, a psychoanalyst practicing in Tallahassee, Florida, who was helpful with the theoretical background to Chapter 3. Any mistakes I make in presenting psychoanalytic theory are my own, however.

My literary agent, Faith Hamlin, provided friendly encouragement, as always, plus a thorough knowledge of the bizarre world of publishing. Glenn Young, the lively publisher of Applause Theatre Books, gave enthusiastic support for the book and helpful editing of its manuscript. Finally, I want to express thanks to my students, to my acting teachers of years ago, and to my directors and fellow actors over the years, from whom I have learned so much about the strange and wonderful art of acting.

Three of my doctoral students in the School of Theatre of Florida State University, David Klein, Cheryl Nuzzo, and Donna Rigdon, helped with research for the book. I am grateful for their assistance. Cheryl Nuzzo compiled the bibliography of acting textbooks; the annotations are my own.

I have retained traditional usage with regard to gender, in which *he*, *him*, and *his* apply universally to women as well as to men, as do *man*, *men*, and *actor*. Initially, I tried desperately to write *his or her*, *actors and actresses*, etc., or to use the plural pronouns *they* and *their*, but found myself again and again backed into awkward corners. George Orwell advised breaking any grammatical rule to avoid writing something barbarous; I finally decided *not* to break one, even though it is arguably sexist, for the same reason. To those who are offended, I ask forbearance. Because of the subject matter of the book, personal pronouns and collective nouns popped up frequently, and there was no easy way of dealing with them.

ONE

INTRODUCTION: BREAKING OUR IDEOLOGICAL SHACKLES

Acting theory in America remains pretty much where it has been for the past sixty years. This theory has its roots in Stanislavski's ideas, as taught by Maria Ouspenskaya and Richard Boleslavsky at the American Laboratory Theatre in New York City in the 1920s, and then as radically interpreted and taught by Lee Strasberg at the Group Theatre and later at the Actors Studio. Entrenched today at American acting conservatories and university theatre departments (with a few significant exceptions), it is a mimetic theory, reflecting the influence of the realism that prevailed in the theatre during Stanislavski's early years, but has been adapted to suit the needs of a highly individualist, capitalist society.

The result generally ignores Stanislavski's later work, specifically his "Method of Physical Action," which is why I prefer to call it Strasbergian[1] rather than Stanislavskian; it is never tested and rarely challenged. In sum, it is more ideology than theory, and like other ideologies it is mindlessly and passionately espoused, and faithfully defended against earlier theories, long after all the adherents of those theories are dead. It shackles American acting.

The tenets of this ideology can be summed up as follows: Theatre imitates life, the more closely and directly the better. The good actor therefore repeats on stage what he does in everyday life, drawing on his personal experiences, but, more important, reliving his emotional traumas. Strasberg specifically maintained that an actor, through an interesting process called affective memory, should learn to stimulate in himself a dozen or so real-life emotions, which he could then call up singly or in combination for all possible acting situations. The actor plays himself, not somebody else; acting is basically a form of emotional release. Actor training is primarily a process of coming to know yourself, and of removing emotional inhibitions.

The Strasbergian actor must be constantly on guard against any kind of artificiality in his performance. He may recognize that many plays, particularly those from earlier periods, contain elements that are not found in everyday life; blank verse in Elizabethan drama is an obvious example. But he sees such elements as mere externals; stylized plays, if they are any good, are supposed to have a realistic core. The actor's work still consists of introspection and self-projection, but style will now be added as a veneer. In recent years, more attention has been paid to that veneer than was done forty years ago, in the heyday of the Actors Studio, but the model of the actor is still strongly dualistic. Speech and movement, for example, are now extensively taught, but separately from classes called "Acting." And no matter what the role, no matter what kind of play, the actor is always expected to provide a richly emotional, well-rounded, highly personalized performance.

There are several corollaries to this ideology, which are not usually stated, but which follow logically from the foregoing, and thus affect actual practice: First, seeing a play as a collection of individualized character portraits means that plot, themes, images, rhetorical figures, metrical forms, poetic motifs, and intellectual content of any kind become unimportant; they are, again, externals. As dozens of actors and directors have earnestly told me over the past three decades, "You can't play an idea." You can only play real, live, independent persons, so the theory goes, not literary constructs.

Second, there is therefore little need for actors to study theatre history or dramatic literature. Since good plays are all realistic in their essentials, the particulars of their historical periods may even be distracting. Besides, the actor's main source of inspiration is his own emotional life rather than the character or the play itself. Thus, even in our university theatre departments, acting students are not required to study much theatre history or read many plays. For that matter, they rarely *perform* many plays, since self-expression can be taught more efficiently and quickly through improvisations, monologues, and short scenes.

Third, comic acting is seen as less important than serious acting. Since comic acting is not based on emotion or self-exploration, it is at best something suited to stand-up comedians or show-business hacks. Hence, despite our rich comic tradition in America, it is almost never taught. Character acting is similarly devalued. In Hollywood, it means you are too old to play romantic leads; in the theatre, it means you lack the courage to play yourself. "Hiding behind the character" is another kind of artificiality to be avoided.

Finally, acting, in this view, has little to do with other art forms. Even ardent Strasbergians do not suggest that painters, composers, or sculptors should take up affective memory. Writers do draw upon personal experience, and create characters with emotions, but what teacher of creative writing would suggest that things like plot and theme or imagery and tone are externals that should be taught by specialists in separate classes? Who would teach painting or sculpture or musical performance by exploring the student's personal life? In a backhanded way, the affective memory approach of Strasbergian actors validates the long-held claim of aesthetic purists that acting is not an art form at all.

The method of affective memory is not worthless. The Group Theatre and the Actors Studio produced many fine American actors, some of whom are still capable of rich and complex performances.

Nevertheless, several provisos apply: First, many actors associated in the popular press with the Studio actually had little to do with it. Marlon Brando, for example, played only a single role there; he received his major training from Stella Adler, a superb acting teacher who studied with Stanislavski himself, and who has received far too little recognition. Second, these actors did, and do, most of their work on film, where, for reasons I shall outline later, affective memory is far more valuable than on stage. Finally, and perhaps most important, these actors came up at a time when there was a great tradition of classical acting in America; the older generation of actors, with whom they saw themselves in opposition, were noted for a polished technique. "Method" actors tended to scorn that technique, but it nonetheless set a standard that they could not ignore. The great Method actors therefore all have a good deal more technique—not just "speech and movement," but clarity, simplicity, and precision—than is commonly recognized. But now, in a sense, that capital is spent. Young actors do not have a tradition of polished acting—particularly stage acting—against which to test themselves. Nor does their acting theory, as derived from Strasberg, give them any way of thinking about things like speech and movement except as "externals." For Strasberg, they were at best necessary evils. The internal/external dichotomy, like realism and affective memory, is another ideological shackle that hinders young actors' artistic development.

In recent decades, there have been sweeping changes in aesthetic theory, which have had as yet little influence on theatre training and practice, but which seriously call into question every aspect of our standard acting ideology. Structuralism, poststructuralism, semiotics, deconstruction, feminist criticism, psychoanalytic criticism, and phenomenological criticism all have one thing in common: a rejection of *mimesis* (how art imitates life) as a basis for understanding how works of art are created or how we respond to them. All these theories see a work of art as a system of conventionalized signs, communicating with its audience something

8

like language (though differing from language in significant ways); whether the work reflects life, is close to it, far from it, or somewhere in between, is of little interest. The important thing is not how lifelike—or unlifelike—a work of art is, but rather how the work functions, how it affects us. This turns out to have little to do with mimesis.

The time is long overdue for applying some of these new theories to acting. Two approaches are potentially very profitable: psychoanalytic criticism, which explores the unconscious processes that energize art, and phenomenological criticism, which rigorously examines art as a subjective experience, i.e., what creating a work of art, or responding to one, actually feels like. Applying these approaches to acting theory will expose the serious weaknesses of the standard ideology. Their application will also radically change the way acting is currently taught in the United States, and will greatly expand the range, flexibility, and impact of our actors in performance.

This is not to say that we have no good actors now; we have many, including some great ones. But as an avid theatregoer for thirty-five years, I can testify that the general level of American acting, at least *on stage*, has noticeably declined, despite vastly expanded training programs. In contrast with British actors, particularly in classical roles, we are no longer in the same league. Thus, while traditionally many American actors performed successfully in England,[2] today almost all the traffic comes the other way. Of course, every British actor is not better than every American actor, but on average, the British actor today is more flexible, has a broader range, is more imaginative, and even has more emotional intensity (once our fallback quality) than his American counterpart.

Nothing less than a radical attack on Strasbergian ideology, going right to its assumptions, will break its shackles. We need to get back to fundamentals: What acting is, why it moves us, what its purposes are, how it relates to other art forms, what it is like actually

9

to be there as an actor acting or as an audience member watching him. If we look at these questions freshly, avoiding the rigid rationalism that characterizes the standard ideology, a number of themes will emerge that are central to this book:

1. Acting has deep psychological roots; good acting consists not of copying what you do in everyday life, but of tapping a certain kind of energy.

2. Acting has important personal and social functions. Character acting—portraying somebody else—is not only valid, it is the essence of the acting experience. (Stanislavski actually maintained that all good acting was character acting.)

3. Actor training should be broadly humanistic, involving the study not just of dramatic literature and theatre history, but of languages, literature, and history generally, and should be centered on acting in plays rather than just exercises, improvisations, monologues, or even scenes.

4. Most important, acting is a great art form, not only sharing significant characteristics with other art forms, but providing an essential component for all of them.

TWO

_____

THE PSYCHOSEXUAL
BASIS OF ACTING

"Masks, masks.... One puff and they are all gone
to make room for other masks."
– Luigi Pirandello

Everybody, as Jimmy Durante used to say, wants to get into the act. Each year, thousands of young men and women move to New York City or Hollywood in search of acting careers. Some have no experience or training at all, but more and more of them do; there are currently over eighty master's programs in acting at American universities, and over three hundred bachelor's programs, plus hundreds more non-degree-granting programs at conservatories ranging from the prestigious Juilliard School to fly-by-night establishments offering to make you a star in six weeks.

An uninvolved observer might conclude from all this activity that there was a serious national shortage of actors, requiring crash programs to meet an enormous demand. Of course, the opposite is true: Film, television, and the stage combined have openings for only a few hundred new actors per year, so that well over ninety percent of the young hopefuls will never earn a cent from acting. Only a few will ever earn a living at it. There is little demand for

11

actors, but a tremendous demand to become one; many are called, but few are chosen.

The desire to act is so notorious that it has often been dramatized itself, especially in Hollywood films. In the popular imagination, it is simply a variation on the American dream—the drive to achieve fame and make a fortune. But do fame and money provide adequate motivation for something so compulsive as acting? After all, other fields provide these things too, yet people do not seem star–struck about them. The desire to escape obscurity or poverty may drive young people to become real estate tycoons or surgeons or politicians, but not in such numbers, and not against such hopeless odds. Nor do filmmakers turn out romantic movies about them.

Besides, fame and money are possible only for *professional* actors. Throughout the ages there have been amateur groups that put on plays for fun, as thousands of such groups in America do today, devoting enormous time and effort and sometimes even personal expense to perform before small local audiences. There is no such thing as an amateur real estate tycoon or surgeon or political leader. Furthermore, young acting hopefuls are not limited to the poor and obscure; plenty of middle-class and even wealthy individuals go into acting, often against the wishes of their families. Maurice Barrymore, for instance, the father of John, Lionel, and Ethel, was a graduate of Harrow and Oxford and a member of the bar in London before going on stage, where he eventually became an outstanding actor. He can hardly be said to have done it for wealth or esteem, since he stood a much better chance of achieving both right where he was, as a lawyer.

However much actors may want money or fame, clearly their chief motivation must be an inner one, something more basic, tied in to fundamental drives that eclipse any external goal. Additional evidence for this can be seen in the strange, ambivalent way society regards actors: On the one hand, the successful ones are the modern equivalent of royalty, idolized, celebrated, and highly rewarded. On the other, they are considered infantile, petulant, prone to drug-taking and sexual excess of every kind. Acting is the one art form that nearly everybody sees (at least on film or television, though less often today on stage), yet it is the least valued. Many would deny that it is an art form at all. There is little interest in how an actor trains or rehearses or what actual techniques he uses in performance; the average educated person has a good idea of how a painter paints or a musician practices, but even theatre critics usually have only a vague idea of how an actor creates and sustains a role. Other art forms also have an extensive literature dealing with their theory and history, but although there are plenty of acting texts of the how-to-do-it variety, there are very few historical or theoretical works like the one you are reading now. Acting remains a largely unexamined art form.

The theatre historian Jonas Barish has noted that there has existed an "antitheatrical prejudice" extending over many cultures throughout history, including some of the most glorious periods of theatre, such as ancient Greece or Elizabethan England. This prejudice is directed primarily toward actors; they are attacked on the usual grounds of being libidinous, thievish, vulgar, etc., but the deepest emotional intolerance (to which the other attacks are usually associated) appears to be directed toward the fact that *they pretend to be persons who they are not.* Such attacks come not just from crackpots of the Moral Majority type, but from major writers like Plato, Saint Augustine, Rousseau, and Nietzsche. Plato, for example, impugns performers in his dialogue *Ion* for stimulating emotions (a very bad thing for Plato), and in *The Republic* for portraying wicked acts on stage, which he feels will inevitably affect their real-life behavior. His main thrust, however, is that people just should not change roles; in his ideal state, "we shall find a shoemaker to be a shoemaker and not a pilot also, and a husbandman to be a husbandman and not a dicast also, and a soldier a soldier and not a trader also, and the same throughout." As Barish notes, this horror of multiple roles is puzzling.[1] What is wrong with versatility?

Both the compulsive nature of acting and the ambivalent attitude we express towards it strongly suggest that there is a psychosexual component to it. We feel the same way about eating, or defecating, or having sex, all fundamental, pleasurable activities that are sometimes considered shameful. (Eating is less shameful than the other two, but even that makes us feel guilty if we overindulge.) Pretending to be somebody else is a fascinating yet frightening thing, often associated in people's minds with swindling, cheating, and faking in real life; in this view, the actor is a kind of liar. Yet, on the other hand, relatively few people are compulsive liars, while most people feel the itch to become actors at some time or another. Everyone enjoys play acting at least occasionally, not only in amateur theatricals but in festivals like Halloween, Mardi Gras, costume balls. Children playact in their games, of course, and there are even adult games that make great use of role–playing. In real life, having to lie, say, in order to avoid hurting someone's feelings, makes most people uneasy, but acting, even when considered a bit naughty, is *fun*.

To understand the ambivalent attitudes about acting, and about role-playing generally, we need to understand the nature of human identity itself. How do we know who we are? When a Strasbergian acting teacher demands that his student play himself on stage, he implies that this "self" is a given, but is it? After all, philosophers have pondered the question of the self for thousands of years; to "know thyself" was the highest goal of the ancient Greeks, implying that we can only know who we are after rigorous education and experience. Similarly, in modern times, a person undergoing psychoanalysis takes years to come to know himself, ultimately realizing that he can never know himself totally.

In a trivial sense, of course, the actor can only play himself, by definition. Who else can he play? He cannot literally turn himself into someone else, but can only draw upon his own resources and experiences. But on the other hand, one's self is a fluid thing, changing in different circumstances. You are different with your

14

parents than you are with your spouse, and different again with your children—not only in their eyes, but in your own. Our sense of self is an *idea*, a mental model, which changes from time to time. I feel that I am the same person that I was at age five, because I have continuous memories going back to that time, but on the other hand, my image of who I am has changed drastically.

In his later years, Freud considered the problem of human identity at some length. One of his insights was that the newborn infant's identity is a kind of blank tablet. The infant has no identity, no model of self, because he has not learned the earliest and most fundamental lesson in life, the distinction between self and other. By the time we are adults, we have long since taken it for granted that we have a self, a fixed "thing" that never changes (some religious people believe it continues even after death) in a world that is constantly changing. Even though, as I have noted, we frequently adjust or modify details in our model of ourselves, we assume that there is an invariable core of our identity that is *me*, as opposed to a lot outside that is *not* me. But that is not how the infant experiences it at all. To him, there is just *sensation*. In *Civilization and Its Discontents*, first published in 1930, Freud wrote:

> When the infant at the breast receives stimuli, he cannot as yet distinguish whether they come from his ego or from the outer world. He learns it gradually as the result of various exigencies. It must make the strongest impression on him that many sources of excitation, which later on he will recognize as his own bodily organs, can provide him at any time with sensations, whereas others become temporarily out of his reach—amongst these what he wants most of all, his mother's breast—and reappear only as a result of his cries for help. Thus an "object" first presents itself to the ego as something existing "outside," which is only induced to appear by a particular act.[2]

From this first instance, the infant gradually learns to define the boundaries of its ego, developing a sense of self. Identity is something human beings have to *learn*, and the learning is an inherently painful process. The infant cannot control his mother's breast. Sometimes it is there, sometimes not; it is an "other" that is totally beyond his control, except insofar as he can induce it to appear by flailing and screaming. It is a terrible lesson: There is a world beyond yourself, which you need, but which you can never fully dominate. Most of the time it dominates you.

Freud went on to write that "the tendency arises to dissociate from the ego everything which can give rise to pain, to cast it out and create a pure pleasure-ego, in contrast to a threatening 'outside,' not-self."[3] The mechanism is thus similar to that of sexual repression, as we learn to limit our desires through contact with what Freud called the *reality principle*, the harsh fact that reality is a source of pain as well as pleasure, and that pleasure must be severely limited, in contrast to our drives, which were originally limitless. In developing an identity, we are similarly forced by reality to limit our sense of self, which was also originally without limit:

> Originally the ego includes everything, later it detaches from itself the external world. The ego-feeling we are aware of now is thus only a shrunken vestige of a far more extensive feeling—a feeling which embraced the universe.[4]

There are times in our later lives when we return to this infantile state of "limitless narcissism." Under the influence of alcohol or drugs, lost in the raptures of love, carried away by religion, we experience an "oceanic feeling,"[5] as Freud called it. This is very pleasurable, in contrast to the rigid, confining sense of identity that ordinarily burdens us. The boundaries of the ego seem to dissolve, and we feel at one with the universe.

As we go through life, we must continually redefine who we are, as we are called upon to take different roles—boy or girl, daughter or son, student, adolescent, youth, adult, lover, worker, parent, grandparent, "senior citizen." The psychoanalyst Erik Erikson identified eight such stages for human beings, each of which involves an *identity crisis* as the individual has to redefine himself or herself.[6] In such a crisis, the disparity between your image of yourself and reality becomes ever greater, until you must redefine yourself or collapse into neurosis. For example, a "midlife crisis" occurs in your late thirties, when you must confront the fact that you are no longer the young person you have been all your life. Half your life is gone; what was potential has become actual; your once boundless opportunities have dwindled to a very few, often meager ones. People around this age often exhibit bizarre behavior—throwing away careers, suddenly taking drugs, getting divorced—as the identity crisis overwhelms them.

On a small scale, identity crises happen every day. One of my students, receiving a failing grade on a report, cried, "That's not *me*! That's not *me*!" She either had to resubmit a much improved version of the report (which in fact she did) or give up her self-image as a good student. There is a joke about a golfer who boasted that his usual game was around 75; when he went out and shot 95, he was forced to admit that he had previously shot his "usual" game only once. Your image of yourself is always an *ideal*, which must be lived up to. If you cannot live up to it, the result is a crisis, which leads either to a redefinition of yourself or to neurosis, a compulsive self-delusion.

Here, then, is the pain/pleasure mechanism that produces enjoyment in role-playing. In a safe, socially approved situation (at a party, on a holiday, or in a play) you are allowed to drop, temporarily, the *pain* of living up to your idealized self-image. You can even be a despised figure—an idiot, a villain, a coward—and not only not be abused or ridiculed for it, but even receive laughter and applause. There is also the *pleasure* of reconnection with the oceanic feeling, when there was no differentiation between self and other, no alienation from the world, only complete integration and harmony. I shall later cite studies quoting actors who speak of how exhilarating acting is, even during the characters' saddest or most terrified moments. The character weeps, but the actor feels ecstatic (from the Greek *ex histanai*, which means, literally, out of one's place) because he is liberated from his usual cabined, cribbed, confined everyday personality.

A safe, socially approved situation for putting aside everyday identity is important. Most people would be uncomfortable about changing identity in everyday life situations, where it is usually part of some antisocial act like lying or swindling. Strasbergians, with their realistic obsession with making acting "truthful" and "honest," overlook that it is the very fact that the stage is *unreal* that liberates the actor. Because he knows it doesn't really matter, he feels free to do wild, outrageous things that he would never dare to do in real life.

Role-playing is sexual in the broad Freudian sense of providing pleasure, and we feel an ambivalence about it in the same way that we do about sexual matters generally. The antitheatrical prejudice is an expression of this ambivalence, which is the reason that moral philosophers have often been made uneasy by theatre, and also the reason that actors, in addition to being castigated for playing with their identities, are popularly characterized as being libidinous. We learned our identity by a process of *repression*. As we grew, we constantly had our identity limited, from an original oceanic feeling to one that was a narrow ideal. ("A good little girl doesn't do that," was a constant refrain, sometimes backed up by physical punishment. "A good little girl *must* do this.") Learning identity was part of the same process by which we learned sexual restraint—not to suck our thumb, not to urinate or defecate in our pants, not to masturbate in public. Thus, later in life, we unconsciously fear that letting down the boundaries of identity will lead to letting down all constraints for our animal impulses, leading to loss of control, to unlimited promiscuity and perversity.

Bisexuality is a particular threat associated with acting, since gender identity too is something that human beings have to learn. The infant is bisexual by nature, having no notion that there are two kinds of people, and that it is one or the other. Gradually, it is forced to define itself as a little boy or a little girl, and to behave in the manner expected for males and females. Henceforth, taking on the role of the opposite sex, reverting to the undifferentiated bisexuality of infancy that Freud described as "polymorphous perversity," remains forever a fascination and a threat. In many periods of theatre history, women have been played by men. Furthermore, playwrights from Euripides to Shakespeare to Shaw have explored gender identity in their plays; men playing women and women playing men make extremely potent theatre. With the rise of the women's liberation movement in recent decades, there have been many contemporary films and plays, such as *Victor/Victoria*, *Tootsie*, *Yentl*, and *Switch*, that similarly explore gender role-playing.

The antitheatrical prejudice is thus rooted in powerful unconscious desires and fears. These fears are, of course, largely irrational. Sexual drives need outlets as well as constraints; sexual promiscuity is neurotic behavior, but sexual impotence or frigidity are also neurotic. Similarly, if people remained forever in a state of limitless narcissism, never developing any sense of identity, they would be unable to function or even survive, but to be unable *ever* to let down the mask of one's identity would be equally bad, since life requires us continually to redefine our identities. Furthermore, societies themselves change the ground rules for role-playing from time to time, as in our society today, where the feminist movement is changing the way we define masculine or feminine behavior. Thus all societies have identity safety valves, including masked balls, public festivals like Halloween, or religious rituals in which participants apparently become possessed by gods or spirits. Societies also have theatre.

Theatre, in which actors take on changing roles, has among its many functions the examination of identity. For the individual, theatre is a kind of identity laboratory in which social roles can be examined vicariously. In a safe environment, detached from everyday life, the audience member can forget his own identity for a while, and identify with the characters he sees. Both performers and audience members are in a sense "actors" in the theatrical experience, dropping their regular identities and trying out new ones. This is valuable for both the individual and for society. Just as the individual must revise his identity at crucial times throughout his lifetime, so too must a dynamic society frequently revise the way in which it wants its members to perform. The roles of male and female in our society have been undergoing radical redefinition in recent years, which is the reason for the many plays and films dealing with gender. But even in static societies, where roles change slowly if at all, theatre is still an important device for teaching what it means, in a given society, to be a man, a woman, an adult, a worker, a parent.

There is an additional individual and social value in learning to identify with others. To see another person as a full-fledged, conscious human being, capable of thinking and feeling and suffering, is the first step toward true morality. Christianity embodies the process in its Golden Rule, "Do unto others as you would have them do unto you." Much of the evil in the world is caused by seeing individuals or groups of people as objects, as "other," rather than as yourself. Theatre teaches the skill of *identifying* with others rather than objectifying them—to recognize the humanity they have in common with us, rather than treating them as mere things to be shoved aside or stamped out.

Philosophers of aesthetics have long noted the quasi-religious nature of the artistic experience. Like religion, a work of art takes us out of our ordinary selves by reminding us of our connections with larger things—with others, with our society, with history. We should recall, too, that actors in many cultures have been considered shamans, magicians, or priests. David Cole has described how, in such cultures, the shaman, a sacred priest-actor, takes his audience back to the time of myth—"a time of origins, the period of Creation and just after, when gods walked the earth, men visited the sky, and the great archetypal events of myth ... took place."[7] The time of origins for the universe can be seen as a metaphor for the time of our own personal origins, the state of limitless narcissism again. The actor toys with role to help us temporarily rediscover rolelessness.

Freud seems to write disparagingly of the oceanic feeling; the very phrase *limitless narcissism* suggests that it is something unseemly. Nevertheless, this concept is a rare case where science, art, and religion all meet. Although it is literally a regression to infantilism to experience the oceanic feeling, it is wrong to consider it therefore to be trifling or neurotic. To re-encounter our origins, to be reminded of who we truly are, creatures of, rather than merely in, the universe, is valuable whether considered mystically or scientifically.

To summarize, the essence of the acting experience is the feeling of becoming somebody else. Providing both conscious and unconscious pleasure, this self-transformation has deep psychological roots that explain the compulsive nature of acting and also explain the antitheatrical prejudice that makes individuals suspicious of it. To insist that an actor merely play his everyday self instead, as the Strasbergians would have it, is an extremely dubious approach. It is, as Jonas Barish pointed out, an example of the antitheatrical prejudice ironically coming into the theatre itself.

Strasberg himself displayed a deep suspicion toward acting, which appeared over and over again in his teaching and writing. Of Laurette Taylor's performances, for example, he wrote, "It was the fact that it was not acting which made it great acting."[8] As a statement about acting, this is a common enough metaphor, meaning that it did not *seem* like acting to those watching; Strasberg does not qualify this remark by explaining what Taylor was *actually* doing, however, and when you are the most famous acting teacher in the country, such statements tend to be taken literally. To an acting student Strasberg made a remark that has often been quoted: "If you want to be an actor, don't *act*. *Be*."[9] Such an admonition may have been useful in dealing with an actor who was straining too hard, or who was too fond of acting clichés. In the same vein, a teacher of English composition, dealing with a student whose writing is exaggerated and overly rhetorical, might suggest that he simplify his style by trying to write the way he speaks. But as a general rule, acting is not the same as everyday behavior, just as writing, even when it seems colloquial, is not the same as everyday speech. When "Don't act, be" goes beyond being a method for taming excess and becomes instead a central principle (as it commonly is in American theatre training), it not only produces the difficulties commonly ascribed to it, like inaudibility on stage or a lack of precision, it also cuts the actor off from the very source that energizes his performance.

One thing that needs to be recognized is that an actor's self is not so rock-solid as it seems. It is in fact fluid; in a sense, all the world *is* a stage, and we are all playing roles in it, although that is not how we commonly see ourselves. Our everyday self is a narrow construct, but it has more range than people imagine; our *total* self is far broader still, and ultimately infinite. Actors who seem to be playing themselves, when they are successful, are actually playing roles they have become so skillful at that they seem pure and natural. Rock Hudson, a homosexual, had thousands of women sighing over him because of the convincing way he played romantic heterosexual men. Humphrey Bogart, son of a wealthy doctor who gave him a fancy prep school education, had audiences convinced that he was a real gangster. Marlon Brando, of solid midwestern, middle-class background, achieved his early successes playing elegant roles like Marchbanks in Shaw's *Candida*; when his performance as Stanley Kowalski in the film of *A Streetcar Named Desire* became a big hit, he had to start wearing a torn T-shirt in everyday life in order to live down to his fans' expectations. In each of these cases, the actors were thought of as "just playing themselves"—and even condemned for it!

The difference between everyday role-playing and role-playing on stage is that our everyday roles have important emotional connections for us, being ideals that must be lived up to rather than masks that we put on for fun. When an acting teacher insists that his pupil play "himself," he is automatically provoking all kinds of conscious and unconscious fears about that self, triggering repression mechanisms that usually spoil the performance. Telling a young man in a love scene that he must play it as himself, with all his adolescent shyness, inexperience, and acne, will doom him to failure; telling him that he is Don Juan, with irresistible powers over women, gives him a chance of success! Just as much bad writing is the result of being too *close* to everyday speech, with all its redundancy, disorganization, and imprecision, so too is much bad acting the result of being too close to the actor's everyday self, confining him in its rigid mold.

In other words, *character acting* (which Stanislavski himself considered essential to all good acting) needs to be valued much more highly than it is in the United States. This kind of acting, in which the actor plays a role significantly *different* from his everyday self, is neither taught nor much appreciated in this country, with the result that our acting so often seems timid and narrow. At recent auditions held by the University Resident Theatre Association (URTA), which are used by most major theatre schools in the United States in selecting students for admission, the instructions insisted that auditioners perform only pieces that corresponded to their own age and type; they also solemnly warned against using dialects. A brilliant character actor like Peter Sellers would not only never have succeeded in our theatre, he would have had a hard time even getting training.

The situation in the Broadway theatre or in Hollywood is similar. The commercial theatre shares with serious theatre a contempt for character acting. The commercial actor is supposed to have a "personality," a gaudy identity created for him by agents and publicity people, which he must cling to at all times, in real life as well as in films and plays. The results are pernicious: Our actors have a much narrower range than those in England and continental Europe. They perform far less frequently. They make much more money, but are typically much less happy. Just watch any talk show on television for a tiresome listing of their woes. Again, if they are just in acting for the fame and money, why are they so worried and uneasy? Is it not ultimately because American acting practices leave them unfulfilled? They went into acting in order to experience self-transformation but now find themselves more self-limited than a bank clerk or a word processor operator, who can at least play a wide range of roles at their local community theatre.

There are significant exceptions, of course; Dustin Hoffman, for example, despite being a major star, has refused to limit himself, and as a result has become a great character actor. Meryl Streep is equally courageous, though critics regularly attack her for using accents (i.e., for *acting*). But the star/personality system still prevails in the United States, in both film and theatre (whether commercial or not), and, worst of all, in our university theatre departments and acting conservatories. In the large theatre school where I taught for a decade, students are "typed" early on, and their roles severely limited. They act mostly in contemporary American plays (it is a battle to get even standard classics included in the repertory, much less something adventuresome), taking roles as young Americans. Older roles are played by faculty or townspeople. Of course, one can argue that the teachers are simply preparing the students for the American theatre as it exists, but that becomes a vicious circle. Students are prepared in a degraded way for a theatre that is degraded. If change does not come from the theatre schools, where will it come from?

The advantages of stressing character acting, whether in training, casting, or rehearsing actors, or even in non-acting fields like drama criticism or playwriting, are many: First and foremost is the fact that it is the psychological root of the impulse to act, the very thing that makes people want to be actors in the first place. The feeling of temporarily becoming somebody else is what makes acting pleasurable, what gives good acting its vitality. (Bad acting is accompanied by the feeling of not being able to escape your everyday self, of not being able to "find" the character.) Actor training should give students the opportunity to portray characters wildly different from their everyday selves and employ transformational techniques like mask work, animal studies, and impersonations. Acting teachers should be particularly alert for the kind of actor (Peter Sellers was apparently one) who *needs* such a radical change in order to perform well; I have seen talented young students destroyed as actors because they were not allowed to perform anything but their everyday selves, which they simply could not do.

Casting directors must also liberate themselves from excessively realistic practices. In particular, the "color-blind casting" practiced at liberated theatre companies like the Long Wharf Theatre in New Haven, the New York Shakespeare Festival, or the Folger Shakespeare Theatre in Washington, D.C. needs to be widely emulated. Realistic type–casting, besides cutting off from consideration individuals who might be best in a given role, has a vicious, racist side-effect. Blacks and other minorities are excluded from performing, even in non-realistic classical plays where their race could easily be accepted as conventional.

Critics, too, must free themselves from the shackles of realistic casting. A few years ago, James Earl Jones, a great African-American actor, played the role of Judge Brack in an otherwise all-white cast in a production of Ibsen's *Hedda Gabler*. The critics' reaction was predictable: While some bent over backwards to be nice to Jones, they couldn't help pointing out that there were, in case you didn't know it, no blacks in nineteenth-century Norway. At the same time, no critic took issue with the fact that the cast was speaking English, though nineteenth-century Norwegians actually spoke Norwegian. Speaking English was simply a convention, a neutral means for American actors to convey the play to an American audience, something that quickly slipped into the background if you thought about it at all. Accepting the conventionalized nature of the stage (which, as I shall argue, by no means implies that it is sterile and unemotional) would free us to accept minority actors in a similarly neutral way, with great benefit both to the actors and to their audiences.

Finally, American playwriting could benefit from a broader concept of characterization. Our stage is now dominated by realistic playwrights—Michael Weller, Tina Howe, Wendy Wasserstein, Marsha Norman, Beth Henley, Lanford Wilson, etc.—who write small plays that are little more than psychological case studies. It is Ibsen without his social and metaphysical dimensions, Strindberg without his mystery, Chekhov without his poetic orchestration. Brecht once called this kind of theatre an emotional striptease, as the actors are called upon to reveal their inner selves, but to reveal nothing outside, no wider significance, whether social, historical, or existential. By writing only such plays of emotional self-exposure, American playwrights help to perpetuate a narrow, realistic acting style that is of little help when actors come to perform great plays from the past—or the great ones that might get written in the future.

THREE

ARE ACTORS NEUROTIC?

"Acting is exhibitionism." – Otto Fenichel

*"One prominent characteristic of the professional actor
is his failure to develop identity."* – W. Henry and J. Sims

*"Actors have failed to develop a normal sense of identity
and body image during the early maturational
phases of infancy."* – Philip Weissman

Freud's interest in identity spawned a whole area of modern psychoanalysis called *ego psychology.* In fact, while the popular view of psychoanalysis still focuses on the repressed desires of the unconscious mind, as Freud did in his early work, analysis of the ego (more or less equivalent to the conscious self, manifested as the personality and its relationships) has long been a predominant form of psychoanalysis, particularly in the United States. Psychoanalysts like Erik Erikson, Heinz Lichtenstein, Donald Winnicott, Edith Jacobson, and Heinz Hartmann have written about how the normal ego develops and how this development can become disordered. Treatment of ego disorders rarely consists of simply having the patient confront unpleasant hostile or sexual feelings, as in the simple, dramatic cases that Freud originally treated. Instead, ego psychology takes many years of careful reconstruction of the patient's sense of identity.

Oddly, such psychoanalysts have rarely had much to say about the theatre. For example, Lichtenstein's major work, *The Dilemma of Human Identity*, does not mention theatre, acting, or actors at all; Erikson's equally major *Identity, Youth, and Crisis* has a section on Bernard Shaw's identity problems (though nothing on his drama), and another on the character of Hamlet, but nothing on what it means to act in a play or film. In general, identity psychoanalysts seem to be avoiding the subject of theatre, even though it immediately raises fascinating questions about their central concerns.

Perhaps this avoidance is because the phenomenon of the actor seems to challenge the basic premise of ego psychology, which is that a strong ego, a firm sense of your identity, is a healthy thing to have. The whole goal of ego psychology is to provide a solid, realistic sense of self for patients who lack it. Actors, on the other hand, would seem to have a weak sense of self, since they change their selves with every role. From this, it is easy to conclude that actors are simply neurotic, as some psychoanalysts have done. A classic example is the analyst Philip Weissman, who writes in his *Creativity in the Theater: A Psychoanalytic Study* that actors are individuals who "have failed to develop a normal sense of identity and body image during the early maturational phases of infancy."[1] Weissman goes on to run down actors in even worse terms: They fear being castrated, they typically suffer from depersonalization, exhibitionism, "and related perversions," and they may develop severe acting-out neuroses or even psychoses. (When they are not ignoring actors, psychoanalysts disparage them.) Yet it is hard to imagine an actor seeking treatment for the very thing that provides him with his livelihood, and for which he may have trained and sacrificed for years. Nor does it seem proper to condemn performance as neurotic behavior, when in fact it is highly valued and rewarded in most societies. Neurotic behavior, by definition, is supposed to be out of keeping with reality; if acting is delusional or neurotic, it also provides fame, admiration, and wealth—hardly unrealistic achievements. (A good question for someone like Weissman would be, "What would you not give to be a Laurence Olivier or a Marlon Brando, no matter how much they may have 'failed to develop'?") Furthermore, as noted in the last chapter, acting has a valuable social function—releasing us from self-centeredness, reminding us of our connections with larger things—while neurosis has none. The neurotic helps neither himself nor others.

There are also notable subjective differences between the unreality of acting and that of neurotic behavior. The unreality of an actor's role is fully understood by both the audience and the actor himself; it is an agreed-upon fiction. The unreality of, say, an obsessive-compulsive person washing his hands a hundred times a day is far from understood; such a person actually feels that the washing is necessary. Moreover, in contrast to the actor, who enjoys performing, the neurotic has strong feelings of anxiety and unhappiness that accompany his behavior.

Seeing the actor as neurotic, then, is simply another variation of the antitheatrical prejudice. Of course, individual actors may suffer from neuroses, just like individuals in other professions, but these neuroses are by no means central to their work; indeed, just as with other professions, a neurosis is an illness that *hinders* the actor from functioning well. A good example of the actor-as-neurotic was Marilyn Monroe. An actress of genuine though limited talent, her neuroses have been catalogued in dozens of books and articles. Certainly her neurotic behavior—lateness or absence from the set, promiscuity, drug-taking, tantrums, fears, not to mention her ultimate suicide—cannot be said to have *helped* her acting! She would have been much better off if, like most successful actors, she had been stable, reliable, and mentally healthy. Yet to psychoanalysts like Weissman, there is no distinction between pathetic individuals like Monroe and the outstanding artists whose consistently fine performances of countless roles over many decades entertain and enlighten millions of us lesser creatures.

Neurotics, in fact, usually make bad actors. Their own sense of identity feels so perilously weak that they find it threatening to take on another. Successful actors, on the other hand, typically have a strong sense of identity, which is why they can safely put it aside for a while. Psychoanalysts have been so concerned with the value of a strong identity that they have avoided the subject of acting, but it in fact tends to verify their theory. In general, it is the sign of a *strong* identity to be able to put it aside for a time; a person who is secure in the role of parent, for example, has no trouble getting down on the floor and romping with his children, knowing that he can easily reassert his authority if it should become necessary. It is the insecure parent who is likely to be aloof and authoritarian, because he fears that showing another side of himself to his children would lead to a total loss of control over them. Similarly, there is a world of difference between a successful actor in the theatre, who can easily put aside his everyday identity (with genuine benefits to both himself and society), and the neurotic in real life, whose sense of self is so weak that he dare not. The existential psychoanalyst R. D. Laing has used the term *elusion* to describe the process by which a person with a weak identity impersonates himself, feeling that he must play the role that he in fact actually has.[2] A fictional example taken from drama is Hector Hushabye in Bernard Shaw's *Heartbreak House*, who tells endless romantic lies about his personal heroics, though in fact he actually has saved people's lives and won medals for doing so. The life of such neurotic individuals seems an endless, sad masquerade. But elusion is no more real acting than sexual frigidity is normal self-restraint. Unlike elusion, good theatrical acting is a result of having a strong ego, not a weak one.

It is ironic that actors are popularly characterized as being arrogant and egotistical, but also as being weak and childish. Yet these apparently contradictory disparagements embody a subtle truth. To be successful as an actor, you must indeed be strong and confident, because only then can you become again like a child, playing at artificial roles with all the intensity and delight of childhood. A paradox of acting is that to fear making a fool of yourself guarantees that it will happen, because only by letting go of your ordinary, dignified, ideal adult self can you succeed. A person cannot let go of that self, however, if he fears that it will thereby vanish forever. The actor's "childishness" comes from his self-esteem, from his firm sense of being fully adult.

The French psychoanalyst Jacques Lacan took issue with ego psychology. The ego, he reminded his colleagues, "is an imaginary function."[3] He saw the strengthening or perfecting of the ego as a ridiculous goal, since the ego is not the self, but only a construct, an ideal. It is interesting that most of his opponents, the identity psychoanalysts, are American. It is in American actor training that we also find an emphasis on the conscious self, the ego, which is to be exhibited on stage in role after role. There is the same resistance to a fluid concept of the self as in ego psychology, which suggests a cultural connection: The weak sense Americans have of themselves as a people, in a young, melting-pot country, exhibits itself on a social level by excesses of patriotism like a proposed constitutional amendment to make it a crime to burn the flag. On a personal level, witness the amazing popularity of self-help books and self-development courses, the T-Groups, encounter sessions, Esalen, Rolfing, est, and so on. Americans act as though their identity would go out like a candle if they were not constantly guarding and enhancing it.

It is therefore no surprise that there should be a prejudice against character acting in this country. The antitheatrical prejudice is especially strong where the sense of identity is weak. Thus, where a Frenchman is always a Frenchman, be he a criminal or a fool or even a traitor, an American is only an American if he lives up to popularly conceived ideals. There has never been an "Un-French Activities Committee," not because the French are more democratic or freedom-loving than we are—in many ways they are less so—but because, even when chopping off one another's heads, they always know who they are. In the long-established countries of the world, character acting is typically more admired than it is in the United States, because it is not seen as a threat. A strong sense of identity provides the base from which to act a wide range of roles. The American actor seems condemned always to act the same "self," even though it is only a small part of his total persona; the fear hovers that should he stray from his accepted "self," not only will the public be confused, but his acting will become hollow and artificial.

In this regard, we should remember that the founding members of the Group Theatre and the Actors Studio were the children of immigrants or immigrants themselves. (Strasberg himself came to America from Austria-Hungary in 1909, at the age of seven and a half.) Their turbulent, shifting backgrounds, the suffering from prejudice, and the experience of speaking a different language at home from that spoken at school and on the streets, meant that their youth was one long identity crisis. It is understandable, then, that they would have embraced a theory of acting that stressed a rigid, unchanging self, which would have seemed like an oasis in a bewildering desert, or that "honesty" in emotion would be prized, when so often in real life they had had to hide their true feelings.

A legacy of this approach is that American actor training, and rehearsal techniques as well, have often come to resemble psychoanalysis itself—or a parody of it (which is also what the T-Groups, etc., resemble). Since the actor must show real emotion on stage, and since he is typically inhibited, it becomes the job of the acting teacher or director to release him from his inhibitions. The teacher or director interrogates the actor about his emotional life, often in the most intimate and intrusive way, reducing the poor individual to hysterics or uncontrolled weeping as a triumphant "breakthrough." That such experiences do *not* transfer to the stage, and may even damage the person's ability to act, somehow never deter the practitioners of this approach. Certainly, the hysterical moments are "dramatic" in the popular sense, and impressive to those watching, and even to the student himself, who feels that something so devastating must add up to something.

An extreme example of the emotional release approach to actor training was reported in New York in *The Village Voice* in 1979. An acting teacher named Paul Mann, whose classes included such techniques as group nudity, allegedly had sexual relations with his students as a method of "releasing" them. Had he been bisexual he might have gotten away with it, but students noticed that the "special sessions" in his private office were limited to the female members of the class, and the more attractive ones at that. Interestingly, after the *Voice* exposed this outrageous "teacher," other acting instructors were quoted as saying that Mann's approach was perfectly reasonable; they too had sex with students.[4] In this they were being logically consistent; if the goal of actor training is the release of real, honest emotions, then rape by deception is certainly one way of achieving it.

Incidents of this sort are reminiscent of what Freud called "wild" psychoanalysis. Early in this century, as his ideas were just becoming known, Freud learned of the case of a divorced middle aged woman suffering from states of anxiety, who was advised by her physician that her sexual desires were the cause of her problems. Citing Freud, the doctor (an American!—how often these excesses are associated with us) gave her three choices: she could be cured only if she would return to her husband, take a lover, or masturbate. When he met the woman and heard her story, Freud was appalled. In an essay published in 1910, he pointed out that psychoanalysis had extended the term *sexual* far beyond its usual range, to include "all expressions of tender feeling, which spring from the source of primitive sexual feelings, even when those feelings have become inhibited in regard to their original sexual aim or have exchanged this aim for another which is no longer sexual."[5] He pointed out that it was possible to engage regularly in sexual intercourse and still suffer from neurosis, and went on to note that "the idea that a neurotic is suffering from a sort of ignorance, and that if one removes this ignorance by telling him facts (about the causal connection of his illness with his life, about his experiences in

33

childhood, and so on) he must recover, is an idea that has long been superseded."6 Though these passages were written eighty years ago, they have failed to alter the popular view that psychoanalysis consists of having the patient confront unpleasant facts about his early life, or that the cure for neurosis consists in the removal of inhibition. They have similarly failed to prevent American acting teachers from treating their students as if they were neurotics whose inhibitions must be removed, if necessary by methods even more "wild" than those Freud had to confront.

Though psychoanalysts like Weissman and teachers like Mann might have been surprised to find an underlying agreement, both deal with actors as if they were mentally ill. Both are implicitly denying that acting is an art form, or else have an implicit definition of art itself that sees it as a neurotic symptom. Both would "cure" an actor by having him stop acting: The psychoanalyst sees acting as neurotic behavior resulting from arrested early development, while the "wild" acting teacher sees it as a shallow form of performance that must be rejected in favor of the expression of honest, real emotion. The only difference between the two is that, while the analyst presumably understands the techniques of psychoanalysis, the "wild" acting teacher still conceives of it in the crude terms of removing inhibitions that Freud long ago rejected.

Emotional release was never the goal of actor training in the past, nor is it the goal of training in most other countries today. (This may be changing, however; recently a Strasberg Institute was established in London, which is like bringing ashes to Newcastle.) Of course, acting involves emotion. This has long been recognized; Plato even *attacked* acting because it induced emotion in both the actor and his audience. An actor's ability to emote has been highly prized at many times in history, in many countries besides the United States. (In some times and places, however, emotional *restraint* in acting has been prized.) Our approach is different, however, when we stress *real* emotion, drawn from the actor's personal life, rather than imaginary emotion drawn from the play.

Although "wild" acting teachers often invoke the name of Stanislavski as justification for their methods, he nowhere suggested that an actor's main problem is learning to overcome inhibition in his *personal* life. The young acting students depicted in his book, *An Actor Prepares*, are diverse in their backgrounds and abilities, but none is neurotic, and Stanislavski's work with them (in his persona as "Tortsov," their wise old acting teacher) in no way resembles psychoanalysis. The closest he comes to exploring their personal emotions occurs by accident: An actress playing the role of Agnes in Ibsen's *Brand* turns out to have had a child who died, just as the character has. In the scene, Agnes finds another child on her doorstep. Stanislavski is impressed by the intensity of the actress's weeping, but points out that her emotion is actually wrong for the character and the scene: "Weeping for one who is gone is not the weeping called for in this particular scene where sorrow for what is lost is replaced by joy in what is found."[7] Rather than dwell on her personal trauma or exploit it for sensational effect, Stanislavski typically relates it *to the play*, which is always paramount in his theory, rather than to the students' private lives. The actress playing Agnes is not experiencing some kind of "breakthrough" of her emotions; there is no suggestion that she has had difficulty expressing her grief in real life. Instead, she is discovering how to perform a particular character in a particular scene, where, in fact, her recollected personal emotion brings unsatisfactory results.

Freud's theories provide a useful basis for understanding the psychology of the actor. The theories must be applied with full understanding and care, however; it is particularly dangerous to treat the actor as if he were a patient undergoing psychoanalysis. We must look deeper, at some of the psychological mechanisms underlying all human behavior. At the same time, we must look honestly at the phenomenon of acting, how it really operates, rather than fitting it to the procrustean bed of ideology. Acting is *not* neurotic behavior; release from inhibition in everyday life is *not* a typical acting problem; an actor's principal source of inspiration is *not* his own personal life, but the role itself, and the given circumstances of the play.

FOUR

ACTING AND SPEECH

Acting has traditionally been associated with oratory. Actors study speech as part of their training; indeed, at times they have studied little else. On the other hand, orators have often learned from actors. There are stories going back to ancient times of orators studying acting; Plutarch tells us that the Greek orator Demosthenes studied with the actors Neoptolemus and Andronicus, and that Cicero studied with Roscius, the Roman comedian, and with Aesop, a tragedian. It is important to remember, too, that until recent times oratory, or "rhetoric," was a major area of education. Anybody in public life—a minister, a teacher, a politician, a lawyer—had to be a good public speaker; even military officers studied how to address their troops before going into battle.

Rhetoric was even taught in universities; in the Middle Ages it was one of the seven "liberal arts"—arithmetic, music, geometry, astronomy, grammar, logic, and rhetoric—which were the only subjects offered. Rhetoric, however, involved much more than speaking per se. It included everything involved in speech–making, including both how to write one and how to deliver it. In studying delivery, the orator learned everything that would also interest an actor, including vocal development, intonation, emotion, and gesture. (Andronicus specifically taught Demosthenes "action."[1]) Even characterization could be involved, since imitation, usually for satiric effect, could be a potent feature of a speech. (Cicero warned that such imitation should not be too extravagant; here, he felt, the orator needed to be more moderate than the actor.[2])

In the twentieth century, rhetoric has for some reason declined as an area of study. It is still necessary for public figures to make speeches, but not to make them well. There have been some striking exceptions, like Winston Churchill and Adolf Hitler, but most are like Walter Mondale, who maintained that his poor speaking ability was something he was born with and could do nothing about, thus helping to hand the election over to Ronald Reagan, a much better speaker. It is hard to imagine any politician in the past having such a ridiculous attitude. It cannot be blamed on the electronic media; people still *speak* on film, radio, and television, though of course the techniques for effective delivery are sometimes different from those of a lecture hall. The prejudice against oratory is perhaps vaguely connected with the antitheatrical prejudice; Mondale may have thought that his remark would distinguish him in voters' minds from Reagan, a "mere" actor.

The decline in the study of speech is not limited to Mondale, however, nor to politicians, nor to the United States. It seems to be part of a general cultural shift, and such shifts are often largely arbitrary. There can be no doubt that politicians, ministers, teachers, lawyers, etc., in many countries do not speak as well as they used to. Nor do actors. Here, however, there are signs of change; a generation ago, in the heyday of the Actors Studio, speech was not taught at all in many acting programs (including that of the Studio itself), and the mumbling American actor was a standard joke. Now, it is more and more being taught again, though, as we shall see, often in a manner that produces poor results.

It does seem, however, that speech and acting are inescapably mixed. Auditioning actors are typically asked to *read* from the script, rather than act it out fully. Rehearsals usually start with readings. But most importantly, the key to characterization is often through speech—a dialect, a manner of intonation, a lower or higher pitch than normal, a special rhythm. Peter Sellers said that when he got the voice right, "the person takes over," with the walk, gestures, and even the look of the character following almost automatically.[3] There is something about speech that seems *fundamental* when it comes to acting. In the beginning is the word.

Freudian theory helps to explain why this is so. A common criticism of Freud is that he "reduced everything to sex." This is in fact true, except that, as we have seen, his concept of sex was much vaster than just sexual intercourse. In the essay already quoted, he wrote that "in psychoanalysis, the term 'sexuality' comprises far more; it goes lower and also higher than the popular sense of the word."[4] It goes lower because it includes *all bodily pleasure*; higher, because in displaced or substituted forms, it projects itself into all aspects of mental life. In particular, the infant's pleasure from the erogenous zones of the mouth, the anus, and the genitals are all important aspects of sexuality. The sensations experienced from these areas in the first few years of life have profound consequences for all our later psychology.

The infant in its first year or so of life is in what Freud called "the oral phase," in which its main source of pleasure is the mouth. Later, it shifts its interest to the anus, and later still to the penis or clitoris, but in this earliest phase, when it lacks the muscular ability to deal with the other areas, the mouth is the center of attention. Any parent can recall the passion with which the infant sucks, whether on a breast, a bottle, or a pacifier, and how, as it develops, it tends to put everything it possibly can into its mouth. What is important for acting theory is that it is in this oral phase that the infant is also learning identity. As Freud noted in *Civilization and Its Discontents*, the first distinction between self and other occurs when

39

the infant realizes that there is a major source of pleasure—his mother's breast—that is beyond his control, which reappears "only as a result of his cries for help."[5] Equally important, as the infant develops in the oral phase, he develops aggressiveness with the mouth, biting and spitting in addition to crying, all of which are attempts to express power and individuality. It is also in this late oral phase that the infant begins to learn language.

All of our erogenous zones have a bearing on our sense of identity, but the mouth, being the first, has special importance. Language development is crucial. For Jacques Lacan, language *is* the self; there is no identity without language, and no language without identity. He wrote, "It is not a question of knowing whether I speak of myself in a way that conforms to what I am, but rather of knowing whether I am the same as that of which I speak."[6] As we learn to speak, we define not only the world, but ourselves in relation to it. Before, we saw, but now we have a *viewpoint*; before, we heard, but now we *comprehend*, according to the system for comprehension that language provides.

We learn to speak by a kind of sorting out process. Tests have shown that the infant in his earliest experimentations with speaking can make all possible phonemes (the smallest distinguishable units of sound in a given language) in all known languages. By the time he has achieved a basic mastery of his own language, however, around age three or four, he can only make the phonemes of that language. Like adults, he now finds it very hard to reproduce sounds from another language if they are not in his own; the French *l* and *f* are easy, because they are the same as in English, but the *r* and *u* are difficult if not impossible. It is thus very hard for anyone to speak a foreign language without at least some accent, no matter how long he studies it or how fluently he otherwise speaks it.

Moreover, his language now seems intimately connected with himself. It seems not just one language out of many, but *normal* language, *neutral* language. I remember, years ago, walking through Paris with a young Englishwoman I had met there. She stepped out

40

into the street, looking in the wrong direction (which of course was not wrong to her, since she was used to cars traveling on the other side of the road). "Look out!" I shouted. "The cars are coming the other way!" She looked at me, baffled, and finally stepped back up on the sidewalk just in time to avoid being hit. I wondered why she had moved so slowly. "I couldn't understand what you were saying," she explained. "With your American accent, it took me a while to figure out what you meant." I was shocked, because I had never before thought of myself as having an accent—*she* had an accent, not me! Also, as an actor, I was proud of my clear, resonant voice. How could a native speaker of English have trouble understanding it? Such lingocentrism is typical of all speakers of all accents and all languages everywhere. No matter how sophisticated you are about language (and I had studied several foreign languages, plus linguistics), there always remains the vague feeling that anyone who speaks differently is speaking artificially, while your own way of speaking is just plain, clear, and "natural."

In learning language, the infant is undergoing a constant process of correction. "Good" sounds yield a positive feedback; the parent expresses understanding and delight, and may even give physical rewards, like a hug, a kiss, or the named object. "Bad" sounds yield indifference or even ridicule. Gradually, the reward/punishment system is internalized in a mechanism of *repression*, which is of course the same mechanism as is being internalized for all the infant's behavior. Desirable activities are rewarded, undesirable ones ignored or punished, until the infant learns almost automatically to do the former and avoid the latter. (The impulses toward the latter remain in the unconscious mind, however, and are notoriously troublesome.) This is the reason, then, that the infant can no longer make the sounds it used to produce so easily; it has repressed them.

Peter Handke's contemporary German play *Kaspar* is a little fable about the repressive process of learning language. The title character undergoes speech torture, starting off uttering one sentence, "I want to be someone like somebody else was once,"[7] and gradually becoming swamped with words, indoctrinated by aphorisms like, "No one may bite/the fork with his teeth/no one may cite/the names of murderers at/dinner,"[8] until he is fully brainwashed. In real life, the process is more subtle; words define and limit us, in such a way that we do not know we are being defined and limited. We are not tortured, but conditioned. It does not feel as though someone, or something, is forcing us to pronounce the English *r*, or preventing us from making the French one; the former just seems natural and the latter contrived, though of course to a French person the reverse is true, and in infancy we pronounced both equally well. Nor does it seem that anyone is preventing us from walking around naked; it is just something we don't want to do, though in infancy we reveled in it. (There are laws against public nudity, but these are the result, not the cause, of our feelings about it.) Repression is unconscious, occurring so automatically that it does not seem to be happening at all.

My way of speaking, then, simply seems part of me, like my arm or my ear. A General American accent, which I learned growing up in New Jersey and which served me well as an American actor, seems normal, while a southern, midwestern, English, or Irish accent seem *other*. When I speak with one of these other accents (which is not easy for most people, and outright impossible for many), I have the strange sensation of being somebody else. This feeling of otherness, this transformation, is of course the essential quality of the acting experience. It is distinctly pleasurable, because it reconnects us with the oceanic feeling, that time when our self was without limit. Speaking with another accent is liberating, which is why actors like Peter Sellers find that other aspects of characterization, like movements and gestures and facial expressions, seem to come easily once the new voice is achieved. Self-transformation, or rather, self-*expansion*, can be achieved in ways other than through the voice, but changing one's manner of speaking remains the commonest route for actors.

This feeling of otherness, achieved through speech, underlies many psychological phenomena besides acting. Learning to speak a foreign language (an overlooked but potentially valuable part of training for actors, by the way) involves an expansion of the self; a person who speaks more than one language often has noticeably different personalities in each of them. Indeed, the principal benefit of foreign language study as a "liberal" (i.e., liberating) art is that it broadens the student, with concomitant gains in increased tolerance, sensitivity, and imagination.

There is also the phenomenon of "possession," which occurs in primitive, shamanistic rituals. In traditional societies, the feeling of otherness is taken literally, as if another person, or spirit, were speaking through you. David Cole, writing of such practices, notes that "total and eerie transformation of the voice seems to be a universal characteristic of possession experience."[9] The change is so dramatic that the possessed shaman seems, both to those watching him and to himself, to be merely a passive transmitter. With our more civilized, sophisticated viewpoint, we do not believe in literal possession (though the belief continues in some of our religious cults, as with the practice of glossalalia, or "speaking in tongues"), but the vocal transformation is no less dramatic, spreading beyond the voice itself to all behavior. The actor, who may be a rather conservative or even retiring person in real life, suddenly becomes bold, boisterous, agile. The shy young man, who would die of shame before he would ask an attractive young woman for a date, suddeny comes on to her as a passionate lover in a scene on stage where he has a French accent. Peter Sellers "couldn't sing a bloody note. Yet when he sang Caruso, he took high Cs like Caruso."[10]

This is the reason that speech training for the actor, and dialect work in particular, must be integrated with regular actor training. There are far more important objectives in teaching speech to actors than audibility or correctness. When speech is conceived of as a mere external, a means of projecting nonverbal emotional experiences that are supposed to take place inside the actor first, the results are hollow. The kind of empty intoning that led American actors and acting teachers to ridicule speech work a generation ago is the very thing that is likely to occur when speech is taught in separate classes, in a purely mechanical fashion, with projection and diction the only goals.

Speech work for the actor, of course, extends beyond dialect work. Every character, just like every real person, has his own unique, individualized way of speaking. His speech will be "centered" somewhere, resonating primarily in the nose or the throat or the front of the mouth. He will characteristically slur certain words, or perhaps overenunciate some. His vocal range in singing may be more than two octaves, but in speaking he will restrict himself to a few notes. (American English is notoriously restricted in pitch, in contrast to British English, but even a British speaker will have a *basic* pitch from which he ranges up and down.) Finding a manner of speaking is always part of building a character, even if the character is very much like your everyday self in age, nationality, period, and accent. It is useful in a rehearsal or an acting class to experiment with changes in pitch or placement or enunciation, no matter how subtly, until the character seems to come to life and starts to speak through you.

Nor does this kind of speech work have to be limited to realistic considerations. It is fun to speak like a robot or a space invader or an animal in a fable. In real life, such creatures do not exist, or do not speak when they do, but actors are called upon to play them at times. They come to life in the same way that more realistic characters do: A spasmodic, mechanical-sounding voice will stimulate a spasmodic, mechanical walk, and spasmodic, mechanical gestures.

Verse is another nonrealistic speech element that an actor must often play. American actors have trouble with it because they again tend to think of it as an external, something to be added after the basic emotional work is finished. There is even a cliché, widely heard among benighted actors and directors, that if the emotional values are right, "the verse will take care of itself." This is equivalent to an opera singer thinking that if the emotional values are right, the music will take care of itself. Of course it will not. Verse, whether spoken or sung, is the key to the emotion, the very *source* of the character. The verse must first be analyzed carefully, according to its principals of construction (all those supposedly dull things like iambics and alliteration and assonance). It must then be spoken correctly, with all the proper emphasis, rhythm, and coloring. Of course, if the actor does no more than this, merely chanting mindlessly, he will never rise above the level of "intoning" that Americans so desperately fear (though one never hears an American actor actually doing it anymore). But if, instead, the actor sees this verse work as a means to an end, that he is searching for a "sound" that will come to life, possessing him the way a spirit seems to take hold of a shaman, he will be dealing with verse the way it is supposed to be dealt with. Acting verse is actually *easier* than acting prose if you make yourself its instrument, letting it act through you. One of the ironies in theatre history is that, where the Elizabethan actor performing Shakespeare looked upon the verse as an *aid*, the modern American actor sees it as an obstacle! The very thing that is there most to help him is treated as something to be got around, or postponed, or avoided entirely.

In sum, speech for the actor should never be considered an "external." There is nothing more *internal* than speech, nothing more intimately associated in our conscious and unconscious minds with our sense of self. I speak, therefore I am, and how I speak is what I am. How a character speaks is what he is, and finding the way the character speaks is fundamental to acting. Being heard clearly in all parts of the auditorium is probably the *least* important goal of speech training (a lot of great actors could not be); becoming attuned to the marvelous artistic potential of one's voice, its tremendous range and almost magical power of self-transformation, is of primary urgency.

FIVE

ACTING AND ARTISTIC CREATION

Is acting an art form? Certainly not, if it is considered as just the immediate expression of real, honest emotion. All the arts involve emotion, both in the artist who creates and the reader or viewer or audience member who responds, but in no other form than acting is the claim made that the artist must actually feel the emotion he is portraying, here and now, as the basis for his work. It is generally accepted that, however emotionally intense artistic creation may be, the artist also operates through conventionalized means that must be mastered through long study and employed with great precision. Even romantic views of the artist, which stress emotional expression, do not limit themselves to emotion alone. Wordsworth's often-quoted definition of poetry as "the spontaneous overflow of powerful feelings" comes perhaps the closest to the notion of the actor as emotional resonator, but that is not the entire quotation. Wordsworth went on to say, "it takes its origin from emotion recollected in tranquility"[1]; the emotion is not present here and now, but is something pondered and shaped. To put it bluntly,

47

Wordsworth did not expect someone to come into his study and kick him in the pants or kiss him on the mouth in order to get his creative juices overflowing. Elsewhere, Wordsworth stressed that, for the good poet, "our continued influxes of feeling are modified and directed by our thoughts."[2]

Even if we accept that the actor does not directly experience the emotions he is portraying, however, one often hears other reasons for demoting acting from the ranks of art. Anyone can do it, goes one argument; playing the violin, say, or painting a recognizable portrait, require talent and years of training, but anyone can get up on stage or before a camera and act. The trained actor is more likely to do it better than the untrained one, but after all, there have been examples of individuals with no experience at all giving successful performances. Nor are trained actors immune to failure. Another argument is that acting is ephemeral, disappearing the moment it is born; art is long, but acting is short. Shakespeare's texts live on, but Burbage's performances of them have vanished forever. A related argument is that the actor does not *create* anything; unlike a painter or sculptor or playwright, he merely follows the instructions someone else has written down, making the actor no more an artist than someone doing one of those paint-by-numbers hobby kits.

These arguments have some validity, but are they really all that important? The naive but successful actor is actually rather rare, and besides, his counterpart is not unknown in the other arts. A "primitive" painter or poet will occasionally burst on the scene to great acclaim. Nor are trained painters or poets any more failure-proof than their acting counterparts. The main reason for the anybody-can-do-it attitude, which is actually just another version of the antitheatrical prejudice, is that a good actor often seems to be doing very little; making it look easy is part of his craft. But again, other artists can make their art look easy too; according to Ben Jonson, Shakespeare scarcely blotted a line. In fact, good acting is quite difficult, which is why, if you think about it, you will recall that most performances you have seen have been mediocre or worse. If anybody can do it, why is it so often done so badly?

There is a sense in which anybody can, and does, do all the arts. Everybody sings; everybody sketches; everybody tells stories. The professional is just someone who, because of superior talent and training, does these things for a living. Anybody can act, just as anybody can run a bow over the strings of a violin, but by and large, the trained professional is the one most likely to create something enjoyable in the process. The Puritan work ethic does not apply to the arts, however, so that there will always be examples of amateurs doing better than professionals. Black people in New Orleans after the Civil War picked up the musical instruments that were readily available and cheap because of the many military bands that had been operating there, and, without any training or experience, created the greatest American musical form—jazz. David Garrick in England in the eighteenth century decided to leave the family wine trade and go on stage, where he immediately played leads and became one of the greatest actors in history.

Not only is professionalism no guarantee of success in the arts and amateurism no guarantee of failure, but also there is no proportion between the work expended and the quality of the results. A poem tossed off in a few minutes may turn out to be better than one labored over for months—in fact, is more likely to be better, because laboriousness is usually the sign of failure in artistic composition. Certainly if the *results* seem labored, the work is no good!

The lack of a work ethic is one of the reasons that there exists an anti-arts prejudice, of which the antitheatrical prejudice can be seen as merely a part. The artist is often perceived as a loafer or a wastrel—which he sometimes is—who does not have to "work" like other people. What he produces butters no bread, meets no payroll. (It also pollutes no rivers, but we are only gradually coming to see that as something positive.) There may also be deeper psychological reasons for our prejudice, however; like acting, all the other arts have strong infantile components. Children learn to sing, paint, dance, tell stories, from the time they are learning to speak. These activities are thus associated in our minds with pleasurable but childish behavior. The arts are *play*, and adults are supposed to *work*. Thus professional moralists, when they are not attacking theatre, are usually attacking some other art form. Plato would have banned nearly all the arts from his ideal city; both Jews and Moslems banned the painting of pictures; Christians smashed statues; American censors are forever attacking literary works as dirty, blasphemous, or seditious. The artist himself is seen as lazy, promiscuous, irresponsible—in a word, a child.

The anyone-can-do-it attitude, then, is related to a much broader prejudice. Acting is particularly vulnerable here, because the actor's instrument is himself, instead of some arcane device. In fact, there is a good deal of *craft* involved in acting, with specialized techniques that must be mastered through long experience, which I shall be discussing later, but the techniques are not obvious and not well known among non-actors. Furthermore, acting is ubiquitous. It is one art form that everyone, no matter how philistine, is likely to encounter, especially in these days of television. The average American watches it seven hours a day, most of the time in dramatic programs (plus endless commercials, most of which are dramatized with actors). Anything that common can not be very special! Also, because television is dominated by small, elite commercial interests with little concern for quality, performances are usually slapdash, so that the acting that people are most likely to encounter gives little sense of its high artistic potential. Americans may idolize TV stars as personalities, but not as artists.

As for the charge that acting cannot be an art form because it is ephemeral, this too is part of a broader prejudice. All art is ultimately intangible. Of course a book or a painting or a statue has substance, but its substantiality has nothing to do with its artistic nature. Michelangelo's David is not just a hunk of stone; a collection of Shakespeare's plays is not just a pile of paper. The nonmaterial nature of art makes it seem, when considered in a certain frame of mind, trivial. Thus a conservative newspaper columnist in the university town where I work demanded that art, music, drama, dance, etc. be dropped from the curriculum. They were "nonessential," and hence unworthy of taxpayers' money.

Antonin Artaud, in his 1933 article "No More Masterpieces," actually *celebrated* the ephemeral nature of acting, which he saw as having deep metaphysical significance, since it reflects the transience of life itself. Masterpieces, on the other hand, the great dramatic works of the French tradition, "are literary, that is to say, fixed; and fixed in forms that no longer respond to the needs of the time."[3] This outlandish attitude, which has had enormous influence on theatre practitioners of our time, might be called an "antiliterary prejudice." This prejudice has a lot to do with the poor quality of productions of classical plays today; some directors, particularly American ones, have developed an outright contempt for playtexts, which they feel free to alter, adapt, update, or otherwise emasculate.

Whether seen as something negative or something positive, however, the ephemeral nature of acting is only relative. Ultimately all works of art disappear, destroyed in war or natural disasters, forgotten because of political upheavals, lost because of carelessness, eaten up by termites or beetles or microbes or fungi. And, of course, at the end of the lifespan of the earth, *everything* will disappear, "the cloud-capped towers, the gorgeous palaces, the solemn temples, the great globe itself" shall dissolve, or rather, be incinerated by an expanding sun and leave not a masterpiece behind. Besides, considering an art work as a "durable" is to see only its materiality, which, again, is not its essential aspect. If we consider the work of art as an *experience*, as it appears to the viewer or audience member, the situation is very different. A work of art is recreated every time someone responds to it, and dies when the experience ends, although its material existence continues unchanged. (Or so we assume. Bishop Berkeley in the eighteenth century maintained that *everything* exists only by being perceived, but no one lives his daily life on that assumption, and even Berkeley had to explain the continuity of the existence of things by saying that God was perceiving them.) The stony materiality of Michelangelo's David has a continuity of existence, but its aesthetic nature exists only as something perceived by a human being. An animal looking at it will certainly experience its stoniness, and may even bang its head against it, but it is in no way a work of art for the animal. The *art* in an art work does not reside in the thing itself, but in a transaction between the observer and the thing. It is common to speak of responding "to" a work of art, but really, the response "is" the work of art.

This response varies from time to time, and from individual to individual. We do not see Michelangelo's statue the way his fellow Renaissance Florentines saw it, as the embodiment of the civic virtues of *fortezza* (strength) and *ira* (anger), and a symbol of the victory of the republic over the Medici tyrants.[4] We are more likely to respond to its erotic potential, as an ideal of male human nudity; it has also acquired the patina of a cultural artifact, blessed by centuries of adoring critics, so that we now validate ourselves and our culture when we look at it. Lacking a shared, cohesive Christian religion, we do not respond to Shakespeare's plays the way his contemporaries did, in the context of the Great Chain of Being where everything had its place, church and state were inseparable, and all men were created *un*equal. Thus, for example, Caliban's cries of "high-day freedom!", which had an ominous significance for the original audience, have more ambiguous resonances for us, since freedom is now considered a good thing, particularly for enslaved natives like Caliban. This does not mean we have to take a totally relativistic view, in which all readings of Shakespeare are equally good (or bad), nor a solipsistic view that we can never share anyone else's reading. We can indeed share our readings (or else centuries of Shakespeare criticism and generations of school classes are meaningless), but it takes an effort. It is not automatic. If both you and I bang our heads against the stone of a statue, nothing needs to be said, but if we wish to share our aesthetic response, we need to say a great deal. In fact, not only do aesthetic responses vary from time to time and from person to person, but even the *same* person will have differing responses; I have read, seen, and even taught *Macbeth* dozens of times, and it always means something different.[5] Literary though it may be, the play is not "fixed" for me, as Artaud would have it, but alive and changing.

Considered as an experience, then, acting is neither more nor less ephemeral than the other arts. Burbage is dead, while Shakespeare's texts sit on my shelf, but I have to recapture the experience of those texts, reinvigorate them with an informed and imaginative reading, or they remain just pieces of paper with black marks on them. Moreover, Burbage's performances have not vanished without a trace. They too can be imaginatively reconstructed, using contemporary accounts, memoirs, pictures, and the playtexts themselves. With modern actors, we can go even further, because we now have films or tapes of performances, either as recordings of stage productions or as art works in these media themselves. The traditional attack on acting for being ephemeral really only applies to the stage, since films and tapes do endure. Moreover, we now have photographs, theatre programs, critics' reviews, and feature pieces in periodicals to help us recapture performances from the past. I did not see John Barrymore's Hamlet, but, as a student of theatre history, I know a great deal about it through indirect means. Of course, my experience of his performance would have been vastly more intense and significant if I had been there, but I would argue that it still amounts to something, and is in fact more intense and significant than it was for some of those who *were* there.

Finally, the attack on acting as being uncreative betrays a lack of sophistication about the nature of creativity itself. If creativity is defined as "coming from nothing," then acting is indeed uncreative. The actor starts with a script; even in an improvisation, he starts with a character, or a situation, or perhaps a line of dialogue. But all the arts start with something; even a blank canvas imposes limitations and suggests possibilities. Mikel DuFrenne, the French phenomenological critic, maintained that "all the arts require a

53

performance: the painter executes or 'performs' a portrait, the sculptor a bust." The artist does not create a work in his brain, *ex nihilo*, and then "realize" it on canvas or in stone. "The creator does not see, he feels," Dufrenne went on, "he feels a desire which answers to a call: something wants to come into being."[6] This urge, this itch, leads to initial strokes on the canvas or a rough outlining on the stone. These beginnings suggest further strokes or more chipping; there is a kind of dialogue between the artist and the evolving work. *The work itself is his main inspiration.* "The artist is an artist only through his act. He does not think the idea of the work but rather about what he is making and what he perceives as he creates."[7]

The actor goes through a similar process in preparing his role. Unlike the painter or sculptor, he does start with a role in a script, but he too goes through a process of dialogue with the role as the role emerges in rehearsal. There is a similar process of trial and error, hesitations, feeling his way, as the performance comes more and more to feel right. (Sometimes it never does, in which case the role is a failure.) The actor has his role assigned to him, while the "creative" artist is free to start where he wishes (though we should remember that artists often start with assignments or commissions), but in both cases creativity is an ongoing process. Only the starting points are different; after that, the manner of creation is the same.

Furthermore, the actor does not just slavishly follow what the playwright has written down. If that were all there were to it, then not only would two actors play a role exactly the same way, but there would be no reason for any actor ever to fail. The actor must always breathe life into the role, make it his, make it seem an independent, living being. Even when the playwright is very specific with both dialogue and stage directions, there is still an enormous amount of work to be done; the playwright cannot possibly foresee everything, but even when he is very clear in his demands, they cannot be followed like a blueprint. The playtext must be explored and experimented with, in a long and often agonizing process, until the actor's performance is not only true to the text but independent of it, so that the audience does not think about the text behind the performance, but only about what they see and hear.

The playwright Arthur Miller has written cogently on his own creative process, and the similar one of an actor performing in one of his plays. At the beginning of writing *Death of a Salesman*, he says, "All that I had was the first two lines and a death—'Willy!' and 'It's all right. I came back.' ... 'It's all right. I came back,' rolled over and over in my head." The work evolved in the way that DuFrenne described, by trial and error, with the driving inspiration being the lines themselves, which suggested other lines, and whole scenes, until finally the whole play was finished. (Note that Miller did not start out with a full-blown, philosophical concept like "I shall prove that capitalism is heartless," or "I shall create a tragedy of the common man.") Miller goes on to describe Lee J. Cobb's similar slow evolution in the role of Willy: "Lee seemed to move about in a buffalo's stupefied trance, muttering his lines, plodding with deathly slowness from position to position, and behaving like a man who had been punched in the head.... It seemed as though Lee's sniffing around the role for so long recapitulated what I had done in the months before beginning to write."[8] Cobb was eventually magnificent in the role, but his rehearsal certainly did not consist of merely following Miller's instructions in the script! The same kind of process of seeking inspiration, finding it, and building on it, which characterizes all artistic creativity, was as fully evident in Cobb's approach as it had been in Miller's, as Miller himself notes.

The "uncreative" argument, then, like the "ephemeral" argument, is a canard. We would do well not to focus on aspects that make acting, at most, only different in degree from the other arts, rather than in kind, and instead consider the similarities between acting and the other arts. We have already noticed some in passing: The other arts, like acting, have their origins in infantile activities; the artist, like the actor, is widely viewed as childish; there is an anti-arts prejudice as well as an antitheatrical one; the creative processes are similar in all but the starting points. But there are other similarities as well, which have important implications for the teaching of acting and our understanding of theatre.

Acting entertains and enlightens. In this country, we tend to notice only the former with regard to acting, and to notice the latter with regard to the other arts, particularly when we talk of the high or "fine" arts. In fact, all the arts exist on many levels, so that if Hollywood or Broadway sometimes present us with degraded, vulgar acting, there are similar cultural forces creating degraded, vulgar music or pictures or novels. The prevalence of low, trivial acting should not blind us to the potential for actors, "the abstract and brief chronicles of the time," to educate us on the complexities and depths of human behavior, to bring great literature to life on stage, to instruct us about our society, our history, our destiny. In many cultures, actors are not worshiped as quasi-royalty nor paid fabulous salaries, but instead are revered as teachers and as transmitters of cultural values. Actors in Europe typically have long-term relationships with great repertory companies, where they regularly perform the classics. In Japan, the best actors are honored as "Distinguished National Treasures." All this may seem a sentimental appeal, but it is worth remembering when even our best theatre schools seem only concerned with preparing actors for a degraded theatre, rather than challenging them to improve that theatre. Acting is potentially just as great, high, or "fine" as any other art form, and at some times or in some places it has been or continues to be so.

Furthermore, like other art forms, acting has a history and a theory. Garrick's King Lear, Edmund Kean's Shylock, Edwin Booth's Iago, John Barrymore's Hamlet are all capable of being studied and appreciated; they are as much a part of our cultural heritage as Van Gogh's sunflowers or Tolstoy's *War and Peace*. As with other art forms, there is a *tradition* in acting, with identifiable styles and trends and influences. In addition, there is a recognized body of theory associated with acting that goes back thousands of years, which, as with other art forms, helps us to understand, cherish, and teach it. This book is an attempt to explore and expand that theoretical tradition.

There are also similarities between acting and the other arts in how they are created and in how we respond to them. In the previous chapter, I noted the phenomenon of possession in acting, how the initial stimulus (often the voice, although there are other possibilities) takes on a life of its own; we speak of the actor playing a role, but actually, the role plays him. This feeling of passivity *vis-à-vis* the role has its counterpart in all artistic creation, in the phenomenon of inspiration. Again, in pre-industrial, pre-scientific societies, there is usually a belief in a spirit, a god, or a muse who is the actual author of the artistic work, operating on or through the human artist. The classical epic poem traditionally started with an invocation to a muse, which is exactly like an actor in rehearsal trying to find the character, to achieve that feeling in which the performance is moving of *its* accord rather than the actor's. The painters of Russian icons prepared for their work with prayers and rituals; they did not even sign the paintings, since they were not the actual painters, God was! The feeling was that God was guiding the brush and that they had to be worthy of his guidance. The Japanese Noh actor spent an hour before performance staring at his mask, so that the spirit of the mask would enter him and perform the role.

In our time, artists typically do not speak of being literally possessed, but there is still that search for the (often elusive) inspiration, and a feeling of passivity when it is achieved. For Mozart, composing was a matter of writing down the music that was already playing in his head. Rossini, similarly, maintained that in his youth, tunes sought him out; later, alas, he had to seek them, which is why he stopped composing. Ibsen said that when writing his plays it was as if he were *watching* them in a theatre and simply recording the characters' speeches and actions.

For the artist, then, the work of art has what Susanne Langer called a "virtual life,"[9] existing independent of him. Even the literary artist has this feeling about his work; although his medium is words, the experience of literary creation is very different from that of ordinary discourse. It is not a matter of saying something, but of creating something, which takes on a life of its own from an early stage in the creative process. This is why it is false to speak of a writer (or any other kind of artist) as having a "message," of trying to demonstrate or prove something. That is not what artistic creation is all about. In fact, when a playwright or a novelist announces that his latest work will expose the evils of racism or prove that government is corrupt, we feel that something is amiss. It is not that we believe, on the contrary, that racism is a good thing or that governments are pure as snow, but rather that it does not sound as if he is creating a literary work at all, but a newspaper article or a sermon instead. Nor is there anything wrong with newspaper articles or sermons, but they are different from plays or novels in important ways. Articles, essays, lectures, and sermons do not have "virtual life"; far from seeming to be independent from their author, they are an extension of him, written or spoken in his own voice, while plays or novels or poems, or pictures or statues or musical compositions, or performances by an actor, if they are any good, do have such life, seeming to be an autonomous other.

The independent life of a work of art is an amazing thing, if you think about it. There is a strange, all-in-all quality about what is being portrayed. A painting, for example, is not just a collection of shapes and colors, but seems to be a world of its own, complete unto itself, which is just *there*. Even abstract expressionist paintings like those of Jackson Pollock are more than just splotches of paint; there seems to be pattern, coherence, completeness. Likewise, a musical piece is not just a collection of sounds, but a coherent organization that seems complete and to which we respond emotionally. In other words, the viewer or reader or audience member also has a feeling of passivity toward a work of art, which is independent of him, as it had been for the artist who created it. The feeling is passive because the art work seems just to be "speaking" to you; there is no conscious effort being made to decipher or organize it, although of course you are unconsciously doing these things or it would seem incoherent.

Similarly, a performance by an actor has independence and coherence. Although it is common for critics to discuss an actor's looks or voice or gestures (some critics can discuss little else), his performance is both more than these things and none of them. The character just seems to be alive, even though both we and the actor know it does not really exist. It seems to be self-governing, though in fact the actor is governing it. The play too seems to have independent existence, even though it is just a bunch of actors walking around on stage or in front of a camera saying words that someone else has written. This explains why there have been great actors who were not particularly handsome or beautiful, like David Garrick or Glenda Jackson, or whose speech was indifferent, like Edmund Kean or Marlon Brando. It also explains why theories of acting that stress real, raw emotion are woefully inadequate. The actor is not merely displaying his face, body, or voice, any more than a painter is just displaying colors; nor is he displaying his emotions, any more than a poet is displaying words. Instead, the actor is creating a work of art.

Emotional release by itself, no matter how real, "honest," etc. the emotion may be, is never enough by itself to create a character, as Stanislavski emphasized in the anecdote about the young woman playing Agnes in *Brand*. As Susanne Langer has pointed out in discussing musical composition, such release not only has no artistic form, it requires none: "A lynching-party howling round the gallows-tree, a woman wringing her hands over a sick child, a lover ... trembling, sweating, and perhaps laughing or crying with emotion, is giving vent to intense feelings; but such scenes are not occasions for music, least of all for composing."[10] Nor are they occasions for acting. Such intense moments are rare (many roles do not have them), and brief in relation to the performance as a whole. Complete within themselves, they carry with them no compulsion, no "itch" to create something further. Peak emotions do not serve as a basis for a character, but, when properly performed, are instead the *result* of the characterization, in the overall context of performance. Similarly, the audience does not judge a performance by the honesty or intensity of peak emotions. (It is amusing to imagine a set of judges, like those at a diving or skating contest, raising numbers—5.6, 5.8, 6.0, etc.—while the actor on stage thrashes about weeping.) The audience responds to the characterization as a whole, in the context of the play as a whole, so that it is perfectly possible to give a bad performance no matter how powerful the emotional heights.

The emotional release approach to acting, then, considers only a few isolated moments, rather than the character as a whole. All the false theories of acting—"emotional release," "anyone can do it," "acting is ephemeral," "acting is uncreative"—tend in some way to ignore the actor's work of art, which is the character. Creating a character is something "anyone" can *not* do (though ordinary individuals may from time to time hit upon *one* character that they can play well). Playing oneself is never adequate to create a character, though at times the persona one plays in real life and the one depicted on stage or on screen may be so similar as to seem to coincide. But even in such cases, it is closer to the truth to think of the actor's real-life self as a role than to think of the actor's stage or screen self as a non-role. If the performance on stage or screen is successful, it is still a character, regardless of its relationship to real life, and seems to be self-governing, rather than guided by the actor. And rather than judge it by the actor's personal life (of which we may know nothing), we instead judge it by its own coherence, intensity, and appropriateness to the play.

Similarly, although a performance by nature is ephemeral, the character created by it can have lasting substance. It may even live on for centuries. It may influence other performances, and may be recapturable by various means. (It can never be fully recaptured, but then, neither can the original responses to any other art form.)

Finally, acting is not uncreative, because the actor must definitely *create* his character, even though it already exists in the script and even though other actors may have already performed it. Just as the reader must reinvigorate a literary classic with an informed and imaginative reading, so too must an actor restore life to the character through a process that resembles in most essentials that of creation in other art forms. The actor is not a neutral, mechanical transmitter of the playwright's conception, like a tape recorder or a film projector, but a living artist who engages with the author's conception in a complex and difficult process, to emerge, when he is successful, with something unique and vital. In the end, the performance must seem *independent*, both of the script and of the actor himself.

There are ways in which acting does differ significantly from other art forms, but these in no respect diminish its artistic validity. For one thing, an actor works with other people. Artists and writers in the past often collaborated, but nowadays they usually work alone. Actors, however, almost always work with other actors in a play, and even in a one-person show usually have a director guiding them. If the actor's work of art is his character, that character must exist in the context of a larger work—the play. That context is both a challenge and an inspiration; the actor's performance must fit in with the rest, rather than going off by itself, but if the actor looks upon the performances of his fellow actors, and the demands of the play as a whole, as sources of inspiration rather than an onerous burden, then they actually enhance rather than limit his creativity.

One of the problems with our extremely individualist culture is that it makes it hard for us to imagine creativity as occurring anywhere except within the fevered brain of the lonely artist. In fact, as noted, artists in the past often collaborated, and there is no reason to believe that the only alternative to total individualism in art is hack work. Every artist is inspired by his materials, and by his evolving art work, in addition to his subject matter; the actor's materials and art work happen to include other actors, as well as properties, costumes, settings, and lighting, in addition to the character as presented in the script. Stanislavski's concept of "communion" (sometimes translated as "relating"), which I shall discuss in Chapter 11, stresses this synergy. Creativity should never be considered as implying total newness, coming from nowhere; it is more like *discovery* than it is like willing something into being. Rather than withdrawing into himself, the artist needs to become sensitive to things around him. The actor is no different. He creates with the help and inspiration of others, who make him more of an artist, not less.

Another element that differentiates acting, at least on stage, from most other art forms is the presence of an audience. All artistic creation is aimed ultimately at an audience, but only in the performing arts, including music and dance in addition to acting, is that audience present at the moment of creation. Of course, this creation has been prepared, in rehearsals where there was no audience, but nonetheless the character and the play must be recreated for each performance, where the audience definitely affects the work.

It is important to distinguish, however, between performing *for* an audience and merely performing *to* an audience. In this, the actor resembles the artist in his studio or the novelist in his study, both of whom hope that an audience will eventually appreciate their work, but who certainly do not think of themselves as directly persuading, titillating, cajoling, or otherwise eliciting some response. Their primary attention, as always with genuine artistic creation, is on the work itself; they actually become like audience members themselves as the work progresses. Yes, they aim to please the audience—to the extent that they are part of it!

Similarly, an actor in a play is not trying to move the audience directly. Unlike a lecturer or a classroom teacher or a stand-up comedian, the actor does not play *to* an audience, focusing on their immediate response. Instead, he plays to his fellow actors or to the other imaginary goals in the play. Even in a play where an actor addresses the audience, he does so in character, in the framework of the play, which is vastly different from speaking to them as himself in some unframed context like lecturing.

Nevertheless, the audience is important in theatrical performance. For example, actors typically say that the experience of acting in films is less intense and satisfying than on stage. Furthermore, stage actors definitely respond to the audience; a "good" audience (i.e., one that is alert, sensitive, and appreciative) will draw out a better performance than a "bad" one. A production will sometimes improve spectacularly when it finally plays to a public; late in rehearsals, there is often a feeling that the play *needs* an audience, that performing has become stale and listless without one.

The function of the audience, then, is surprisingly active. In a sense, they *verify* the performance. When the audience at a lecture is unresponsive, the lecturer feels that it is his fault and works harder to get his points across; when the audience at a play is unresponsive, the actors often feel that it is the *audience's* fault. It is the audience that is "bad," not the performers. The audience is not fulfilling its role, not appreciating what is there on stage, not verifying it with laughter, applause, or (most satisfying of all) hushed silence.

An analogy can be seen in sports. The spectators at a sporting event provide the athletes with a sense of playing "for keeps." Good plays will be cheered, bad ones scorned. Everything will be noticed, responded to, and remembered. In practice, with no spectators, mistakes can be corrected, and plays improved; in a game, with spectators, it is always now or never. This heightens the experience, makes it seem more alive and real. Athletes usually perform better with an appreciative audience, which is why playing on one's home court or field is a definite advantage. On the other hand, the athletes are not performing to their audience; in fact, "grandstanding"—making something look fancy or difficult—is recognized as detrimental. The athletes' attention must be on the game, and the spectators actually help them to focus their attention on it.

In the theatre, the audience has exactly the same function. During rehearsals, one can go back, correct, improve. This has obvious advantages, particularly early on, but it ultimately becomes frustrating. The actors need an audience, need to play for keeps, in order to do their best work. The same problem of rehearsing occurs in film, where one can do one "take" after another. Only one take is needed for the final film, but knowledge of that very fact is often inhibiting, so that take after take is necessary for a scene that would achieve success very quickly on a stage with an audience. In recognition of this, many television shows are taped or filmed before a live audience, to draw the actors out.

Nonetheless, just as the athlete's attention is on the game, so the actor's attention is on the play. The audience is not merely passive, receiving what the actors send them, but instead is active, providing the actors with the focus they need. Just as the audience identifies vicariously with the actors, so too do the actors identify vicariously with the audience. Both actors and audience feel good when something goes well, and feel bad when something goes badly. But worst of all for the actors is when the audience does not *notice* something, good or bad; they have failed as an audience, have not lived up to their responsibilities to provide focus because they are not focusing themselves.

For the stage actor, then, the audience is actually *part* of his creative process. The actor responds to them, as he does to his fellow actors and to the given circumstances of the play in performance, but it is an indirect kind of response. A good actor does not grandstand to them, any more than a good athlete does. The actor who is always thinking in terms of dazzling the audience is a ham—or worse. The good actor comes before the audience as an artist, not as a pitchman, and the audience are the actor's collaborators, rather than his customers. By verifying the actor's performance, they enhance his creativity, making him more an artist than he would be without them.

SIX

THE ACTOR'S SUBJECTIVITY: THE CREATIVE STATE

In all of the vast acting literature—the textbooks, the memoirs, the anecdotes, the biographies and autobiographies, the interviews, the historical studies, the theoretical speculations, the manifestos—it is rare to find any mention of what acting feels like. What could be more important than to know what it is like *to be there*, on stage or before a camera? Yet actors themselves seem reluctant to talk about it; their memoirs, autobiographies, and interviews will often not refer to acting at all, but instead focus on their personal lives. David Niven, a fine actor who eventually wrote several popular books about his life, provides a classic example. His books are full of delightful gossip about Hollywood, but they seem forever to be talking *around* acting. We are partying with actors, seeing them in intimate moments (including very disturbing ones, like a total emotional breakdown in Vivien Leigh), spying on producers and agents and gossip columnists and hairdressers, playing practical jokes, pursuing beautiful women, boozing with directors and fellow actors. But somehow we are never—acting. Niven takes us into restaurants and bars, on yachts, in swimming pools, in mansions and beach houses, even into dressing rooms, but we never quite get in front of a camera.

It is easy to dismiss these as popular writing with no pretense at teaching anything about the nature of acting or how to do it. Cert nly the books were best-sellers. Yet there is something both typical and telling about them. To the actor, his successful performances seem wonderful, but mysterious and volatile. They come from someplace beyond his control, part of him (obviously), yet strange and different. Stage actors thus fear that they will not be able to repeat good performances night after night; all actors fear that they will not be able to go on finding successful characterizations in new plays and films. Actors are thus understandably reluctant to dissect their creative processes. Examining your own methods can lead to "paralysis by analysis," like the golfer who could no longer hit the ball when he had to figure out whether he breathed in or out during his backswing. Thus, when pressed to explain how he works, an actor will typically send up a smokescreen. He will prefer to reveal (or invent) the most intimate details of his sex life, his drug taking, his latest divorce, in hopes of diverting attention from acting itself. If the subject seems unavoidable, however, he will try to placate the interviewer or reader with what the actor thinks they want to hear. This means fitting his acting into one of the standard myths in our culture. One of these is the romantic myth of the suffering artist—what torture it was to play King Lear, what agony to act Hedda Gabler! What does acting feel like? Pain!

The other myth introduces the realist, holding a mirror up to nature, analyzing the behavior of his fellow human beings. There is a long tradition of observation and analysis—David Garrick observed lunatics in Bedlam Hospital as preparation for King Lear, just as, more recently, Dustin Hoffman observed autistic patients in California as preparation for his role in the movie *Rain Man*. The contemporary American actor, however, is more likely to stress how he held the mirror up to his own nature, analyzing his *own* behavior. Uta Hagen, an outstanding American actress and a good acting teacher, has written a textbook in which this is even developed into a method, which she calls "substitution":

> At eighteen, when I played Nina in *The Sea Gull* with the Lunts, many elements of the part existed for me in life. Nina is a young, unsophisticated, middle-class girl from the country who is thrown in with a famous actress of whom she is in awe and a famous man (a writer in the play) whom she hero-worships. That *was* my relationship to the Lunts, so I was able to use them head-on.[1]

Anticipating the obvious objection that such coincidences between role and life are unusual, she goes on to insist that there are nonetheless always similarities, so that substitution can and should be used for every moment of a role. With Blanche in *A Streetcar Named Desire*, for example, she notes that she never had a sister like Stella. Nevertheless, she maintains that she can still recall her relationship with a girl who "felt" like a sister, or a friend she depended on for love and comfort. "I may even use a dozen elements from a dozen different relationships from my past."[2] What does acting feel like? Remembering something, or someone.

Theories like this are dubious. Agonizing, observing, or remembering are not really central to an actor's work, though all actors do these things occasionally. To stress them as a basis for acting is misleading, especially in teaching, where it can lead to disastrous results. The theory of the suffering actor is of course just the "real, honest emotion" approach all over again, though, if consistent, its advocates should give equal time to the pleasure of playing happy moments. Because this would not fit the myth of the tormented artist, however, the emphasis is always on negative emotions. A teacher of mine used to insist that an actor had to "dig into his guts" if he wanted to be any good, reliving all the pain and suffering of his life. This raises the question that if acting is such a horrible experience, why do it? The proponents of the acting-as-pain school are the very ones who would scorn the idea of acting just for the money or fame. Are actors masochists?

In fact, acting is not painful at all—*good* acting, that is. Bad acting is what is painful, not only to the audience but to the actor himself; nothing is more frustrating than not being able to "get" the character, the feeling of forcing something that just will not happen. But good acting is exhilarating, all the more so when portraying moments of intense suffering. When these are going right, everything seems to be moving of *its* own accord, my tears flow without my having to force them, I howl in agony with astonishing intensity, and I am thrilled by my own performance, enjoying it in exactly the same way that the audience does. It is sometimes a delightful surprise when it comes out, unplanned, with an unusual sound that is so bizarre yet so *right*. I am, again, like one possessed. It is not like crying in real life, but it is far from being a cold, mechanical experience. It is almost indescribable joy.

Theories that overemphasize the actor as observer, whether of others or himself, also ignore his subjectivity. Of course actors observe, and sometimes make use of what they encounter, but remembering things from offstage is not central to their work. Acting, like sports, is a here-and-now experience. As with a sport, there is a good deal of training and preparation involved, but just as the baseball player at the plate is thinking about the *ball*, rather than his coach's advice, so too is the actor, when performing, thinking about the character and the situation, including the realities of props, costume, and the other actors. Observed real-life behavior may be useful in creating detail; it may even be a stimulus that gets a characterization started; but it is not what one *plays*.

It is unlikely that consciously recalled, postinfantile experiences ever have much to do with acting or any other kind of artistic creation. The actor is tapping unconscious energies, recapturing the oceanic feeling. This does *not* mean that preparation for a role consists of quasi-psychoanalysis, but it does mean that acting, as it is *lived*, is not so much something you do as something that happens to you. The consummation of the acting experience needs to be triggered, somehow. The trigger might well be a recalled personal experience or an observed behavior in someone else, but it can also be something that has nothing to do with these things, like a change in voice, or a piece of costume, or a poetic image in the dialogue. And, of course, even in marksmanship finding the trigger is not the same as hitting your target. A gesture or a dialect or a way of tilting the head might bring a role to life, but the role must still be brought to a fully characterized performance. Mikel Dufrenne, quoted in the last chapter, explained how, after the initial inspiration, the artist undergoes a kind of dialogue with the evolving art work, adding, discarding, shaping, in response to what he sees and hears. In other words, *the actor's main source of inspiration is the role itself.* By opening night, if all has gone well, the trigger that got it all started may be, if not actually forgotten, long since swallowed up into something larger and far more important.

Stanislavski's greatness as a theorist of acting is partly the result of his willingness to examine his own subjectivity on stage, rather than deriving a theory from imagined axioms about what acting ought to be. At the beginning of his textbook, *An Actor Prepares*, he describes the experience of a young acting student, "Kostya" (obviously Stanislavski himself, in his youth), playing a scene from *Othello* for a classroom exercise. Despite its length, the passage is worth quoting in its entirety, especially since descriptions of the actor's subjectivity are so rare. It starts with the moment when Kostya entered the theatre:

> I was filled with a complete indifference until I reached my dressing room. But once inside, my heart began to pound and I felt almost nauseated.
> On the stage what first disturbed me was the extraordinary solemnity, the quiet and order that reigned there. When I

stepped away from the darkness of the wings to the full illumination of the footlights, headlights and spotlights, I felt blinded. The brightness was so intense that it seemed to form a curtain of light between me and the auditorium. I felt protected from the public, and for a moment I breathed freely, but soon my eyes became accustomed to the light, I could see into the darkness, and the fear and attraction of the public seemed stronger than ever. I was ready to turn myself inside out, to give them everything I had; yet inside of me I had never felt so empty. The effort to squeeze out more emotion than I had, the powerlessness to do the impossible, filled me with a fear that turned my face and my hands to stone. All my forces were spent on unnatural and fruitless efforts. My throat became constricted, my sounds all seemed to go to a high note. My hands, feet, gestures, and speech all became violent. I was ashamed of every word, of every gesture. I blushed, clenched my hands, and pressed myself against the back of the armchair. I was making a failure, and in my helplessness I was suddenly seized with rage. For several minutes I cut loose from everything about me. I flung out the famous line "Blood, Iago, blood!" I felt in these words all the injury to the soul of a trusting man. Leo's interpretation of Othello [a fellow student had spoken of his sympathy for Othello with such sensitivity that Kostya had almost wept] suddenly rose in my memory and aroused my emotion. Besides, it almost seemed as though for a moment the listeners strained forward, and that through the audience there ran a murmur.

The moment I felt this approval a sort of energy boiled up in me. I cannot remember how I finished the scene, because the footlights and the black hole disappeared from my consciousness, and I was free of all fear. I remember that Paul [playing Iago] was at first astonished by the change in me; then he became infected by it, and acted with abandon. The curtain was rung down, out in the hall there was applause, and I was full of faith in myself.[3]

The passage begins with a description of stage fright, which, for the actor, typically occurs *before* a performance. (Stephen Aaron has a book that deals with stage fright as experienced *during* a performance,[4] but this phenomenon is more likely to be experienced

70

by public speakers than actors, unless, as here, the acting is going badly.) The moment Kostya could "cut loose," the feeling of emptiness and shame, the constricted throat, the powerlessness, all disappeared.

The good performance was triggered by serendipity; Kostya's very frustration paradoxically released him. His strength as an actor was in recognizing that triggering had occurred, and to have pursued the experience. The line, "Blood, Iago, blood!" became central to the scene. The line sounded so good, that, as Kostya says, he felt *in the words* all the injury of Othello. A chain reaction was set off; where before, anxiety had led to more anxiety, now good moments led to more good moments, so that even Kostya's partner was infected by his playing. Although there was a moment of recollection, it was a memory of something felt *about the character* (or Leo's interpretation of it), rather than a memory of something in Kostya's personal life. Also, although Kostya forgot about the footlights and the "black hole" of the proscenium, there is no implication that he felt that he was really Othello and that the events of the scene were actually happening. Far from being oblivious to the audience, he gained "a sort of energy" from them, as he sensed their attention and approval.

The creative state described here was Stanislavski's goal for all the actor's preparation in classes and rehearsal. At one point, unwittingly anticipating Freud's term *oceanic feeling*, he actually used the phrase "the ocean of the subconscious" to describe this state of inspiration.[5] Stanislavski believed that one could not always achieve this creative state; acting is not a branch of engineering, but an art form, in which there are no guarantees of success. He did maintain, however, that although an actor could not always be inspired, role after role, night after night, he could always act adequately, in a manner that was interesting and easy to watch, which was logical in terms of the character and his circumstances in the play. In other words, there is a *craft* to acting, which can at least guarantee an acceptable performance, just as there is a craft to drawing that can at least guarantee a recognizable portrait. "One cannot always create subconsciously and with inspiration.... Therefore our art teaches us first of all to create consciously and rightly."[6] Stanislavski did feel, however, that when a role was prepared in this logical manner, with the actor trying always to talk as the character would talk, do as the character would do, etc., an inspired state, though never assured, was most likely to occur. When the actor works in a conscious and right manner, "that will best prepare the way for the blossoming of the subconscious, which is inspiration."[7]

Stanislavski elaborated this logical process with what he called the *magic if*; playing a scene in which there is a mad killer behind a door, the actor does not try to convince himself that there is really a madman there, but only asks himself what his character would do *if* there were.[8] This distinction is important, because one popular misconception of Stanislavski is that he wanted actors to hallucinate that the events of the play were actually happening, when in fact he only insisted that they examine their behavior rigorously and in detail, in terms of the given circumstances of the play. He wanted to propel the actor *into* the play, which is equivalent to achieving the state of inspiration. Although Stanislavski does not make the equation, the actor's involvement with the play during the state of inspiration is, of course, exactly equivalent to the *audience's* involvement. The goal is to have the actor carried away by the play, just as the audience is to become carried away.

For Stanislavski, then, the play was definitely the thing, wherein to catch the inspiration of the actor. A stress on real, honest emotion would definitely *not* achieve this goal. When Kostya tried to "squeeze out more emotion," he became powerless, but when a line from the play recalled his empathy with the character, inspiration flowered. For all Stanislavski's reputation for stressing emotion, his texts are full of warnings like the following: "When you are choosing some bit of action leave feeling and spiritual content alone."[9] "In the beginning forget about your feelings."[10] Stanislavski did in fact believe that good acting was full of emotion, but that the emotion was an end point rather than a starting point, the result of carefully prepared, logical, and ultimately *involved* acting. Emotion is the result, not the cause, of good acting.

The stress on the play and the character, then, rather than on the actor's emotions or personal life, is crucial in understanding Stanislavski. One word he liked to use a lot to describe good acting was *truth*, which in this country has been usually interpreted to mean true to life, or else real, true emotions. In fact, Stanislavski could not have been more plain about what kind of truth he was talking about: "To play truly means to be right, logical, coherent, to think, strive, feel and act in unison *with your role* [emphasis mine]."[11] The actor does not "reality test," checking everything he does against real life; nor does he churn himself up into a "truthful" emotional frenzy. Reality testing not only makes all nonrealistic drama impossible, even with realistic material it takes the actor's imagination away from where it ought to be, on the role itself. Trying to become emotionally worked up leads only to the kind of paralysis that Kostya experienced; instead of seeking to commune with the character and his situation, the actor is communing only with himself, unwittingly triggering repression mechanisms that choke off the very things he seeks, leaving him isolated from the play and impotent. The testing that the actor does should not be of outside reality, but of the play itself, via the *magic if*; the emotions that he feels should not be his own, but those of the character, which he feels not directly but vicariously, in an intense kind of empathy.

Shelley Russell-Parks, in her recent study of the actor's process, interviewed dozens of actors at all levels, from stars like Derek Jacobi to undergraduates at her university. She found that "most actors agree that some sort of perceptual transformation does occur and that their means of access, while highly individualized and seldom entirely dependable, is an artistic method."[12] This changed perception is not a feeling of actually being the character—one successful actor scorned the very notion of becoming the character as "method bullshit"[13]—but of being in the character's head as a kind of observer. It is an expansion of the self rather than a transplantation; the actor retains his everyday self and adds another. This altered state has the following characteristics:

1. It is always pleasurable, even when the emotions being portrayed are painful.
2. It is not a withdrawal into oneself, but instead involves a heightened awareness of one's surroundings, including set, properties, costume, and fellow actors.
3. One does not lose a sense of one's real, everyday self, nor of the mundane reality of the set, costumes, etc., but all these things take on an added aura.
4. The experience of transformation cannot always be achieved, and cannot always be maintained when it is achieved.
5. This self-transformation is nonetheless a *sine qua non* for the best acting.

Freudian theory provides an explanation for all these attributes. The experience is pleasurable because it is a return to an infantile state, when there was no boundary between self and other. In this state, we still see and hear the same things around us, but have entered into a new relationship with them; they are now part of us rather than separate, which gives them a new aura. It is an elusive state, because there are repression mechanisms operating to take us back to our ordinary self; our earliest lesson was the distinction between self and other, which has since then been drummed into us over and over until the separation has become an automatic way of thinking that is hard to escape. Nonetheless, when we do escape that way of thinking, there is a tremendous sensation of liberation and power. The actor feels as if he can literally become anybody and do anything; he becomes inventive and compelling, and, amazingly, everything he chooses to do turns out to be right. Sam Waterston described the experience as it happened to him during a production of *Waiting for Godot:*

> Everything was just working perfectly, and I wasn't thinking about it anymore, and suddenly, I had a sense of taking off.... As I was doing the speech, I was thinking things that were brand new. I had never thought of the character in the way that it came to me to think of it at that moment. All the thought processes were being changed, and I had the sensation that every single one of them was being communicated explicitly to the audience.[14]

There is a quasi-religious quality to descriptions like this; Waterston was "born again." Mystical religious experiences of a certain type resemble acting to a considerable degree. Western religious mystics have usually sought enlightenment introspectively, by looking inward, but oriental religions at times have stressed an external kind of mysticism. Alan Watts notes that, in this tradition, "the content of the liberation experience—*satori*, *Nirvana*, etc.,— ... is the physical world, seen in a new way."[15] This liberation experience, like that of self-transformation in acting, is elusive, tending to come suddenly and often unexpectedly. The Buddhist monk may experience it without warning after long periods of frustration, from trying to answer a *koan*, a question posed by a master that really has no answer, like, "What is the sound of one hand clapping?" Similarly, Kostya, after a period of frustration in playing Othello in which nothing went right, suddenly became liberated and performed superbly. Both mystical enlightenment and the experience of self-transformation in acting are overwhelming, the ultimate goal, yet, unfortunately, are beyond our complete control and baffling.

David Cole found similar forms of mysticism in primitive religion. He distinguishes two kinds of primitive priests: the *shaman* who imaginatively travels to the world of the gods in his rituals, and the *hungan* who is imaginatively possessed by the gods. Cole notes that the actor resembles both; in the initial phase, where the actor is seeking the character, he is like the shaman, but when the character is found and self-transformation achieved (as when Kostya cried, "Blood, Iago, blood!"), he becomes like the hungan. Cole calls this reversal "rounding," where the actor goes "from masterful explorer to mastered vehicle."[16]   The actor seeks the character until the character finds him.   Although we speak of playing a role, in good acting the role actually plays you.

Good acting, then, resembles other semi-voluntary human experiences, like sexual arousal or falling asleep, where there is a shift from being active to being passive.   Becoming aroused or falling asleep are activities that *you* are doing (who else?), but which seem to be happening *to* you.   As with self-transformation in acting (Cole's "rounding"), they may at times happen unawares, but at other times may be sought fruitlessly.   They are beyond our direct control—we cannot "turn on" sexually nor "turn off" and fall asleep the way we can switch a light on and off—but we can do things that will increase the *likelihood* that these experiences will occur.   We are more likely to fall asleep if we retire to a quiet, dark room than if we stay where it is noisy and bright; we are more likely to become sexually aroused if we are focusing on our lover than if we are still thinking about the worries of the day.   In fact, if we list the circumstances under which sleep or arousal are most likely to occur, they resemble the circumstances that are equally conducive to acting:

1. Isolation
2. Relaxation
3. Focus
4. Responsiveness

That both sex and sleep need *isolation* is obvious.   Both undertakings are carried on separately from ordinary, everyday activity and are unlikely to occur when there are interruptions.   *Relaxation* is equally critical; tension, fear, or worry all inhibit proper functioning, while excessive striving may nullify the very thing sought.   The need for *focus* is less obvious, but no less important: in sex, one focuses on one's partner (or, in masturbation, on some fantasy).   A common cause of sexual failure is lack of focus; one is distracted by the cares of the day or, commonly, by one's self—a sure way to sexual failure is to be constantly monitoring your own arousal (Am I getting an erection? Am I starting to have an orgasm?) rather than monitoring your partner's arousal. In trying to sleep, too, the experience of insomnia is one of being compulsively distracted; unable to sleep, your mind races with a thousand thoughts, but as sleep approaches, your mind typically attaches to some simple image, which subtly turns into a dream. Finally, *responsiveness* is related to focus. To fall asleep, it is best to respond to the warmth and comfort of the bed, luxuriate in the peace and quiet of the darkness, enjoy the daydreaming that will soon turn into actual dreaming. In sex the way to escape awkwardness and self-consciousness is to become other-conscious, responding to your partner as in a dance, delighting in his or her look, touch, smell, sound. Sex is, after all, supposed to be enjoyable.

If we consider acting in terms of these characteristics, we note first of all that acting is carried on in *isolated* spaces. A theatre building functions to isolate both actors and audience from the everyday world; even when performances are outside, they are typically in some secluded place like a park. Furthermore, the stage itself isolates the actors from the audience. In recent decades, directors have experimented with a wide range of spatial arrangements that not only remove the proscenium arch but may place the actors amidst the audience or even shift the audience itself around. Nevertheless, at any given moment, the performance space is well defined via lighting, furniture, platforms, or simply the way the actors relate to their surroundings. Even when actors and audience interact, as in some avant-garde productions, there is a clear sense of the audience being drawn *into* the actors' space rather than (as is sometimes said) the audience/actor relationship breaking down entirely. There are good psychological reasons for the isolation of the theatre and of the stage from their surroundings. It makes the point, spatially, that the performance is *not* real, that there is no threat of danger, that what is taking place has no practical consequences and hence can be indulged in freely. Isolation, then, helps to make the stage into a magical space where anything can happen. Our inner "censor," as Freud called it, allows us to behave there in sometimes wild and outrageous ways because it knows that it does not matter. Artaud, similarly, maintained that the actor's performance "remains enclosed within a perfect circle," so that it "frees itself and dissolves into universality."[17] The avant-garde director Peter Brook insisted that "I can take any empty space and call it a bare stage,"[18] but the point is that it must be—empty.

Many actors find both acting classes and rehearsals for plays frustrating because there is no "magic" space. Acting classes are typically held in drab rooms under ordinary lighting; the teacher, who may consider things like setting and lighting to be "mere externals," not only does not provide them but will typically not even delimit a performance area. The actors just stand up in front of the rest of the class and do a scene or a monologue, but it does not *feel like acting* to them in the same way that performing in a play does, so that it may be difficult to experience the same sense of release. Similarly, performing in rehearsal, also in some drab room without a set or stage lighting, will not feel like acting. Often, actors' performances improve significantly the moment they get on the set or the moment stage lighting is turned on. Now the stage is isolated, special, magical, liberating.

The importance of *relaxation* in acting cannot be overstated. Acting teachers and theorists, no matter how widely they may disagree on other things, tend to agree on this point. Lee Strasberg was a fanatic on the need for actor relaxation, but so were Artaud, Jerzy Grotowski, and Michel Saint-Denis. Stanislavski has an entire chapter in *An Actor Prepares* called "Relaxation of Muscles,"[19] and returns to the theme repeatedly throughout his writings; note how Kostya, when he attempted to "squeeze out emotion," became "constricted" and "violent," clenched his hands, pressed himself against the armchair, etc. He only started to act when he "cut loose." Tension is energy turned inward; it is the physical manifestation of psychological repression. Thus, even a little bit of relaxation can help an actor, because it is in a sense paying back double; what was working against you now works for you. The acting teacher will thus work on lengthy exercises in getting the student to relax specific muscles in his face, limbs, and body, and may even (following Artaud, who made much of it) work on breathing. Such exercises always have at least some positive results—it is impossible to be too relaxed on stage—that are immediately visible.

Beyond this, there is a deeper psychological sense in which relaxation is necessary. Excessive striving in acting, like trying too hard to make love or to fall asleep, backfires. Kostya could not act until he stopped trying so hard. In an overreaction to the antitheatrical prejudice, actors will sometimes stress how hard they "work"; the acting-as-agony school is an example of this syndrome. Being overly casual about acting is a bad idea too, of course; discipline, training, preparation, and just plain drill are important. These things are not ends in themselves, however, but are means of achieving the liberation of self-transformation. Acting, like sex, is supposed to be pleasurable—and is ultimately only good when it is.

Many acting teachers stress the need for concentration, or *focus*. Kostya began to act when the line, "Blood, Iago, blood!" focused his attention from the many things that were distracting him. Bad acting feels very much like insomnia, in that one's thoughts and feelings seem scattered and out of control; in good acting, the actor (like the audience watching him) is riveted. Stanislavski has a chapter entitled "Concentration of Attention," in which he describes an exercise where the student is surrounded on stage by a circle of light: "The effect on me was like magic. All the little knick-knacks on the table drew my attention without any forcing or any instruction on my part. In a circle of light, in the midst of darkness, you have the sensation of being enti~ly alone. I felt even more at home in this circle of light than in my own room."[20] In performance, the actor can imaginatively achieve this "circle of concentration," which might vary in size from the entire stage to a single point or object. Similarly, Viola Spolin, the noted improvisation teacher, centers her method on what she calls the "point of concentration," "a chosen agreed object (or event) on which to focus," which transports the player, giving him energy, yet also provides artistic detachment.[21]

It is ironic that the way to achieve focus is not through trying to exclude inappropriate thoughts and sensations, but by achieving greater *responsiveness* to appropriate ones. For example, the actor should not try to blot the presence of the audience out of his mind, a negative approach that is doomed to failure. Short of death, thinking can never be turned off—try not to think of your mother for the next five minutes! Instead, if he finds the audience distracting, the actor should increase his awareness of his stage environment, including props ("all the little knick-knacks" for Kostya), or the way the lighting falls on a piece of furniture, or the sound of his partner's voice. Stanislavski tells an anecdote about a Hindu maharajah who chose a minister by announcing that he would take only the man who could walk around the top of the city walls holding a dish filled to the brim with milk, without spilling a drop. Various candidates attempted the feat while the maharajah's soldiers yelled at them and fired off guns. The candidate who finally succeeded explained his method: "I was watching the milk."[22] He did not try to exclude the sounds of the shouting and gunfire from his consciousness, but instead focused his attention on the point of concentration, the bowl of milk itself.

Techniques that take the actor's attention away from the performance, like Uta Hagen's hypothetical substitutions, are damaging to focus. Images drawn from personal life may be of help in rehearsal, when you are still seeking the character, but they are not good to *play*. Not only did the maharajah's minister not try to blot out the sounds of the soldiers, he also did not try to think about things extrinsic to the event—the teachings of his religion, say, or the love of his parents. He watched the milk.

Isolation, relaxation, focus, and responsiveness, then, tend to stimulate the creative state in acting, while their opposites tend to hamper it. The unconscious mind is complex, containing both drives and repressions whose results cannot be easily predicted; thus every actor, no matter how good, will sometimes have failures even when all the conditions seem to be right, and will also sometimes have successes, even when they may seem all wrong. In other words, these conditions are means and not ends. Years ago, I had a friend who was working backstage for the American tour of a British play with an all-star cast. It was amazing to him that, in a long technical rehearsal, the actors could nevertheless always perform at peak emotion. Conditions could not have been worse; there was much stopping and starting, it was very late, there were many annoying delays. The actors would often have to start cold in the middle of a scene, yet still managed to come on with a bang. But of course, they had successfully performed their roles many times in London already. When the character is that well established, you can play him almost anywhere—in the shower, on the golf course, in the subway. If the actors had initially had to rehearse under the same kind of trying conditions, they would certainly not have been able to perform at their peaks, if at all. But once your character has been found, and has begun to play you, it is if anything hard to get him out of your head.

SEVEN

THE ACTOR'S SUBJECTIVITY: FINDING THE CHARACTER

Freud distinguished two types of mental functioning, which he called *primary-process* and *secondary-process* thinking. The former is characteristic of the unconscious: it is associative, using various techniques of *displacement*,[1] in which one mental image quickly and easily shifts to another; it ignores space and time; it is wish-fulfilling, being governed by what Freud called the *pleasure principle*. The latter is characteristic of the conscious mind: It is analytical, obeying laws of grammar and logic; it observes the categories of space and time; it is governed by the *reality principle*.

Primary-process thinking occurs first, both in evolution and in the developing human being. Thus, it resembles the way an animal "thinks," not by analyzing events but by responding to them. When a chipmunk sees the shadow of a hawk, it does not sit around analyzing it, but immediately runs for cover. The shadow "means" danger in a direct, associative way. The developing infant first learns to make associations of this direct and immediate kind and only much later learns the more formal way of thinking, in the secondary-process mode. Nevertheless, Freud maintained that primary-process thinking continues in the unconscious mind, where it emerges in things like dreams, slips of the tongue, and jokes, all of which express displacement rather than logic.

Freud's view of these two modes of thought has been criticized as too narrow. He tended to see secondary-process thinking as the better of the two, more mature, advanced, and civilized, with primary-process characteristic only of relatively trivial mental activity. The psychoanalyst Charles Rycroft writes:

> Of the two types of mental functioning he was describing, one, the verbal mode, was characteristic of the ego, of consciousness, of health, of rational adaptation to the environment, and the other, the non-verbal, iconic mode, was irrational and characteristic of dreamers, neurotics, lunatics, infants and primitive peoples; ... the capacity to use the former was dependent on repression of the latter.[2]

Rycroft goes on to insist that instead, "primary and secondary processes co-exist from the beginning of life and ... continue to function in harmony with one another, one providing the imaginative, the other the rational basis of living."[3] Both types of thinking are equally important, though for any given task one or the other may predominate. Even so, neither is ever completely excluded: Mathematics obviously involves secondary-process thinking, but mathematicians use far more imagination and intuition in solving problems than was once believed. Artistic creation (something that Freud always had trouble with, though he was no philistine) involves primary-process thinking, but logical analysis plays a part too. In this chapter, I want to discuss the actor's inspiration, his "finding the character," which, as we have seen, is so crucial to good acting. This mainly involves primary-process thinking, but, as we shall see, secondary-process (though it can actually be destructive when improperly applied) is important as well.

When the actor is in the elusive creative mood discussed in the last chapter, he is then responsive to some trigger, something that gets the character started. Before this triggering occurs, his acting feels labored and false; afterward, there is a feeling of rightness and a flow of creative energy that can carry him through to a finished characterization. He seeks the character until, if all goes well, the character finds him. This triggering can occur at any time (or never!): before rehearsals even begin; at the first reading, when the actor hears his own voice speaking the character aloud in the context of the other actors' voices; at an apparently random moment during rehearsal when things are going especially well; late in the rehearsal period (to the relief of the actor and director!) when props or lighting or the costume are added; opening night, when the presence of the audience provides a special impetus; or even (God forbid) during a performance *after* opening night. It often happens very quickly, at a single rehearsal or performance, which is why I have described it as triggering, but it can also happen more gradually, as the character sneaks up on you unawares.

Stanislavski maintained that all good acting was character acting. Although the Actors Studio made Stanislavski their idol, when they promulgated the myth of "playing yourself," with real, personal emotion, they were actually going against one of his basic principles. In this regard, Stanislavski's biographer, Jean Benedetti, has noted that although Stanislavski was a tall, handsome actor who might have been considered a leading-man type, "he was not a personality actor and was never good at playing himself."[4] Benedetti quotes him as saying, "Deprived of the characteristics of a role I felt completely naked on stage and it was pure embarrassment for me to stand in front of an audience as myself."[5] Based on his own experiences, and his loathing of the star system, which exploited actors' personal attributes, Stanislavski repeatedly condemned personality acting in his writings.

Nevertheless, the myth of playing yourself continues to survive; there are many who would insist that, although character acting may indeed be the best kind, some fine actors do not change when they perform. Robert Brustein, writing on the occasion of the death of Sir Laurence Olivier, was merely expressing a commonly held view when he compared him with Sir John Gielgud: "Gielgud lacks Olivier's art of transformation.... Gielgud is open to new material, but invariably imprints it with his own personal style."[6] Maybe so, but this is not how it feels to Gielgud. In fact, he maintains that only after he began to think in terms of finding the character did he begin to succeed as an actor:

> Of course, all acting should be character acting, but in those days I did not realize this.... My own personality kept interfering, and I began to consider how I was looking, whether my walk was bad, how I was standing; my attention was continually distracted and I could not keep inside the character I was trying to represent. In Trofimov [in Chekhov's *The Cherry Orchard*, with the Russian director Theodore Komisarjevsky] for the first time I looked in the glass and thought, "I know how this man would speak and move and behave," and to my great surprise I found I was able to keep that picture in my mind throughout the action, without my imagination deserting me for a moment, and to lose myself completely as my appearance and the circumstances of the play seemed to demand.[7]

Photographs of Gielgud as Trofimov do not show him looking noticeably different from his other roles; nor did he apparently change his voice much. For some actors, the self-transformation into the character is subtle—a tilt of the head, a new part in the hair, a slightly slower way of speaking. Merely wearing the character's costumes can be a strong stimulus. (Think how differently you feel when you wear clothes that are unusual for you.) Nor do we automatically rate impressionists like Rich Little or Arte Johnson as great actors just because the changes they make in themselves are drastic. And what does the audience care whether the actor is much different from his ordinary self? There may be some pleasure derived from noting the change, but that is secondary to the experience of the play in front of us. The crucial thing about finding the character is in the actor's subjectivity. With good acting, the actor *always feels different*, as Gielgud did here in playing Trofimov, suddenly knowing what to do when he intuitively identified with the character's image in the mirror.

Thus, although Gielgud maintains that all acting "should be" character acting, in fact, all good acting *is* character acting, as Stanislavski maintained. Even Hollywood movie stars who never change from role to role tend to speak in terms of the character when they discuss performing. Henry Fonda, for example, wrote, "One of the beautiful things about the theatre for me is that it's therapy. I don't have to be me. I've got the mask on."[8] For him, the "mask" was not a physical or vocal one, but rather the opportunity to become exciting and heroic. Such a characterization need not be mere wish fulfillment, however; Robert Redford, a personality actor but also a very fine one, spoke of having been drawn to a recent film role by the fact that "something in him that he can't articulate knows he's gone as far as he's going to go with this life."[9] He simply found the idea of a down-and-out, antiheroic character intriguing. He was not drawn by the character's looks or the sound of his voice, but by his situation.

Thus, even good personality acting is character acting. Although the actor's looks and behavior change little, if at all, from those of his everyday life, his actions take on an aura; they have a "shape." Drinking a cup of tea is no longer just drinking a cup of tea. It now happens in response to imaginary drives, in an imaginary situation; it *means* something to the actor, just as it will mean something to the audience. The fact that the action is now framed changes its nature drastically, just as, say, placing an old pair of shoes on a lighted pedestal in an avant-garde art show changes their nature. The shoes have *become* a work of art, though they were anything but that when they were simply lying in the back of somebody's closet. The personality actor still has to find his character, which is not just his everyday self but an aesthetic transformation of it.

Finding the character is clearly an example of primary-process thinking. It is wish-fulfilling and pleasurable. It is direct and intuitive, a displacement of your sense of self. It is nonlogical, in the sense that it happens by "feel," but it is certainly not irrational. The bias toward reason, science, and technology that is characteristic of our culture (a bias that Freud shared) means that we tend to believe that all thinking that is nonlogical (i.e., primary-process) must be *il*logical, but finding a character is anything but that. It has order and coherence, and is directed toward the rational goal of performing well.

The impulses that trigger a characterization are likely to be primary-process in nature—direct, associative, imaginative. For the same reason, lengthy, logical analysis (i.e., secondary-process thinking) is *not* likely to be effective. This is the root of the anti-intellectualism heard among actors, the notion that "you can't play an idea." Like all clichés, this is largely false—not only is a character an idea, but your concept of your everyday self is an idea as well—but does contain some truth. There are actors who can talk a character to death, who describe it with great sensitivity and even literary sophistication, but who cannot *do* it. In fact, there is a genuine danger in talking about a character too much before you have found it; your creative energy is being channeled into words, descriptions, when it should be channeled into *actions*.

Similarly, there are directors who will also describe the character to death . I recall attending a workshop in which a famous (though not very talented) director spoke for twenty-five minutes about the character of Hamlet in his scene with Gertrude; the actor, who *was* very talented, was in agony, practically begging to be allowed to get up and perform rather than have to listen to more verbiage. Stanislavski, early in his career, indulged in this kind of thing, sitting around a table for weeks reading the play and discussing it with the actors. This no doubt was a relief from the crass, hasty way that plays were usually put on in his day, but he nevertheless came to believe that it was a mistake. Actors need to get up to *speak* and *do* as soon as possible, after only one or two readings to familiarize them with the play; Stanislavski did not believe that plays should be thrown together hastily, but did believe that the extra time should be spent with the actors on their feet performing, with a minimum of discussion, aimed at immediate results. The notion that an actor must first have a full-fledged intellectual model of the character, a mental blueprint which is then merely concretized, is a false view of artistic creation. Instead, the actor must first have an impulse, a mental itch, a trigger, with results that are explored and shaped in rehearsal.

There are three things that commonly provide that first impulse:

1. The actor's own voice
2. An image
3. A gesture.

By the actor's voice I mean the *sound* he produces, which might be as formal as a dialect or as informal as a personalized manner of speaking, like a slight stammer, a rapid tempo, or a high pitch. Voice in the sense of speech, that is, as ordinary, logical discourse, is not likely to prove inspirational. You cannot talk yourself into a role. Some acting teachers have touted a method whereby the actor talks to himself in character throughout a performance in an "inner monologue." Thus, while your partner is speaking, you say to yourself, "Gad, sir, you are a scurvy knave. By heaven, you shall not escape me this time. I'll have you out." Then, on cue, you shout aloud your line from the script, "*En garde!*" It is hard to imagine a stupider approach to acting. For one thing, it assumes that all real thinking is secondary-process—verbal, discursive, tidy. It also assumes that human beings carry on such an inner monologue with themselves all the time, which they certainly do not. Worst of all, it takes the actor's attention away from the play itself into an imaginary inner play of his own (inept) construction, when his attention ought to be on his partner and the meaning of what he is saying. In general, anything that takes the actor's attention away from the play itself in performance is, at best, a dangerous technique, and at worst, an outright destructive one.

With dialect work, it is important to stress that accuracy, per se, is not usually too important. Simon Callow, in his excellent biography of Charles Laughton, remarks that Laughton possessed "an ear that was good without being great (fortunately for him: perfect mimicry is a terrible curse for a creative actor: no great actor has ever possessed it)."[10] Strictly speaking, this is not true: David Garrick was a superb mimic who could regale his friends at parties with impressions of their mutual acquaintances (including both Samuel Johnson *and* Johnson's wife). Marlon Brando is known for practical jokes in which he calls up friends and convinces them he is someone else, using impeccable foreign accents. Nevertheless, Callow's point is a good one. For the actor, mimicking someone's manner of speaking is never an end in itself, as it is with night club impressionists. For one thing, to do a dialect or a stammer too accurately can make a role incomprehensible; the reason that there is a "stage Irishman" or a "stage cockney" is because the real thing would not be understood by most audience members. Far more important, however, is that the goal in doing a dialect or other specialized manner of speaking is not realism but inspiration. The actor seeks that feeling of being different, of having someone else speak through his mouth, which will help him catch fire as the character. Uta Hagen writes that "Laurette Taylor, in *The Glass Menagerie*, did not have an authentic southern speech, but she thought she did, so we believed it too!"[11]

The second kind of effective stimulus for an actor is an *image*. Michael Chekhov, a great acting teacher, stressed image work in his teaching. The student was to seize some image at random in his imagination, then let it change and develop:

> Make a bewitched castle transform itself into a poor hut,
> and vice versa; an old witch become a beautiful young princess;

a wolf turn into a handsome prince. Then start working with moving images, such as a tournament of knights, a growing forest fire, an excited crowd of people, a ballroom with dancing couples or a factory busily at work.[12]

Chekhov later sums up the exercises in imagination as follows:

1. Catch the first image.
2. Learn to follow its independent life.
3. Collaborate with it, asking questions and giving orders.
4. Penetrate the inner life of the image.
5. Develop the flexibility of your imagination.
6. Try to create characters entirely by yourself.
7. Study the technique of incorporating characters.[13]

This is a beautiful evocation of the possibilities of primary-process thinking; it is valuable not just for actors but for any creative artist. Note how it is similar to the process of falling asleep, where one first creates and controls an image, which then turns into a dream, in which the image takes on an independent life. It is characteristic of primary-process thinking for thoughts to seem to become independent from you; though you are actually making them, they seem to be making themselves. Note too how words and phrases like *follow, collaborate, asking questions, giving orders, penetrate* parallel the process of artistic creation that DuFrenne was talking about, in which the artist does *not* start with a fully realized image, but instead has a kind of dialogue with the image as it develops.

In preparing a role, the actor might use almost anything as his image: a portrait from the historical period of the play; the sight of his own costume; the sight of a prop; the sight of his own face, especially as it is made up. The Japanese actor in the traditional Buddhist Noh theatre gazes at his mask for a long time before putting it on, with the goal of having its spirit possess him. We do not today believe that possession literally happens, but it certainly happens in his imagination, and can happen to a modern actor even when his "mask" is his own face seen in a mirror, made up for a realistic role. Gielgud's looking in the dressing-room mirror and "seeing" Trofimov is an example of this imaginary possession. Although the face he saw differed little from the one he had seen in the bathroom mirror that morning, he still felt that he was seeing the character rather than just himself.

Many actors, however, require a drastic physical change as a basis for characterization. Laurence Olivier liked striking makeups, often including a false nose of some kind. Marlon Brando has worn a variety of mustaches, darkened his skin, taken off weight, put it back on again, bleached his hair, shaved it off entirely, put plastic inserts in his nostrils, put cotton inserts in his cheeks, and worn an amazing range of costumes, including the famous T-shirt, a toga, the uniform of an eighteenth-century British naval officer, and a woman's dress. Through it all he has somehow retained the reputation for just playing himself, which shows that even critics are affected by the Strasbergian ideology.

The image may also be verbal. Some actors respond well when directors use metaphors or similes, such as describing the character as a "raging bull," or "like a flame." Even though the director is using language, he is using it in a poetic, primary-process manner, rather than a logical, secondary-process one. It goes without saying that the character is not *literally* a bull or a flame. These are figures of speech, or displacements (to use one of Freud's terms), which evoke a sudden, intuitive awareness of a *similarity* between the character and the image, which the actor may be able to convert into action.

A third source of stimulus for the actor seeking a characterization, which is related to image, is *gesture*. Michael Chekhov stressed this as well, with what he called the "psychological gesture," sometimes abbreviated PG. Thus, if, for example, you were to play a willful, domineering character, filled with hatred and disgust, "you look for a suitable over-all gesture which can express all this in the character." Chekhov appends a drawing showing a possible result, a man thrusting his arm downward and outward, while the rest of his body recoils upward and back away from it. Chekhov describes the full-body gesture as follows:

> It is *strong* and well shaped. When repeated several times it will tend to strengthen your *will*. The direction of each limb, the final position of the whole body as well as the inclination of the head are such that they are bound to call up a *definite desire* for *dominating* and *despotic* conduct. The *qualities* which fill and permeate each muscle of the entire body, will provoke within you feelings of *hatred* and *disgust*. Thus, through the gesture, you penetrate and stimulate the depths of your own psychology [emphasis original].[14]

Here the actor responds not only to the image of the gesture (as seen directly or in a mirror), but to the feeling of it. The word *feeling*, so common in discussions of acting, actually has two meanings: *sensation* and *emotion*. Here the two meanings come together; the physical sensation of the gesture stimulates the emotion appropriate for playing the character. Once the appropriate PG has been found (and Chekhov suggests experimenting, trying several different ones, and gives advice as to what kinds of gestures are most likely to work), it is the trigger for the character. It is not only a practical technique, providing a bodily attitude that can actually be used in performance, but is also a stimulus for artistic creation. The whole character can grow from a single, well-chosen psychological gesture.

The methods of using voice, image, and gesture are obviously related. They all draw on the *character* for inspiration, rather than on the actor's personal life. All are designed to work on your imagination in a direct, associative way. The procedure is wholistic, in contrast with logical, secondary-process thinking, which is step by step; the *whole* dialect or image or gesture affects you all at once. (If it fails to do so, it is best not to analyze it, but to go on to try something else.) The procedure is intuitive rather than rational, but is, again, anything but *ir*rational.

The use of voice (in this artistic way, rather than just working for volume and clarity), image, or gesture is of undoubted value in actor training. Furthermore, every actor and director should be aware of their creative potential in rehearsal, where they are unquestionably better than introspective methods that focus on the actor's personal life rather than on the play. Nevertheless, it should be pointed out that most actors, most of the time, do not consciously use voice, image, or gesture in preparing a role. The actor's main source of inspiration, in most cases, is likely to be the role (in the script, and then in rehearsal), and the play in which it occurs. Instead of drawing on these specialized techniques, the actor just plain does it, rehearsing until he is as good in the role as he can be. There is still a feeling of searching for the character, however; still a feeling of having it find you; still a feeling of becoming somebody different, which is a source of energy. Finding the character may happen quickly or gradually, and may be different from or close to your everyday self, but it happens as result of relatively mundane work with the script and your fellow actors, under the guidance of a hardworking director.

I stress this because there has been an attitude among serious American theatre people for some decades that rehearsals ought somehow always to be magical and special, that just blocking and working the play is hack work. Nevertheless, successful directors do function that way, and the best actors usually prefer it. Although any director worth his salt ought to be able to use, say, psychological gesture, when he thinks it might help an actor, ninety-five percent of rehearsing is sweat—blocking, experimenting, correcting, revising, polishing, pacing. Hack directors and actors do these things too, but rarely with the same patience or sensitivity, or an awareness of what the physical work is doing for the actor's *feel* of the role.

When Stanislavski, late in his career, developed what he called "the Method of Physical Action," many of his older actors resisted it. A stress on blocking and business seemed to be a return to the superficial methods against which Stanislavski had initially rebelled.

Blocking and business were externals, which were supposed to take care of themselves after the actor's internal, emotional work had been done. What Stanislavski realized, however, was that *externals affect internals*, that the physicalization of the role affects the actor emotionally more than any other factor. When speech, positioning, gestures, and movements are done haphazardly, they will stifle the actor's emotions, no matter how earnestly prepared those emotions may be; when the physicalizations are done with care, in keeping with the logic of the role and the play, they will draw the actor out, liberating him into the role.

Working with an actor playing Khlestakov in a scene from Gogol's *The Inspector General*, for example, Stanislavski (again as "Tortsov") makes the following critique:

> Your entrance just now was theatrical, done "in general"; in your movements there was neither logic nor consecutiveness.... You did not even look at Ossip or the bed before you said: "You've been lying around on my bed again." Also, you slammed the door the way they do in the theatre when the sets are made of canvas. You did not remember and you did not convey the weight of the door. The door knob was handled like a toy. All these little physical actions call for a certain amount of attention and time.[15]

The difference between Stanislavski's method here and the traditional hack director simply throwing on a play is enormous. A hack would not have paid the same attention to these details, but would have been satisfied if the actor entered at the right time and place and conveyed a generalized emotion. The Method of Physical Action focuses on specifics, in the logic of the situation. The *magic if* is crucial. Stanislavski applies it stringently: *If* you scold Ossip for lying on the bed, you must see him and the bed first. *If* that contrivance of wood and canvas is supposed to be a door, you must handle it like a door. The director and actors continue like this in scene after scene, over and over, throughout the play.

The Method of Physical Action, alas, requires time, a commodity in short supply in America. At the Moscow Art Theatre, now as in Stanislavski's day, a play will be rehearsed between five hundred and a thousand hours. The American counterpart receives less than two hundred. The lack of true repertory companies here, in which actors on salary can perform at night while rehearsing another play during the day, makes long rehearsals financially difficult; actors have to be paid just for rehearsing, before any revenue comes in. Films rarely have more than a week or two of rehearsal, while television drama usually has only one rehearsal per scene—for the benefit of the technicians, not the actors. (An acquaintance of mine with a long-standing role on a soap opera has never received a single comment on his acting from the show's director.) Furthermore, the Method of Physical Action is unspectacular; it superficially resembles the work of hacks. Compared to the work of, say, Elia Kazan, who would take actors aside during rehearsals for mysterious, whispered conferences about their personal lives, it may seem tame and plodding. It may even seem nit-picking. Would the audience even notice whether Khlestakov looked at the bed or not? Would they care how he handled the doorknob?

Such questions miss the point. The purpose of the Method of Physical Action is not to appease an audience of ruthless reality-testers. Most audience members would probably not notice such things. This method is not aimed at the audience at all, but at the *actor*, as a way of inducing the creative state. As Stanislavski put it, "the point of the physical actions lies not in themselves as such but in what they evoke: conditions, proposed circumstances, feelings."[16] It is a good example of secondary-process thinking working in tandem with primary-process, not by trying directly to will a performance into being, but rather by setting up a framework in which primary-process can flourish. Slowly and carefully, the director is making the world of the play *vivid* for the actor, so that he can respond imaginatively to it. (And, of course, the actor is simultaneously doing much the same thing on his own, exploring the given circumstances of the character and his world in detail.) Primary-process thinking responds to *particulars*, things like mussed beds and doorknobs. Secondary-process thinking generalizes, which can be death to creative activity, but it also analyzes. When analysis is put at the service of primary-process thinking, drawing attention to particulars rather than soaring off into generalizations, creative activity is enhanced.

In fact, the Method of Physical Action is simply a formalization of the way good actors and directors have always worked. (Kazan himself worked this way most of the time.) All successful actors and directors, in all periods, in all styles, whatever their political persuasion, aesthetic theory, or personal predilection, whether working in film, radio, television, or on the stage, share the quality of attention to detail. Bertolt Brecht, who considered Stanislavski in many ways to be his nemesis, nevertheless praised his work in these terms: "In the Moscow Art Theatre every play acquired a carefully thought-out shape and a wealth of subtly elaborated detail. The one is useless without the other."[17]

Patient attention to detail implies a respect for the play*script*.[18] A production, of course, will add unique details of its own, but these are based in turn on those in the script, or else the production will be at war with itself. (The mussed bed and the doorknob are not actually in the dialogue or stage directions of *The Inspector General*, but they follow logically from what is there.) This, alas, is all too often the case these days; a production will seem to have little to do with the script, because of either neglect or consciously-taken liberties. American actors and directors are just not used to examining plays intimately. The Actors Studio approach involves very little study of dramatic literature. Even in university theatre departments, analysis of the playscript for its overall shape and elaborated detail is rare.[19] The trouble is that American theatre people, even when they have widely differing approaches, often seem to agree that respect for text is stuffy and untheatrical. Strasberg represented one extreme: His students rarely performed the classics for him, rarely performed entire plays, and were not encouraged to read dramatic literature systematically. In his memoirs and in recordings of his classes at the Studio, he rarely talked about a play per se, instead teaching relaxation, "emotion memory," and devices similar to Uta Hagen's substitution. But at the opposite extreme of the American theatrical spectrum are avant-garde theorists and practitioners like Lee Breuer, Richard Schechner, Robert Wilson, Richard Foreman, or Andrei Serban, who have vigorously rejected the introspective, psychologistic approach of the Actors Studio, but who share its antiliterary bias. Following Artaud, they see literature as something fixed and dead; their productions usually take ruthless liberties with the text, or use no text at all.

With both extremes rejecting the close study of dramatic literature, it is no wonder that American actors have little respect for it. Neither side seems to recognize that the script must be the richest source of inspiration. We should not respect the text of, say, Shakespeare's *Hamlet* because of its reputation as a wholesome cultural icon, but rather because, to perform it well, we must inevitably deal with all its elaborate specifics, which, if explored with any sensitivity, are a constant source of stimulation. At a recent production of *Hamlet* at the National Theatre in London, Michael Bryant, one of the finest supporting actors in the world, gave a superb new interpretation of Polonius; noting among the given circumstances of the text that the character is Lord Chamberlain, that he is constantly intriguing and manipulating, and that he has both power over and respect from most of the other characters (though not from Hamlet), Bryant made Polonius *authoritative*. He was still pompous and foolish, but he was not just the simple dodderer that he always seemed in the dozens of productions I had seen previously. Using psychological gestures like a strut in his walk and a sharp edge in his tone of voice, Bryant became strong and forceful in the role, ordering characters like Reynaldo around like one used to command. This gave new focus to his conflict with Hamlet, and shed new light on characters like his children Laertes and Ophelia, and even on King Claudius and Queen Gertrude. The court becomes an interesting place when we realize that Polonius is running it, and that his death is a cause of its disintegration.

Bryant's performance demonstrates how to devise a bold new approach to a standard play by *using* the text, rather than by changing it or adding to it. His interpretation arose from the *magic if*—"If I were Lord Chamberlain I would actually be running the court. Events like the play within the play would come under my jurisdiction. Matters of protocol, like the length of the period of mourning for Hamlet's father, would be my responsibility. My children would not only owe me respect as a father, but would prosper or decline according to how well I did my job," and so on. An actor could not work in this manner if he had been trained to look first of all into himself rather than into the play, or if he had been accustomed to working with directors who altered the text at every whim.

To use the Method of Physical Action, one need not be dealing with a classical text, of course. The approach is useful with any kind of play, and, as noted, is not limited to what is written down. In recent years, scholarly critics have taken to using the term *performance text*, to include not just the script but the entire enactment, as developed and created by the director and performers. Using this terminology, we can say that the Method of Physical Action uses for its stimulus the performance text, which subsumes the script into something larger, and different in nature. Initially, the actor uses the *magic if* with the written dialogue and stage directions, but in rehearsal, these become spoken words and physical actions in a unique, imaginary world. As the script is memorized, it becomes, in another sense, forgotten; the actor responds to what is around him rather than to what is on the page.

Nor is the text limited to a work for the stage. The Method of Physical Action applies to all forms of acting, in all media. In film, for example, consider the director Alfred Hitchcock. He was not considered an actor's director; although he worked in the heyday of the Actors Studio, he had no use for its approach. Not only did he not like to coach actors, he actually found the shooting of a film boring. To him, the interesting part of filmmaking was in writing the script and developing the "storyboard," drawings of the film's shots that are sketched in advance by an artist, and then placed in sequence so that they tell the story visually. Yet despite Hitchcock's lack of interest in acting as an art, some of Hollywood's best actors, like James Stewart or Cary Grant, worked with him again and again, and some weak ones, like Doris Day or Tippi Hedren, gave their best performances by far in his films. The explanation for this paradox lies in the storyboard technique itself. This was his performance text, making the story of the film so clear and compelling that the actors themselves responded to it. Vividly showing them what he wanted, and then shooting that story with meticulous attention to its details (like all good directors, whether in theatre or film), was worth more than all the psychological gropings and agitations in the world could ever be. The Method of Physical Action recognizes that *knowing what the play or film demands of the actor is more than half the job.* But finding those demands is no easy task; they must be sought with patience and insight and love.

EIGHT

THE MIND–BODY PROBLEM

Sometime in the 1770s, the French *philosophe* Denis Diderot wrote an essay on acting entitled *"Le Paradoxe sur le comédien"* (*"The Paradox of the Actor"*). The exact date is uncertain, since it was not published until 1830, long after his death. In the essay, as the title implies, Diderot maintained that the actor on stage exhibits an important paradox; what he appears to do is not what he is actually doing. In particular, the actor could not be feeling the emotions he displays. "If the actor were full, really full, of feeling, how could he play the same part twice running with the same spirit and success? Full of fire at the first performance, he would be worn out and cold as marble at the third." In place of this apparent impossibility, Diderot proposed a dualistic model of the actor: "He must have in himself an unmoved and disinterested onlooker." The inner actor would be to the outer actor as a rider is to his horse or a puppet master is to his puppet; he commands, guides, and controls, but feels nothing. He must have "penetration but no sensibility."[1]

Like most misleading theories of acting, this dualistic model is based on logical deduction rather than on actual experience. Diderot himself was not an actor, nor is there any evidence of actors of his day, or previously, describing their performing in this manner. (In fact, an earlier French work of the period, which Diderot was trying to rebut, stressed the actor's *need* for emotion.)[2] The closest thing to his theory would be the antitheatrical prejudice—the actor as liar, dissembler, impostor, etc. Nevertheless, Diderot was not antitheatrical. The whole thrust of his essay is to *praise* the actor, to point out his similarity to other artists, and to extol his unacknowledged craft. "At the very moment when he touches your heart he is listening to his own voice; his talent depends not, as you think, upon feeling, but upon rendering so exactly the outward signs of feeling, that you fall into the trap."[3]

The immediate inspiration for Diderot's essay was his acquaintance with the great English actor David Garrick, who visited Paris in the winter of 1764–65. Garrick would entertain friends at private gatherings by putting his head through folding doors and, in a few seconds, express half a dozen widely ranging emotions. No one seemed to find this amusing exercise especially paradoxical, however, until Diderot came along. Garrick obviously could not have felt and then *un*felt such a range of emotions so quickly, at least not at the intensity that they were being shown. Diderot, however, reached the conclusion that Garrick was feeling *nothing at all*, but was in fact controlling his face in an entirely mechanical way, as if by pulling strings.

To describe an actor as mechanical would today be derogatory. (Stanislavski repeatedly uses the term as a rebuke; for him, the only thing worse than mechanical acting is the kind that flaunts beauty or handsomeness for its own sake.) As Joseph R. Roach has shown in his recent fascinating study, *The Player's Passion*, however, the opposite was the case in the eighteenth century. Machines were new and seemed wonderful, almost alive. Moreover, Newton's magnificent accomplishment in formulating the laws of motion led people to extend the concept of mathematically ordered activity to the natural level. Books were written comparing animals and humans to machines.[4] Thus, when Diderot wrote in *Le Paradoxe* of "a machine so complex as the human body,"[5] he was using a standard metaphor for his time, one that expressed amazement and respect rather than disparagement. Only in the Romantic era did writers like Coleridge and Schlegel attack this attitude, contrasting the mechanical with the organic, a distinction that remains in our criticism of the arts today, including acting, where the latter is definitely considered to be superior to the former.

Roach's point is well taken. It is always important to read commentaries on acting in the context of their times; they were always written in response to particular problems or disputes, and also typically reflect background attitudes so widespread that they often remain unexpressed. Thus, Darwin and Freud have had considerable influence on writers on acting today, even though they may rarely quote them directly. Similarly, Diderot was writing under the influence of René Descartes (though he is not mentioned in "*Le Paradoxe*"), the French philosopher who in the previous century had developed a model of the human being that soon gained wide acceptance. Descartes, responding to the rising scientific spirit of the age (especially the mechanical discoveries of Galileo), found himself in a dilemma. As Gilbert Ryle put it, "As a man of scientific genius he could not but endorse the claims of mechanics, yet as a religious and moral man he could not accept ... that human nature differs only in degree of complexity from clockwork."[6] Descartes's solution was to see mind and body as polar opposites, two entirely different kinds of substance. The mind had free will, but the body, subject to the newly discovered mechanical laws, did not. The two interacted deep inside the brain, in the pineal gland.

This dualistic model of the human being, which Ryle called "the dogma of the Ghost in the Machine,"[7] dominated Western thinking for centuries. It is clearly related to our traditional Christian view of the immortal soul as something different from, and separable from, the body, but is even more polarized. Ancient views of the soul, whether Jewish, Greek, or Christian, tended to see it not as a separate "thing," but as a generating principle. In Plato's metaphysics, for example, ideas are the ultimate reality; a particular chair is not as real as the idea of a chair, which the carpenter used to make the physical one. The idea of the chair is perfect, but any particular chair has defects. Similarly, the human soul is the idea of the human being, which generated him; although my physical self is full of aches and pains, not to mention scars and grey hairs, my soul is perfect. It is not *invisible*, however; just as we can infer the idea of a chair from looking at a physical one, we can infer a person's soul from looking at him and thinking about him. Thus, far from considering a person's true self to be hidden, ancient writers composed treatises on how to determine a person's character from his face; Aristotle, for example, maintained that large-headed people were mean, while those with small faces were steadfast, those with broad ones were stupid, and those with round ones were courageous.[8] Descartes's model, however, put mind (in French, his word *esprit* can mean mind, spirit, or soul) in a totally private place. Its workings cannot be seen or inferred by observers. Only the individual knows what is going on in his own mind.

This extreme dualism can be related to the lifestyle in Western civilization. Our culture splits public and private to an extreme degree. We spend far more time indoors than people did, or do, in other cultures. A room of one's own at home or an office of one's own at work is considered highly desirable. Bodily functions are carried on in private; to use the toilet in the building where I am writing this book (note that I am already indoors) requires that I pass through two doors into the men's room, and then enter a cubicle. It is interesting to contrast this with the imperial latrine, excavated at Rome, which has two marble toilet seats, side by side; the Roman emperor required much less privacy than I do! Similarly, we are exceedingly careful about keeping our bodies covered with clothing. In most other cultures, clothing is only an embellishment; nudity is simply the lack of something. Thus, in the ancient world, gods and heroes were always depicted as being naked; their bodies were so perfect that, unlike humans, they did not need clothing. In the same vein, athletes in the Olympic games always had to compete in the nude, which was a puritanical regulation rather than a sensual one. Adam and Eve in the Bible, after the fall, see each other's nakedness and are mortified because they have no adornment; they are not sexually aroused, but only "afraid" *(Genesis* 2:10). Milton's version in *Paradise Lost*, however, has them inflamed with "carnal desire":

> He on Eve
> Began to cast lascivious eyes; she him
> As wantonly repaid; in lust they burn,
> Till Adam thus 'gan Eve to dalliance move. (IX.1013-16)

Adam and Eve are exposing more than their bodies now; they are exposing their secret, sexual selves. This changed attitude toward nudity is part of the same cultural frame of mind that influenced Descartes, Milton's contemporary. In "Cartesian dualism," a human being is believed to have a hidden, private self that is always different from his public self.

Related to this view, and perhaps a cause of it, was the rise of capitalism with its implicit philosophy of extreme individualism. Rather than seeing himself as a member of a fief, a guild, a parish, or a town, with a fixed position in an elaborate social hierarchy, a person under capitalism is an entrepreneur free to advance himself— or to fail!—according to his own worth. Nowhere was this philosophy more eagerly embraced than in the United States, where, in the late twentieth century, it is becoming more exaggerated than ever; traditional ties to family, political party, school, neighborhood, company, or trade union seem to be disappearing, so that the individual floats in a vacuum. It is not surprising, therefore, that the American approach to acting should be so ruthlessly individualistic, stressing self at the expense of text, fellow actors, artistic value, or social benefit. Unlike actors in foreign countries, who typically belong to long-established repertory companies, the American actor is an individual entrepreneur, who sells himself, and looks only to himself in preparing a role.

Diderot's application of Cartesian dualism to acting laid the groundwork for performance theory for the next two centuries. Just as Catholics and Protestants, no matter how bitterly they may disagree, share underlying assumptions about Christianity, so too acting theorists, no matter how much they disputed, accepted Diderot's polarization of the actor. Some were "internalists," some were "externalists," and some called for a balance of the two. Furthermore, as we shall see, the theorists have by no means been consistent as to exactly *what* is internal or external. All, however, tended to take it for granted that an actor comes in two separate parts—a visible, audible exterior and a totally hidden interior.

A famous example is the dispute in the late nineteenth century between the French actor Coquelin and the English actor Henry Irving. Coquelin, following Diderot, published an article in which he maintained that the actor has a dual nature, with a detached internal observer controlling the external persona: "The two natures which coexist in the actor are inseparable, but it is the first self, the one which *sees*, which should be the master. This is the soul, the other is the body."[9] For Coquelin, more than for Diderot, the crucial problem was one of *control*:

> The actor ought never to let his part "run away" with him. It is false and ridiculous to think that it is a proof of the highest art for the actor to forget that he is before the public. If you identify yourself with your part to the point of asking yourself, as you look at the audience, "What are all those people doing here?"—if you have no more consciousness where you are and what you are doing—you have ceased to be an actor: you are a madman. Conceive Harpagon climbing the balustrade and seizing the orchestra by the throats, loudly demanding the restoration of his casket![10]

This is certainly a sensational instance. Such extreme identification would indeed be a disaster (though some avant-garde performers today might find the idea appealing), but the example is fortunately hypothetical. It just plain never happens that an actor becomes so emotionally carried away with the role that he becomes a danger to his fellow actors or, as here, the audience. In thirty-five years in the theatre, I have occasionally come across actors who claimed to have identified so totally with the character that they lost control. In the first place, I never believed them—they were obviously saying it to impress their fellow actors—and in the second place, they were never very good. Perhaps it has really happened somewhere, just as there was supposed to be a frontier audience that got so carried away by a performance of *Othello* that they tried to lynch the actor playing Iago. But the danger of too much emotion that Coquelin was melodramatically evoking is hardly a serious one. Nor did he see any parallel difficulty in having the *audience* become so emotional that they run up and seize *Harpagon* by the throat, though Coquelin could hardly have denied that the actor's aim is to achieve an emotional response in the spectators. And what about the opposite problem? The actor who is too tame and inhibited is certainly more common than the one who is seized with an uncontrollable frenzy. Coquelin assumed that the body, of which the soul should be master, is like a spirited thoroughbred, but what if it is a tired old nag?

Responding to Coquelin's article with one of his own, Henry Irving thus took a more balanced view. The actor should "make his feelings a part of his art," but should have "a double consciousness, in which all the emotions proper to the occasion may have full swing, while the actor is all the time on the alert for every detail of his method."[11] The model is still one of Cartesian dualism and still takes the problem of control very seriously. The assumption is that the mind is a kind of autocrat, capable of exacting immediate, total obedience from the body if it steps out of line. Joseph Jefferson, an American actor contemporary with Irving, supported his position, stating, "I know I act best when the heart is warm and the head is cool."[12] (This, in turn, echoed a slogan of the French actor Albert Lambert *père*, "*le coeur chaud, la tête froide.*") But what cools the head, if it insists on being hot? And, on the other hand, if the heart is cold to begin with (a problem no one ever seems to have acknowledged, though it is a common one), how does a cool head warm it up?

Inspired by the dispute between Coquelin and Irving and by Diderot's "*Le Paradoxe,*" the Scottish critic, author, and translator William Archer surveyed actors of his time to see whether they did indeed feel the emotions they were portraying. He published the results in 1888 as part of a book he called *Masks or Faces?* In it, he pointed out, correctly, that "the controversy is entirely modern."[13] Ancient writers, for all their tendency to attack actors as liars and impostors, assumed without question that they felt emotion in performance. Plato even *attacked* actors for their emotional involvement, which he felt was all too easily transmitted to the audience; emotion was evil and infectious. There is also an ancient anecdote about a Greek actor named Polus who carried the ashes of his own dead son on stage in an urn in order to stimulate himself emotionally when playing Electra, carrying the ashes of Orestes, her brother.[14] Only in modern times did anyone notice a paradox about emotion in acting.

Archer's survey showed, unsurprisingly, that most actors claimed to feel emotion while acting. It is interesting to note that typically their feelings were inspired by the *play*, rather than, like modern Strasbergians or the ancient Polus, by their personal lives. One actress remarked that "I have acted the part of Leah [in Augustin Daly's *Leah the Forsaken*] for twenty-four years, and the tears always come to my eyes when the little child says 'My name is Leah.'"[15] On the other hand, most of the actors also maintained that they felt a kind of double consciousness on stage, watching themselves while they felt the emotions, which seemed to vindicate Diderot and Coquelin. For example, Johnston Forbes-Robertson, a leading actor of the day, wrote of "one stratum, the part, the creature I am for the time; the other, that part of my mind which circumstances and the surroundings compel me to give up to all things coming under the head of mechanical execution."[16] Archer called this phenomenon "Brownies of the Brain."

A crucial factor, however, was that the actors never spoke of the inner, observing self as directly *controlling* the outer self, the way Diderot and Coquelin described it. The relationship between inner and outer was *aesthetic* rather than dominant. The comments of the young actress Janet Achurch (famous for her performances in Ibsen and a champion of "the New Drama") are typical: "The only double line of thought I like to have on the stage is a mental criticism of my own performance: 'I got that exclamation better than last night,' or 'I'm sure I'm playing this scene slower than usual,' and so on."[17] Of course, there is always some feedback from the observing self into the performance; Achurch might well have been able to adjust her acting according to what she was observing. She might have tried to build on the good exclamation in the first instance or tried to speed up her performance in the second. But this is not the same thing as saying that the observing self is *causing* the entire performance.

Confusion arises because, of course, the actress's *brain* is managing her entire body and thus is indeed generating her performance. But brain is much more than *mind*, and mind is much more than *consciousness*. The brain regulates many of the activities of the body, like the beating of the heart or the secretions of internal organs, that are involuntary, and thus completely beyond conscious control. Other activities are semivoluntary; we can consciously control our breathing (though never completely), but most of the time it just happens without our thinking about it. Finally, most of the voluntary behavior carried on by humans, though intelligent and well-organized, operates on a kind of automatic pilot. If I want to, I can think about the movement of each muscle in my legs as I walk across the room (and originally, when I was learning how, I had to), but most of the time I do not; the activity has become habitual and autonomous. This is a good thing, too. If I had to think about

109

everything I did, sending out conscious orders to my body according to the model of Cartesian dualism, I would have a hard time even getting out of bed in the morning.

Besides, if we think of Archer's "Brownies of the Brain" as actually running the performance, that does not really solve the paradox. Are the brownies flawless? When Achurch noticed that her performance was going slowly, did that mean a brownie had made a mistake? Perhaps there has to be another brownie watching the first, to correct it. One of the actresses whom Archer surveyed, Clara Morris, actually maintained she had a *triple* consciousness, but why stop there? The lineup of brownies is theoretically endless. But even if we accept this ludicrous notion, there are still other problems. Take the example of an inexperienced actor who finds simple acts like walking, sitting, and standing on stage extremely difficult and performs them awkwardly. Surely his body is not entirely at fault—he does these things fairly skillfully every day, offstage. The source of his immediate problem is his mental state. And would we not describe this state as one of *self-consciousness*? Here, there is too much observing going on, rather than too little. He needs to get his attention away from himself—get those brownies off his back, as it were—and onto his surroundings, his fellow actors, and the goals of his character in the scene.

The dual consciousness of the actor is a genuine phenomenon. The actor certainly has a feeling of watching himself, and when all is going well, it is a pleasurable sensation that enhances the performance. It does not manage the performance *directly*, however, but instead is part of the creative mood that gives a performance energy. Stanislavski, ever mindful of the actor's subjectivity, wrote:

> I divided myself, as it were, into two personalities. One continued as an actor, the other was an observer.
> Strangely enough this duality not only did not impede, it actually promoted my creative work. It encouraged and lent impetus to it.[18]

Kostya's duality promoted his creativity because he was *enjoying his own performance as he watched it.* The actor responds to his own acting much as the audience does. When a performance is going well, the resultant pleasure induces a general feeling of confidence and delight that relaxes the actor and releases his power. When a performance is going badly, however, self-consciousness is distinctly not pleasurable, and, as in the case of the inexperienced actor, may even be the cause of his poor acting.

Furthermore, even during a good performance, when something goes wrong on stage—a dropped object, a forgotten line, a flubbed piece of business—the observing self does not start pulling strings and shouting orders to the outer self, as we would expect from the Diderot/Coquelin model. Instead, the feeling of doubleness *disappears.* Galvanized into action—or, conversely, paralyzed into inaction—the actor loses his aesthetic appreciation of his own performance.

The American experience with Cartesian dualism in acting theory in the twentieth century contains an unacknowledged paradox of its own. Because of their anti-emotional stance, we have come to call Diderot and Coquelin externalists, but they were anything but that. The performance was supposed to be controlled from *within*, by the conscious mind. What Strasberg and his followers have done is to take over Diderot's and Coquelin's *in*ternalism and give it an opposite value. Before the twentieth century, dualists in acting theory tended to identify emotion with the actor's *body*; reason was inside, emotions outside. Furthermore, they assumed that plenty of emotion was always available; extremists wanted to stamp it out, while moderates only wanted to keep it under watchful control. Strasberg, on the other hand, associated emotion with the actor's *mind*; emotions were now inside, while the outside, the body, was associated with "externals" like speech, movement, and technical polish generally. In other words, he reversed the traditional polarity.

In addition, Strasberg recognized the problem that previous dualists had overlooked: "How do you stimulate the heart to be warm?"[19] Every technique he developed was in answer to that question. As for the traditional problem of controlling emotion, Strasberg simply shrugged it off. He assumed that any good actor would always have plenty of self control, just as his predecessors assumed that any good actor would always have plenty of emotion. When actors went too far in one of his classes (which happened much less often than was popularly believed), he merely scolded them like naughty children. David Garfield, historian of the Actors Studio and a worshiper of Strasberg, writes, for example, "During the late fifties and sixties, on the rare occasion when a Studio actor proceeded to remove all of his clothes, Strasberg would take him to task for indulging in a meaningless exhibition, and tell him to keep away from the exercise."[20] Austere, reserved, and domineering, Strasberg by his very presence forestalled excessive behavior in his classes. Many have noted the paradox that Strasberg, himself emotionally cold and rather prudish, should have laid so much stress on emotion in acting. Actually, this was not paradoxical at all, but consistent: In the theatre, as in his personal life, the problem for him was always to *express* emotion, not to keep it in check.

A major thrust of twentieth-century philosophy has been to reject the mind-body polarity. It is not that philosophers now see mind and body as being the same. Rather, they have objected to Descartes's setting mind and body as equal and opposite kinds of substance. Gilbert Ryle, in his classic *Concept of Mind*, called this a "category mistake." It is wrong, said Ryle, to present facts belonging to one category in terms that are appropriate to another. Mind is not a special kind of substance, it is not a substance at all. He gave an analogy of a foreigner visiting Oxford or Cambridge for the first time: "[He] is shown a number of colleges, libraries, playing fields, museums, scientific departments and administrative offices. He then asks, 'But where is the University?'"[21] Of course, the university is different from its colleges, libraries, etc., considered individually, but it is not some additional, special building or department. Instead, it is *all of its parts*, considered as a whole. Similarly, mind, though not a summation of the parts of the body, is nonetheless a means of organizing body behavior and should not be considered another, albeit special, body part. In Ryle's view, the mind is not hidden; when you see me behaving intelligently, you are seeing the workings of my mind. It makes no more sense to speak of my mind being hidden in my body than it would to say that Oxford is hidden within its campus.

Of course, I can hide the workings of my mind, as I would if I told a lie, just as I can hide my emotions by suppressing them. But as another modern philosopher, Ludwig Wittgenstein, pointed out, the fact that the dualistic model of a mind hidden in a body works well for a person who is falsifying or deceiving does not mean that it is appropriate when he is being truthful. Most of the time, the mind is *not* hidden. It is especially misleading to think of it as always operating behind the scenes, because that leads to a model in which every bit of outward behavior must first be completely formulated inside, which is just plain false. You do not first have to say something to yourself and then say it aloud. (The ludicrous "inner monologue" approach to acting carries this false implication, among others.) You do not first have to feel something "inside," and then merely "express" the emotion outside. And you certainly do not have to formulate a conscious thought of what you intend to do before you actually do it.

Descartes and his followers, in the theatre and elsewhere, put far too much emphasis on human *consciousness*. One does not have to be a Freudian to see that there are unconscious components to the mind. In this regard, Ryle distinguished two kinds of thinking: "Knowing how and knowing that."[22] Either one can exist without the other. Knowing *that* a golf swing is a double pendulum subject to Newton's Laws of Motion does not mean that you know how to hit a golf ball. Learning Newton's Laws might be of some help to a golfer, but most golf champions have probably never heard of them.

Similarly, I know more about acting than Laurence Olivier did—many of his observations on the subject strike me as terribly naive, in fact—yet he obviously knew *how* to act much better than I do. The two kinds of knowing can interact; I have tried to draw upon my limited know-how of acting in formulating the theories in this book, and, conversely, some of you who read the theories may ultimately become better actors as a result. But the causality would not be *direct*. I would certainly never maintain that only through a comprehensive, conscious understanding of acting theory can you become a good actor.

Conscious thought, which is "knowing that," does often take place away from view. I can contemplate Newton's Laws without your having any idea what I am thinking about. But knowing *how* cannot really be hidden. I can hide my ability to play golf well by pretending to be a duffer, but I cannot hide it while I am playing skillfully. There is no way simultaneously to pretend to be bad and to experience being good.

Besides, the actor is not really pretending in this sense. The audience knows full well what he is doing. We can think of him as hiding his true self from us if we wish, but that is not how it usually seems to the audience, nor how it usually seems to the actor himself. I might just as well say that an automobile mechanic, working on my car, is "hiding" his at-home self as a husband and father, since he is not showing me that self. But the mechanic is not hiding his mechanical skill; nor does he achieve that skill by having the unseen husband/father self manipulate his hands. Like the actor in performance, he is absorbed in his work, whose mental component is fully apparent as it progresses.

Acting, then, is a skill, a "knowing how." The actor not only has to know how to act in general terms—how to stand and move on stage, how to hit the mark in filming, how to project his voice, how to articulate well, and so on—but has to learn how to act a particular role, scene by scene and line by line. Trying to find the character is learning *how*. The false model, in which the actor first must have a full-fledged idea of the character in his consciousness, was debunked above in Chapter 5. Dufrenne showed how artists in general do not start with a fully developed concept, but become engaged in a dialogue with the art work as it develops, inspired by the creation itself to develop and improve that creation. The dualistic model of the actor, which comes down to us from Diderot through a variety of shifts of emphasis, is particularly inhibiting to this dialogue. Coquelin, who insisted that the actor should feel nothing, and Strasberg, who insisted on intense emotion, both erroneously believed that the actor's artistic creation takes place entirely inside, as a conscious, fully developed concept, a "knowing that," which is then merely realized outwardly. There is no place in such a model for the outside to affect the inside. Artistic creation flows in one direction only, from within to without. Externals like costuming, props, blocking, and even the playwright's words are unimportant artistically—they are of course unavoidable, but they have no more artistic significance than a printing press has to a poem or a movie projector to a film. The actor has indeed become a ghost in a machine.

In place of Cartesian dualism, we need an integrated model of acting that sees it as a skilled, felt activity. Despite the phenomenon of double consciousness, the actor is not really doing two separate things, and should not think of himself as being in two separate parts. Responding to both internal and external stimuli, he both thinks and feels, but most important, he is *involved* in the activity rather than detached from it.

It is interesting to contrast acting today with sports, a type of performing that has not been affected by Cartesian dualism. No one thinks it odd when an athletic coach shifts easily from an emotional appeal to do or die for Old Siwash to a technical description of how to step into a pitch or to make a tackle. These are simply different *aspects* of the same performance behavior. It is taken for granted that not only does an athlete think, feel, and perform simultaneously, but that his thinking and feeling are readily apparent for all to see and

judge. If the coach compliments an athlete for a "smart play" or
scolds him for a half-hearted one, the player does not indignantly
reply that the coach could not possibly know what was going on
inside him. The thought or feeling were implicit in the action.

With acting, we should similarly recognize that "internal" and
"external" are *only metaphors*, rather than literal descriptions. Instead
of imagining that an actor first thinks and then acts, or first feels and
then acts, we should recognize that, like the athlete, he is thinking,
feeling, and acting *all at once*, with a growing degree of skill as the
role is learned in rehearsal. Furthermore, his thinking and feeling
are implicit in his acting, rather than mysterious entities hidden
behind it. The crucial thing is not to invoke thought and feeling like
elusive ghosts, but to examine his performance for consistency and
potency.

Like the athletic coach, the director or the actor himself should
feel no compunction about shifting back and forth in describing the
work in internal or external terms. There is nothing wrong with
saying both, "Cross down left," and, "Humiliate the bastard." Each
is simply a different rhetorical approach to the same problem of
achieving a good performance. It has become anathema in the
American theatre to suggest that emotional blockage might be the
result of being in the wrong position on stage, or that a different
costume might evoke a better performance, or that the rhythms of
Shakespeare's verse are the key to a character's emotions. Yet in
actual practice these things are obviously true to anyone not blinded
by the ideology of Cartesian dualism. Emotion flows both ways;
externals affect internals as well as vice-versa. Acting is a complex
process, which can be described in many different *ways*, but which is
not many different *things*.

NINE

EMOTION AS PROCESS

Believers in Cartesian dualism have usually implied that the successful actor feels exactly what the character feels, or else feels nothing at all. The former position raises questions of repetition (how can the actor feel something so intense as Othello's jealousy, night after night?) and of control (how can the actor then avoid killing the poor actress playing Desdemona?), while the latter disputes documented evidence not only from William Archer's nineteenth-century survey, but from interviews and memoirs of countless actors since. Attempts at an intermediate position, which describe the actor as feeling the character's emotions under the watchful eye of an autocratic consciousness, also go against documentation; actors rarely describe their experiences that way. Besides, as shown in the last chapter, twentieth-century psychology and philosophy have mustered powerful arguments against that kind of "ghost in the machine" model.

Is there a third possibility, that the actor feels emotions that are *different* from those of the character? Most theorists of acting have never considered such a possibility, but there are exceptions: George Henry Lewes, a nineteenth-century English writer whose book, *On Actors and the Art of Acting*, remains a classic of performance criticism, attempted to resolve the problem of control by suggesting that, although the actor feels real emotion, this emotion is *weaker* than it would be in real life, and therefore controllable. "He is in a state of emotional excitement sufficiently strong to furnish him with the elements of expression," he wrote, "but not strong enough to disturb his consciousness of the fact that he is only imagining."[1] Making the actor's emotions appear tamed and unthreatening does not do justice to the acting experience, which is intense and exhilarating. Nevertheless, Lewes's approach is valuable, particularly in his emphasis on imagining, which suggests that the emotions are of a different nature than they would be in everyday life. Nor does he insist that the emotions the actor is *imagining* are the same as those of the character, stressing only the actor's "state of emotional excitement." The character might be suffering agony, in this view, while the actor felt elation.

Twentieth-century aesthetic theory tends to support the idea that the emotion the actor feels on stage differs from emotions in everyday life not so much in degree as in kind. All the arts are seen as operating through conventionalized signs, no matter how raw, direct, or natural the art work may seem. This does not mean that artistic creation or artistic response is a cold, mechanical, unfeeling process, however. Quite the opposite, in fact; the signification always carries an emotional component. But the emotions involved are not so much directly felt as conceived of intuitively. As Susanne Langer writes, "The feeling in a work of art is something the artist *conceived* as he created the symbolic form to represent it, rather than something he was undergoing and involuntarily venting in an artistic process."[2] Of course, the conceiving is not fully conscious, secondary-process thinking; the artist (like his ultimate audience) has a *sense* of the emotion. Rather than feeling it directly, he *has a feeling about it*.

To understand the difference between the two types of emotion, consider the following situations: In the first case, a director in rehearsal, trying to get a particular emotional quality from an actor, says, "Imagine that your father has just died." In the second case he says, "I hate to have to tell you this, but I have just received a message that your father died this morning." Both statements would elicit an emotional response, but not the same one! The former emotion would be weaker than the latter, but it would be far from trivial. The actor would not just coldly demonstrate some grimaces and shrieks to show, mechanically, how a bereaved person would react. If he had any sensitivity at all, he would be imaginatively moved by the statement, and the emotions stimulated in his imagination would intensify his acting. There might be grimaces and shrieks, but they would be felt rather than merely exhibited. The latter emotion, however, would be completely different. The actor would be numbed, devastated. Rather than being stimulated imaginatively to a better performance, he might be unable to perform at all.

For want of anything better, I shall call the former kind of emotion *imaginary*, and the latter kind *real*. But the idea of imaginary emotion should not carry connotations of emptiness or tameness. Imaginary emotions are, in their own way, powerfully felt. In some ways, they are *more* intense than real emotions, because real emotions often elicit unconscious repression mechanisms that prevent their being fully experienced. The actor who hears that his father has actually died is, as noted, numbed. The actor who only has to imagine his father's death is free to experience the emotion fully, exploring it and drawing upon it.

Distinguishing imaginary from real emotions clears up many problems about acting, including those created by Cartesian dualism, and explodes some acting myths. The differences between the two types of emotion can be summed up as follows: .

119

	Real	Imaginary
Arousal	*Fast*	*Slow*
Subsidence	*Slow*	*Fast*
Response	*Direct*	*Distanced*
Attitude	*Often painful*	*Always pleasurable*
Repression	*Often*	*Never*
Control	*Difficult*	*Easy*

Real emotions are usually aroused quickly. The actor hearing that his father had actually died needed no preparation in order to feel devastated; he would have felt the same no matter where or when he heard the terrible news, no matter what he had been doing. In fact, any preparation the director might have provided would have been aimed at *softening* the emotion—telling the actor to sit down, to take a deep breath, etc. The actor who is told to imagine his father's death, however, would feel nothing unless he was already in the creative state. The imaginary emotion would only occur if he was relaxed, and sensitive to the imaginary stimulus; even then the emotion would be ephemeral. The exercise, in fact, might not even work.

The real emotion, once aroused, would go away slowly. It might be hours or even days before the actor could function normally; weeks or even months before the pain had gone away entirely. Even if, shortly after hearing the news, the actor received another message saying that the first report was a mistake, the emotion would not disappear immediately. He would need at least a few minutes to recover. The imaginary emotion, however, is ephemeral, as noted. It would disappear almost immediately if the director were to say, "OK, break for lunch." An actor who claims to remain overwhelmed in such circumstances is either lying (to try to impress the director and the other actors) or has somehow become moved to real emotion.

Real emotions, then, are a direct response to immediate stimuli. Imaginary emotions, however, involve *aesthetic distance*. This term does not imply tameness or coolness, but rather that the emotion has a *form*, which can be contemplated. As Susanne Langer put it in the passage quoted above in Chapter 5, "sheer self-expression requires no artistic form."[3] A person undergoing intense real emotion, sweating, trembling, laughing, or crying as a result of some traumatic event, is not observing the effects of his emotion aesthetically. To show him a film of himself in the emotional state, even months later, would be disgusting. For the actor in the creative state, however, the imaginary emotion has a form that he contemplates and even shapes. This contemplation is *in the form of action*, but the action has a structure rather than just coming out haphazardly. To tell a person weeping with real emotion to cry a little louder would be callous and ridiculous, but it makes perfect sense to say so to an actor in rehearsal. And, of course, if the scene goes well, the actor would be delighted to see a film made of it.

Real emotions are often accompanied by underlying feelings of anxiety, especially with negative emotions. We wish that the emotions would stop, but, of course, cannot will them away. Imaginary emotions, on the other hand, are always pleasurable, no matter how negative they may be. Aristotle first noted this paradox in the *Poetics*: "There are some things that distress us when we see them in reality, but the most accurate representations of these same things we view with pleasure—as, for example, the forms of the most despised animals and of corpses."[4] Aristotle goes on to develop his theory of tragedy, which is of course a dramatic form depicting all the horrors of mankind—disease, war, famine, oppression, death— which we nonetheless view with pleasure. It is interesting that proponents of the acting-as-pain theory do not insist that the *audience* suffer too. Imaginary emotions are all right for those observing, but not for those performing! Actually, of course, the actor's emotions are of the same order as those of the audience; the actor is, among other things, an audience member at his own performance. If the performance is going well, both actors and audience are enjoying themselves, even during moments when the characters are suffering intensely. The actor weeping on stage does not say to himself, "How terrible, I wish this would stop," as he would in everyday life; instead, he thinks, "How wonderful! I've got it right, I hope I can keep it up!"

The conscious anxiety felt with real emotion often has an unconscious counterpart. Even with positive emotions, there may be repression mechanisms operating that tend to choke off the emotion. Psychologists recognize two kinds of emotional restriction: *suppression*, in which the person consciously tries to choke off the emotion ("I won't think of it now," says Scarlett O'Hara at the end of *Gone with the Wind*, "I'll think of it tomorrow"), and *repression*, where the same process takes place unconsciously and automatically. It is important to recognize that Freud saw repression as an important part of any person's emotional development. Although he lamented that the Viennese turn-of-the-century bourgeois society in which he lived and worked was generally over-repressed, he certainly did not advocate total license. Such an idea would not only be impractical—imagine a child never taught to control its bowel functions, for example—but, he came to feel, literally impossible. A tendency to repress is as much a part of our psychological makeup as any other of our drives. "Wild" acting teachers, like "wild" psychoanalysts, miss this important point, claiming to be above repression themselves and capable of removing it easily in others. Such an attitude is just as arrogant as claiming to be above sexual desire. All actors are repressed, as are all acting teachers and directors, or else they would not be functioning human beings.

There is a problem, then, in stressing real, "truthful" emotions in actors. Real emotions trigger repression; an unconscious "censor," which Freud eventually came to call the "superego," is always ready to choke things off. The director who, say, abuses an actor in rehearsal to the point of making him weep may feel a certain triumph, but it will be short-lived. The actor will not be able to shape the emotion to a performance and may not even be able to repeat it. A naive film entitled *The Method* recently depicted a San Francisco acting student—supposedly a middle-class housewife!— actually having sex for money in order to learn to play the role of a prostitute. Her acting teacher, a somber European despite his wild approach, sees this as a great breakthrough, but if an actress were actually talked into such a scheme she would either be so disgusted as never to want to play the role or so jaded to begin with that the experience could teach her nothing. Was this actress so unimaginative as to be unable to fathom what it is like to be a prostitute without directly experiencing it? What would she have done if called on to play a murderess?

Imaginary emotions, on the other hand, do not trigger repression. As long as the actor is convinced that they are not real, the superego does not censor them. Repression, of course, can occur when the imaginary emotion carries over into a real one. If the actor were told to imagine that his father had just died at a time when the parent was actually on his deathbed, the emotion would probably be artistically uncontrollable and unrepeatable, assuming that the actor was able to perform at all. It would be like the scene from *Brand* that Stanislavski describes, where the actress turned out actually to have had a child who died. The action is powerful, but raw, unshapable, and unsuited to the particular scene. Note too, that an audience member is in exactly the same situation with respect to the emotion; if you were to watch, say, the death of King Lear at a time when your own father was dying, it certainly would not enhance the emotional experience. The play would come to a stop for you. Your attention diverted from the plight of Lear to your own painful dilemma, you would probably have to leave the theatre.

Finally, imaginary emotions have the very characteristic that so confused Diderot and Coquelin: They are controllable. The control has both positive and negative aspects. In positive terms, imaginary emotions can be modified, and they can be repeated. ("I have acted the part of Leah for twenty-five years, and the tears always come to my eyes when the little child says, 'My name is Leah.'") In negative terms, they can easily be held in check. The only danger of their running away occurs if they somehow stimulate real emotions, which means that the actor, and his teacher or director, must be careful always to keep acting in the hypothetical mode. There is a problem with love scenes, for example, where the physical contact of the actors can lead to actual sexual arousal. This does *not* make the scene more intense, but instead makes it impossible to work with. In fact, such situations usually end up with the actors nervous and withdrawn, as their repression mechanisms start functioning automatically.

To sum up, imaginary emotions are genuinely felt. They are felt in a different way from real ones, however. The verb *to feel* actually has several meanings: At the simplest level, it means merely to perceive a physical sensation, as when we feel the cold, or feel the texture of a fabric. It can also mean to be aware of something intuitively—"I feel there is something wrong with this car." "I feel that the author is trying to convince us of something." Finally, it can mean to experience emotion—"I feel sad." "She felt wonderful." The second meaning is more characteristic of imaginary emotions than the third. Stanislavski's famous dictum, "feel the part," is often misunderstood to mean actually to undergo the emotion that the character is experiencing. In fact, the exact quotation (in the Hapgood translation) is "feel yourself in the part,"[5] which clearly suggests feeling in the intuitive sense. *Have the feel of the part* might be an alternate way of putting it.

In this view, you act in the same way that you play a musical instrument or a sport, by intuitive feel rather than by conscious manipulation. A beginner at golf, for example, is taught a variety of positions and moves, but the experienced golfer does not consciously think about more than one or two of these things at a time.[6] Instead, he knows what an effective golf swing *feels* like, and, in fact, checks the individual positions and moves only with the goal of recapturing that feel. Similarly, the actor in rehearsal works to gain the feel of the character's emotions. Once he has that feel, it becomes the basis for all subsequent performances. If he starts to lose that feel, he should not go rummaging around in his personal emotions introspectively, but, like the golfer, should go back carefully through the moves, the vocal placements, and the points of attention that gave rise to the feel of the emotion in the first place. In other words, feeling in this sense is the same thing as what I called "finding the character" in Chapter 7. Feeling emotion, then, *is an end point in the rehearsal rather than a starting point.* To try to work by first churning yourself up into a paroxysm of real emotion results only in a forced, generalized performance. It is almost as silly as a golfer trying to hit the ball by first working himself into a rage. The emotion is not something that happens first, inside; it is felt *in* the action and is the *result* of performing the action correctly. It is actually a test by which you know that you are acting effectively. You feel, "Ah, now I've got it."

Is it necessary to feel emotions in order to make the audience feel them? Oddly enough, the Strasberg approach, if it were logically consistent, would imply that you do not. Strasberg, for example, describes his experience as a youth of seeing the great Jewish actor Jacob Ben-Ami twice in the same role. The first time, it was "purely mechanical." The second time, in the climactic scene, "a shiver ran through my spine because this was something totally different. The gesture was the same externally, physically; yet there was an inner life. It was a kind of scenic communication that we in the theatre would call inspiration."[7] Yet if the gesture was *literally* the same, physically, in both performances, how could anyone tell the difference? If the emotion is something hidden away, part of "inner life," how does it communicate itself? Thinking about acting in this way implies that there is some kind of spiritual, telepathic connection between the actor's hidden mind and the audience, which any intelligent person would have to reject utterly, and which Strasberg himself does not presuppose. The audience responds only to what it sees and hears; if the actor's emotion is an inner, hidden "thing," then of course it is not necessary for him to feel it. To reproduce the outer sounds and gestures, accurately but mechanically, would obviously be enough to affect the audience.

Psychology has long since discarded the notion of emotions having an arcane, spiritual essence, however. A century ago, the American psychologist William James and the Danish psychologist Carl Georg Lange seriously questioned the commonly held notion that emotions originate within us. James wrote:

> Bodily disturbances are said to be the "manifestation" of ... emotions, their "expression" or "natural language." ...
> My thesis on the contrary is that *the bodily changes follow directly the PERCEPTION of the exciting fact, and that our feeling of the same changes as they occur IS the emotion* [emphasis original]. Common sense says, we lose our fortune, are sorry and weep; we meet a bear, are frightened and run; we are insulted by a rival, are angry and strike. The hypothesis here to be defended says that this order of sequence is incorrect, that the one mental state is not immediately induced by the other, that the bodily manifestations must first be interposed between, and that the more rational statement is that *we feel sorry because we cry, angry because we strike, afraid because we tremble* [emphasis mine].[8]

This is the famous James-Lange theory, which acting teachers have long recognized but rarely accepted. The trouble is that James expressed it here in such an exaggerated fashion that he merely seems to be turning the traditional view inside out. He himself admitted this, going on almost immediately to write, "Stated in this crude way, the hypothesis is sure to meet with immediate disbelief."[9] Now, it certainly is crude to say that "we feel sorry because we cry," etc. After all, we can cry from peeling onions and not feel sorry, strike a punching bag without feeling angry, tremble from the cold and not feel afraid. James was using a polemical way to emphasize his belief that emotions are *processes*, not things. The core of his theory is not the statement usually quoted about feeling sorry because we cry and so on, but the following: "Emotional brain-processes not only resemble the ordinary sensorial brain-processes, but in very truth *are* nothing but such processes variously combined."[10] James's more controversial statements were intended to show that crying is *part of the sorrow process*, and not merely its manifestation; that striking out is *part* of anger, and so on. He did not intend to shift the seat of emotions from the inside to the outside, but to reject the duality altogether. *A process has no pinpoint location.* A waterfall is not a particular drop of water.

James was in revolt against what is called *psychological atomism*, the idea that psychic events can be reduced to their separate parts and not change their nature. A process is not just the sum of its parts; more important than the parts themselves are their links to one another. An emotion takes place both inside *and* outside, both in the brain and in the rest of the body. Even when an emotion is repressed so that an observer cannot immediately see it, there are still physical manifestations—increased blood pressure, a faster heartbeat, faster breathing, etc. The process has not gone off to some mysterious spiritual realm, but has simply retreated to hidden parts of the body. It can still be physically observed and measured, but now special instruments are required. We should recall that in the infant, emotions *always* involve strong physical manifestation. We are not born repressed, but howl or shudder or laugh lustily. We gradually learn to turn off the more obvious manifestations of emotions in most circumstances, so that emotions become internalized in a literal, physical sense, but it does not follow that when emotions are actually exposed openly they are just the outward expression of the inner turmoil. They are still part of a total process; if there were no physical manifestation at all, there would be no emotion at all.

When Strasberg watched Ben-Ami for the second time, then, he was actually seeing something physically changed from the first performance. The two processes, though similar, contained subtle but important differences. The distinction is like the one between natural and artificial flavors. The natural flavor of a fruit, for example, is a mixture of several dozen chemical compounds in a delicate blend; an artificial flavor usually consists of one or two of the more predominant chemicals alone. Thus artificial strawberry flavoring tastes recognizably like strawberry, but it seems harsh and phony. In a way it ironically seems *too* strawberry-like. Ben-Ami's first performance had a similar kind of artificiality; in such cases, an actor seizes on a few obvious characteristics of the required emotion—a loud voice, perhaps, or a pout or a sneer—without the accompanying subtler details or the requisite interconnections among them. As with artificial flavoring, the performance manages simultaneously to seem both exaggerated and lifeless.

This kind of bad acting is commonly called *indicating*, which is usually defined as presenting the external aspects of an emotion without any inner feeling, which is how Strasberg describes it here. This again raises the question of how one knows what the actor is feeling if it is supposed to be a purely subjective experience. The actual explanation for indicating arises from the concept of an emotion as a process: The actor who is indicating is not presenting an interconnected process, but is instead only displaying a set of isolated attitudes and gestures. A facial grimace, for example, will seem to float in isolation; the rest of the body will remain uninvolved or the accompanying hand gestures will not match its intensity. The actor's vocal force will not match the grimace either, and his speech rhythms will not be in synchronization with it. Exaggerating the grimace, the weak actor's first recourse, will do no good because it only makes the expression more isolated than ever. The audience is quite capable of picking up the subtle clues that distinguish genuine (though imaginary) emotion and emotion that is merely indicated. Strasberg's genius in his teaching was in his insistence that actors go beyond indicating; the small differences between indicating and true acting loom large artistically. God is in the details.

The actor too can tell the difference between indicating and the genuine article; indicating is very frustrating, as the emotion seems more elusive the more you try to seize it vigorously. In fact, however, indicating is not such a bad thing *in rehearsal*. After all,

Ben-Ami did ultimately get the scene right! Actors should be encouraged to indicate emotion in rehearsal, which is the equivalent of an artist's preliminary sketch for a painting. The important thing, however, is not just to keep repeating the indicating and certainly not to exaggerate it, but rather to feel it, and follow where that feeling leads. Michael Chekhov's psychological gesture is based on nothing but indicating, but as the first step in a carefully planned journey, rather than as an end point. The goal of the psychological gesture technique is the feel of the emotion, in the intuitive sense. Such feeling *is* essential to good acting; such feeling is also perfectly observable because it is inherent in the action itself.

Psychologists in the twentieth century have studied an interesting mental phenomenon called *cognitive dissonance*, which helps to corroborate the James-Lange theory. Cognitive dissonance occurs whenever there is a disparity between attitude and behavior; a person for some reason has to behave in a manner that he does not really believe in. A lawyer may have to defend a client who he believes is actually guilty, a salesman may be given a product to sell that he thinks is worthless, or a person kidnaped by terrorists may be forced to pretend that he believes in their cause. In such cases, the experimental evidence shows that *attitude shifts to suit the behavior*, rather than the other way around. The lawyer begins to identify with the client, the salesman develops genuine enthusiasm for what he previously scorned, the kidnap victim is "turned," becoming an ardent member of the terrorist group. There seems to be a natural tendency for emotion to work from the outside inward; just going through the motions at first can often lead ultimately to genuine feeling. The phenomenon can even yield therapeutic techniques: frigid women, for example, are taught to fake orgasms, which leads, in many cases, to their actually experiencing them!

One famous study showed that when external rewards are given in situations of cognitive dissonance, however, the shift is actually less likely to occur. Subjects were offered cash to convince people that a boring psychological test was actually very interesting. The more money they were offered, the less convincing they tended to be![11] This is further evidence that role-playing satisfies an inner need; it is not something done primarily for fame or fortune.

Acting teachers should reconsider the James-Lange theory. The relation between "bodily disturbances" and emotions is not one of simple causality, as James seemed to imply, but there is always feedback linking the two. The feel of the disturbance is actually part of the emotion. Crying from peeling onions will not *automatically* make you feel sad, but you can tune in to the feeling of crying and use that as a basis for finding the full-blown emotion. Jean Marsh, the noted English actress, once said in a lecture about acting that she had cried on stage by turning away from the audience at a discreet moment and poking herself in the eyes! It gave her the elusive sensation she was seeking to get the emotion right. No one who saw her performances would have called them mechanical or indicating. Her crying became a *felt gesture*, a process fully integrated within itself and within the demands of the play. In other words, she was genuinely acting. The initial, physical sensation is a proto-emotion that can go on to develop into a full-fledged imaginary emotion, or even, in cases of cognitive dissonance, into real emotion. Why should actors and acting teachers not take advantage of this psychological fact? .

TEN

APPROACHES TO ACTING BEFORE THE MODERN ERA: HOW WE GOT WHERE WE ARE

Until the eighteenth century, acting theory appeared mostly in the form of passing remarks or anecdotes. Two themes emerged that I have already discussed: the antitheatrical prejudice, which denounced actors for arousing emotion, or for pretending to be what they were not; and the tendency to associate acting with oratory, so that orators often studied with actors, and vice versa.

The antitheatrical prejudice meant that acting theory never developed to the extent that literary theory did. Actors in ancient Greece had high status, being considered priests of Dionysus, but the fact that Plato, a very influential writer, had denounced them meant that no one took their art very seriously in intellectual terms. Aristotle was a pivotal figure here. Plato and his followers had maintained that tragedy was an inferior literary form because it appealed to the masses (the Platonists were unabashed snobs) and because it required staging to put it over; they had their misgivings about epic poetry too, but at least that seemed to appeal directly to the mind rather than to the senses.

Aristotle's *Poetics* is the first major work of literary criticism ever written. Its influence has been enormous; if, as Whitehead once said, Western philosophy consists of 2,300 years of footnotes to Plato, then Western dramatic criticism consists of 2,300 years of footnotes to Aristotle. Nevertheless, Aristotle was not writing for posterity. To a certain extent, he intended *The Poetics* as an apologia for tragedy, to rebut the Platonists. His defense would, ironically, have profound negative consequences for acting theory. Instead of saying, "What's wrong with being influenced through the senses?", which might have been expected from someone with his scientific inclination, he instead accepted the Platonists' basic premise that sensory stimulation was on a lower mental level than pure cerebration. He went on to a startling conclusion: Tragedy, he said, does not really need staging to be effective, because "even without action it achieves its function just as epic does; for its character is apparent simply through reading."[1] By reading, Aristotle did not mean silently to one's self, a practice that was unknown until well into the Christian era, but public reading by an orator, which was the way epic poetry, and in fact all literary compositions other than drama, were "published." Nonetheless, the implications were clear: Tragedy does not need scenery or actors or even a large audience. Its association with the theatre is a mere accident.

Separating playscript from performance was an amazing insight. Aristotle did much the same thing in separating musical composition from performance in his discussion of music, which gives an idea of the impact his approach must have had. Even today, the ability to read and analyze a musical score is a specialized skill. For most of us, a piece of music is not "real" until we hear it. To suggest that a playscript could stand by itself, rather than being performed in the medium for which it was intended, must have dazzled the ancient Greeks. Unfortunately, however, it left acting out in the cold. In *The Poetics*, Aristotle analyzes tragedy in terms of six elements, which are, in order of decreasing importance, plot, character, thought, diction, music, and spectacle. Acting is conspicuous by its absence, unless we lump it in under spectacle, which is seen as the least important element in any event. (Diction here means not the actor's enunciation in speaking, but the writer's choice of words in composition.) Aristotle barely discusses acting at all, and then only in a negative context: To those who criticize tragedy on the grounds that its audience is too dull to appreciate it unless the performers liven it up with a lot of gesticulation, he replies that this is an accusation about the art of acting rather than poetry. He mentions an actor who was called an ape for overacting, but never mentions any actor who performed well. Thus, with Plato attacking acting and Aristotle seeing it as at most a necessary evil, acting theory languished until modern times.

Nevertheless, if people do not theorize about acting, they do have ideas on the subject. There will always be an implicit theory that can be inferred from the way a society treats actors and the way in which actors rehearse, perform, and generally behave. In the past, people conceived of acting very differently than we do today, which is evident not so much in what they verbalized on the subject as in what they took for granted about it. In the twentieth century, it has become widely accepted that successful actors should be highly paid, living fabulous personal lives that are the object of much scrutiny; they take the place in our imagination that royalty once did. But in the Middle Ages, for instance, acting was a low, vulgar trade, linked in people's minds (and sometimes in actual fact) with beggary, thievery, and prostitution. Actors lived from hand to mouth, eking out a precarious living, traveling from town to town, and performing for meager sums. When they died, they could not even be buried in hallowed ground; the Church considered them unfit.

On the other hand, amateur theatre came to flourish in the Middle Ages. Students performed in the Roman plays of Plautus and Terence (they were considered a good way to learn spoken Latin); members of trade guilds performed "miracle plays," with scripts drawn from the Bible; aristocrats performed disguisings, or "masques" as they were later called, lavish costume pieces with music, dance, and flowery speeches. The Church not only did not object to such performances but, in the case of the miracle plays, actively supported them, even providing the scripts.

Huge sums of money were sometimes spent on medieval productions; there are records of guilds bankrupting themselves in an effort to outdo their rivals. But there was one way money could not be spent: The actors were not to be paid. Nowadays, to call an actor professional is a compliment, while amateur is a term of scorn. In the Middle Ages, the attitude was exactly the reverse. To act for a living was contemptible, but to do it just for fun was perfectly all right.

The miracle plays gradually died out, largely as a result of the Reformation. The Puritans in England, for example, saw them as both popish and pagan; by Shakespeare's day, few were being performed, although he probably witnessed some performances in his youth. On the other hand, the rise of capitalism created a new leisure class in the cities, with plenty of money to spend on entertainment. Enter the professional actor. Professional companies grew larger, more stable, and more prosperous, even performing in specially built theatres rather than innyards, town squares, and anywhere else they could put up a temporary stage. Acting was still a despised profession, but it had become a lucrative one. It is worth noting that Shakespeare made a fortune not as a playwright but as an actor. Playwrights who did not act earned only meager sums.

Elizabethan attitudes toward acting may be discerned from Shakespeare's own *Midsummer Night's Dream*, in which a group of skilled tradesmen actually rehearse and perform a play. The scenes are a satire of the kind of amateur drama then passing into oblivion, with the enthusiastic tradesmen a meager vestige of the great medieval guilds that had performed the miracle plays. The play the "mechanicals" perform, *Pyramus and Thisby*, is not religious, however, but a tragedy drawn from classical literature, and is more or less the kind of drama the professional companies were doing.

(The Greek and Roman classics had become much safer politically than the Bible as sources for plays.) Shakespeare has great fun ridiculing the ineptitude of these actors, who are amateur in the modern sense of the word.

The appendix reproduces Act 1, scene 2 of the play. Since it is satire, it must not be taken too literally as an actual depiction of rehearsal or performance practices of the time. Obviously, Shakespeare's company, headed by Richard Burbage, one of the greatest actors in history, were vastly superior to Peter Quince, Nick Bottom, and the rest of the bumpkins. Nevertheless, the underlying attitudes that are portrayed—the things the actors take for granted—are very revealing.

Some things in the scene seem very modern. When Snug the Joiner says that he is "slow of study," he is using a phrase that modern actors still use; we also find here other modern theatrical terms like *script* (or "scrip," as Bottom puts it) and *properties*. One term that is not in the scene is *director*, a position not really found in the theatre before the mid-nineteenth century. Nevertheless, Peter Quince is clearly in charge, fulfilling many of the functions of a modern director. He has chosen the play, has control of the script, and casts all the parts. Bottom apparently wants to play *all* the roles himself, but Quince has no trouble disciplining him; everyone accepts his authority without question. Quince also sets the time and place for rehearsal, has the final say on costumes and makeup, and will draw up the bill of properties. In a limited way, he coaches the actors.

There are striking differences between Quince and a modern director, however. For one thing, there is no mystique about him; he is one of the actors himself (and, it turns out, not a very good one!) rather than a specialized official. In other words, he is first among equals. Someone has to make certain decisions, and the actors have apparently chosen him to do it. Furthermore, the actors do not ask him how he will approach *Pyramus and Thisby*, what his "concept" of it is, or what style or period he will set it in. The production will succeed or fail on the basis of its script and the acting, rather than directorial interpretation. The means by which the actors will perform the play are more or less standard. If asked how they were going to do it, all they would be able to answer would be something like, "to the best of our abilities."

The actors' attitudes toward performing are also very different from those of their modern counterparts, particularly American ones. When Bottom learns that he is to play Pyramus, for example, his immediate question is, "What is Pyramus? a lover, or a tyrant?" He does not ask about the character's background, his biography, his motivations; the actors are in fact utterly uninterested in psychology. It is assumed that characters come in *types*, and that actors specialize in playing one or more. The joke about Bottom is that he thinks he can play all types. In America today, actors scorn stereotypes, and assume that they will play characters like themselves, or at least find some points of correspondence between the character's individuality and their own personal lives. None of that for Bottom! The more wide-ranging his roles, the better, and although Quince prevents him from playing Thisby, the heroine, it is not so outlandish an idea as it seems to a modern audience. Women's parts were played by males—boys, if possible—and the role goes to Francis Flute, even though he has a beard coming. He will achieve the type with a mask, which no one finds curious.

Until the rise of realism in the theatre in the late nineteenth century, plays demanded types and actors played them. In the English and American theatre, these were known as "lines of business," and might include heroes and heroines of tragedy, of light comedy, fathers and elderly men, witches, clever servants, and even "singing chambermaids."[2] Strong definition, rather than well-roundedness, was the ideal both in acting and in playwriting. Modern actors need to remember this in playing roles from the past, and avoid excessive psychologizing. Bottom himself, for example, is a comic bumpkin, *period*. (He was probably played by Will Kemp, a famous comedian who specialized in such types.) To see his behavior as *caused* by a complex of needs and drives is false to the text and spoils the fun.

Note how, in showing off his prowess, the first thing Bottom does is bellow out a passage of *verse*, and a highly artificial one at that, with elaborate rhyming. It is hard to imagine a modern actor making such a choice. He would probably try to impress a casting director with how subtly and naturally he could read a part, but Bottom instead tries to be "lofty." A modern actor would also probably choose a piece of prose rather than verse for an audition, if he could, but to the Elizabethan Bottom, verse is the first choice, *easier* to act than prose, because it is something to take hold of, "to make all split." In a later scene, he makes it clear that he knows the technicalities of verse writing, arguing with Quince about whether the prologue should be written in "eight and six," or "eight and eight" (III.i.25–27) referring to the syllables of its couplets. Modern American actors, I have sadly found, would not only be unfamiliar with this rather obscure bit of metrical theory, but often cannot even define blank verse, Shakespeare's main poetic form.

It is not that Elizabethan actors like Bottom were incapable of playing realistic dialogue. The mechanicals' scenes in *Midsummer* are themselves written in a slangy, everyday prose. The Elizabethans recognized a wide range of linguistic styles, from lofty to low, for both poetry and prose. Their playwrights and actors had a much more *operative* approach to language than we do; they *did* things with a speech—again, in the manner of an orator—rather than always just trying to be as natural as possible. They were alive to all the poetic devices, not just rhythm and other aural elements like rhyme and alliteration, but poetic imagery and rhetorical structure. The Elizabethan actor made speeches the way an opera performer sings arias. The speeches were the high points, where the acting could shine out; in between were connecting passages (like recitatives in opera) or sometimes whole scenes where speeches were short, being shared among two or more characters. Over the centuries, the recitative kind of scene has become more and more used, until now whole plays are written in which there is no speech of over a few sentences, a kind of playwriting that an Elizabethan actor would have found flat and lifeless, but on which the modern actor thrives.

At the end of the scene, Peter Quince sets rehearsal for the very next night, by which time he wants the actors to memorize ("con") their parts. No one finds this demand onerous. Modern actors learn lines rather slowly, and are often careless about accuracy, a little-known but unfortunate fact. In Elizabethan times, however, rote memorization was the standard means of learning things; students would have thousands of lines of verse beaten into them at school, for example. In America-today, educational theorists reject rote memorization, partly from the recognition that it is less necessary now, with so many ways of cheaply storing information that were not available in the past. One result, however, is that our contemporary actors are much more likely to be "slow of study"; some famous screen actors can act only with cue cards, never daring to go back to the stage simply because they could not remember the lines!

Peter Quince and his company of mechanicals, however, will learn their *entire* parts before they even begin to rehearse, and probably will not have many rehearsals in any case. This is again related to the idea of a role being a set of speeches. Traditionally, actors were like opera singers or symphony orchestra members today, doing most of their rehearsing on their own; they came together as a group to stitch the play together, rather than to create it from scratch. Before the rise of realism in the theatre, a typical rehearsal period was a week or so; in 1860, a widely admired production was described as having had "countless rehearsals"— meaning sixteen![3] But in a realistic play, speeches are mostly short, with a lot of give-and-take, including interrupted lines. The actors have to work together much more than in the past in order to get the performance right. Similarly, roles are no longer defined as types, but by a complex of details, which must be worked out with great care in the company of the whole group. A Broadway play will have about two hundred hours of rehearsal, while in continental Europe five hundred or even a thousand hours are not uncommon, in contrast to about two dozen in Shakespeare's day.

Quince's coaching of the actors consists of explaining the plot and describing the characters. The former is necessary because the actors will not get complete scripts, but only "sides," which show their own parts only, plus a few cue words. To provide complete copies for everyone would have been prohibitively expensive. Using sides (which are still sometimes found today in musical comedy, where the copyright holders want to keep the scripts under strict control) again enhances the sense of a role as a set of independent speeches. Roles are learned by themselves and only then combined into a performance.

The descriptions of the characters that Quince provides the actors are, as noted, unpsychological in the modern sense. Thus Pyramus is "a sweet-fac'd man; a proper man as one shall see in a summer's day; a most lovely gentlemanlike man" (80-82). Usually, Elizabethans thought of characters not in terms of their motivations, but in terms of their *traits*. The "Overburian Characters" of Sir Thomas Overbury, for example, a collection of satirical character sketches published between 1614 and 1622, include a description of eighty-two individuals, such as a pedant, a servingman, and a Puritan. They are all described exclusively in terms of their peculiarities and observable activities, rather than their backgrounds or psychological complexes. A servant, for example, "is commonly proud of his master's horses or his Christmas; he sleeps when he is sleepy, is of his religion, only the clock of his stomach is set to go an hour after his. He seldom breaks his own clothes. He never drinks but double."[4] A modern writer would be interested in *why* a servant behaved in this way, perhaps analyzing his childhood or the social conditions in which he lives. Overbury merely describes.

Insofar as the Elizabethans had a science of psychology, it was based on *humors*—a set of fluids in the body which, when out of balance, supposedly gave rise to extremes of temperament. We still use the adjectives *melancholy, phlegmatic, sanguine,* and *choleric,* which are based on the four humors having the corresponding mental attitudes. But the humors theory is again a static, trait-oriented psychology rather than a dynamic, drive-oriented one. It leads to a categorizing of human beings by type, as writers on humors tended to do. We should therefore not be surprised to find actors and playwrights of that era pigeonholing characters in a similar manner.

In other words, the way in which actors approach roles or playwrights create them will be to a large extent based on the prevalent ideas about what a human being *is.* There is a widespread belief in the theatre today that human nature is ultimately unchanging, that human beings of all times and all cultures are the same beneath the surface. Maybe so, but they certainly do not all *think* of themselves in the same way. Thus it would not offend an Elizabethan to stereotype human beings nor to create literary or theatrical characters based on those stereotypes. That roster of stereotypes summed up what was, for them, unchanging about human nature. The current American cliché that an actor "cannot play an idea" but only a well-rounded, fully psychologized human being would have seemed strange and unnatural to the Elizabethans. As far as they were concerned, human beings were not well-rounded, and their motivations were neither mysterious nor deep. Not only were actors able to play an idea—i.e., a type—they would have found it hard to play anything else.

Joseph R. Roach's admirable book, *The Player's Passion,* already quoted, shows how changing concepts of human nature over the past several centuries has led to differing theories of acting and differing approaches to it. When Diderot in the eighteenth century came up with a new theory of acting, his impulse was coming from the rise of science that challenged traditional notions of body and soul. The new science was dynamic rather than static, stressing motion, forces, processes. Roach cites the French writer Abbé Du Bos, who wrote a treatise in 1719 describing Cartesian and Newtonian mechanics,

Harvey's explanation of the circulation of the blood (which challenged the traditional humors theory), and Torricelli's demonstration of air pressure. Du Bos then put forth a theory of artistic creation based on the idea that our minds react to the air like barometers or thermometers.[5] Thus, Diderot's mechanistic view of acting was based on a prevalent, mechanistic view of what a human being was. Other writers discussed acting in terms of elaborate, detailed physical descriptions, which reflected a similar view of a human being as a mechanical contraption. Aaron Hill, writing in 1746 on how an actor is to express joy, advised him to look in the mirror:

> If ... he has hit the conception, exactly, he will have the pleasure, in that case, to observe in the glass, that his forehead appears open, and raised, his eye smiling, and sparkling, his neck will be stretched, and erect, without stiffness, as if it would add new height to his stature; his breast will be inflated, and majestically backened; his back-bone erect, and all the joints of his arm, wrist, fingers, hip, knee, and ankle, will be high-strung, and braced boldly.[6]

Hill sounds like a modern writer here in conceiving of an emotion in complex terms, rather than as a stereotypical trait or humor. Nevertheless, this is still a notably external view of emotionality. Unlike, say, Lee Strasberg describing the acting of Jacob Ben-Ami in terms of its "inner life," Hill was concerned only with observable details. The emotion was *in* these details, rather than something *behind* them.

Acting in the eighteenth century reflected Hill's attitude, which was, in turn, simply the prevalent view of human nature. A human being was a ghost in a machine; the ghost was the rational, observing self, while the machine was the intricate, scientifically observable clockwork wherein emotions resided. Where we today prize naturalness, psychological depth, and emotional intensity, actors and audiences in the eighteenth century valued polish, intricacy of surface detail, and emotional *control*. Here is a famous description of David Garrick (1717–79) as Hamlet, in his first encounter with his father's ghost:

> At these words ("Angels and Ministers of grace defend us")
> Garrick turns sharply and at the same moment staggers back
> two or three paces with his knees giving way under him; his hat
> falls to the ground and both his arms, especially the left, are
> stretched out nearly to their full length, with the hands as high
> as his head, the right arm more bent and the hand lower, and
> the fingers apart; his mouth is open: thus he stands rooted to
> the spot.[7]

More significant than Garrick's systematized approach to the scene is the observer's (Georg Christoph Lichtenberg) appreciation of it. What critic today would note whether an actor's fingers were together or apart during a single moment of a four-hour play?

Note that Garrick here was anything but cold. Emotion (usually called sentiment or sensibility) was highly valued in the eighteenth century, but it was taken for granted that, both in real life and on stage, it needed to be controlled. Garrick did not just explode with emotion on stage; every move and gesture was planned and carefully executed. In fact, Roach has pointed out that during this very scene, Garrick used a "fright wig," a mechanical contrivance whose hair could be made to stand on end by the actor pulling on a hidden wire![8] A modern actor would use such a thing only as a joke, but for Garrick and his audience it was a serious artistic device. It sums up perfectly the eighteenth century attitude toward emotion, as something intricate, controllable, and *external*.

The romantic movement, starting in Germany in the late eighteenth century and soon spreading to all of Europe, brought major changes in attitudes toward acting, as it did toward all the arts. In playwriting, for example, restraint, decorum, and "the three unities"[9] were tossed aside, in favor of plays (influenced by those of Shakespeare) that were imaginative, variegated, and wide-ranging.

Similarly, in the place of polish and control, actors substituted exuberance, variety, and emotional power. Where John Philip Kemble (1757–1823), a great English actor of the traditional eighteenth-century style who came from a famous theatrical family and who inspired a whole school of acting, was "cold, classical, and correct,"[10] Edmund Kean (1787–1833), the greatest English tragedian of the early nineteenth century, was wild, erratic, and passionate. Kemble was noted for his perfect diction, and took great care with "the disposition of his mantle"[11] even in death scenes, but Kean's diction was slovenly (particularly in his later years), so that lines went unheard, and he was not afraid to cringe or crawl on the floor to achieve an exciting effect. The poet Samuel Coleridge remarked that "to see Kean was to read Shakespeare by flashes of lightning"[12]; moments of great power alternated with periods of somnolence and indifference.

With Kemble's and Kean's careers overlapping, audiences had opportunities to compare and debate the two styles. Thus was born in the romantic era the conflict between contrasting attitudes toward acting that has continued down to our own time. Americans tend now to see it as a conflict between British and American approaches, the former being seen as more polished and better spoken but rather cold, the latter as rough and ill-spoken but more realistic and powerful. A generation ago, the terms *Technique* and *Method* (after the Method of the Actors Studio) were applied to the two supposedly differing styles. Nevertheless, the same controversy has often occurred *within* each of the two countries, or even between England and France, as in the debate between Coquelin and Irving in the late nineteenth century.

Controversies like that between Technique and Method tend to polarize thinking, so that many Americans seem to believe that a blend of the two is impossible, that an emphasis on diction and movement is somehow detrimental to emotion. I know of teachers of Shakespearean acting, and even professional directors of Shakespeare's plays, who actually avoid any analysis of the verse on the grounds that it would automatically lead to sterile intoning. But we should recall that in the past, a careful, polished technique was by no means seen as anesthetizing emotion. Kemble's coldness probably had more to do with his personal predilections than with the theories he espoused or the training he had received. After all, Garrick was anything but cold, and Kemble's sister, Sarah Siddons (1755–1831), was just as dignified and "classical" as her brother, yet was known for her emotional intensity. "Passion is told from her look before she speaks,"[13] one observer noted. As for Kean, he maintained that the impulsiveness and spontaneity of his acting were only an illusion. "There is no such thing as impulsive acting," he insisted; "all is premeditated and studied beforehand."[14]

The Method-Technique controversy (which has been around in one form or another for a long time!), then, is just another variation on the artificial mind-body polarity that dogs so much of our acting theory. The theory is not the thing itself, however; Method and Technique are not so much ways of acting as they are ways of *thinking* about acting, habits of mind that can limit us. Technical skill need not stifle emotion; emotion need not be a formless explosion. As I shall insist in a later chapter, to operate through conventionalized means not only does not inhibit artistry, it is the very basis of it. To insist otherwise is like saying that an infant should not learn how to speak, for fear of later inhibiting him as a poet.

The German romantic critic August Wilhelm Schlegel and the English romantic poet Coleridge used the term *organic form* to justify the apparent disorganization of Shakespeare's plays, which they loved. Critics of the previous era, they believed, had a concept of form that was "mechanical." To insist on pre-existing rules, like the famous three unities of time, place, and action, reduced drama to something lifeless. Coleridge and Schlegel felt that a play should be like a living organism, each one unique, yet perfectly well formed and organized, as evidenced by the fact that it was alive and functioning. Shakespeare's plays *worked* in the theatre; therefore, they had perfectly good form—better, in fact, than the form of the many plays that fit the rules but which were insipid!

The distinction between organic and mechanical is one that has continued to our own day. It represented a sharp break with the past, when organic and mechanical had seemed more or less the same; writers in the eighteenth century were more impressed by the fact that both machines and living creatures *moved*, in a complex but organized manner, than they were by the fact that machines had no minds or souls. Romanticism, among other things, was a reaction against the growing Industrial Revolution, which was seen not only as a destroyer of traditional cultural values but as imposing a ruthless, inhumane existence on people. Machines now seemed enemies of the human spirit. Thus, to write a play that was like a machine or to give a performance like one was a surrender to something evil. It was more important that a play or a performance in it seem *alive*, that it have some vital spark, some soul that animated it.

George Henry Lewes (1817–78), a nineteenth-century English critic whose descriptions of actors are among the best ever written, is an example of how the new ideas of romanticism affected thinking about acting. "Bad acting, like bad writing, has a remarkable uniformity," he insisted, while "good acting ... is remarkable for its individuality."[15] A machine-made object had no individuality; a work of art, by contrast, bore the unique stamp of its maker. Although actors in Lewes's day were still playing lines of business, we see here the origin of the modern prejudice against actors playing stereotypes. The word *stereotype* is itself a technological one, referring to a mechanically cast printing plate. To play a stereotype is to behave like a machine; a machine cannot produce a work of art. Thus, lines of business have disappeared from acting today, and although "type casting" is still widely practiced, it is also widely scorned. Yet before the Industrial Revolution, no one objected to type casting, which seemed like plain common sense. Lacking machines as a model, how could anyone attack machinelike acting?

Understanding the contrast been organic and mechanical requires a familiarity with machines, which an actor in Shakespeare's day, for example, could not have had. Lewes went on to describe the good actor's performance with a typically organic image: "As in all art, feeling lies at the root, but the foliage and flowers though deriving their sap from emotion, derive their form and structure from the intellect."[16] The seat of the emotions, the vital source of a performance, had moved *inside*. Reason, or intellect, was now secondary, an external, which could only shape and guide what the emotions provided.

Far from rejecting technology, as romanticism had, realism was an expression of a scientific spirit, stressing careful observation and objectivity. Science now included human psychology, however, which ironically brought realism back to the realm of the unseen. And while realism is usually portrayed as a revolt against romanticism, in terms of acting it became no more than a revision. Strindberg's play *Miss Julie*, a landmark in dramatic realism, might be seen as a return to eighteenth-century neoclassicism; it obeys the unities of time, place, and action to avoid straining the audience's credulity by keeping the dramatic illusion unbroken. In his attitude toward characterization, however, Strindberg was very different from someone like Hill or Lichtenberg. Strindberg describes his heroine in a preface to the play:

> I see Miss Julie's tragic fate to be the result of many circumstances: the mother's character, the father's mistaken upbringing of the girl, her own nature, and the influence of her fiancé on a weak, degenerate mind. Also, more directly, the festive mood of Midsummer Eve, her father's absence, her monthly indisposition, her pre-occupation with animals, the excitement of dancing, the magic of dusk, the strongly aphrodisiac influence of flowers, and finally the chance that drives the couple into a room alone—to which must be added the urgency of the excited man.[17]

The character of Miss Julie is defined not by a set of traits, but by a history. There is no physical description here at all. Hill's and Lichtenberg's descriptions included minute details of positions, moves, and gestures, but Strindberg's, though equally lengthy, tells us nothing about what Miss Julie looks like. To describe what lies *behind* behavior, he assumed, was enough to define the behavior itself. The actress in the role had to consider Miss Julie's psychological makeup rather than the positioning of her joints or the sparkling of her eyes. If the psychology was right, the physicality would take care of itself. *Miss Julie* is psychological drama in the modern sense—a psychology based not on *traits*, but on *drives*.

The dialogue of *Miss Julie* is in prose rather than verse, using the slangy, disorganized style of everyday speech. "I have avoided the symmetrical, mathematical construction of French dialogue," wrote Strindberg, "and let people's minds work irregularly, as they do in real life where, during a conversation, no topic is drained to the dregs, and one mind finds in another a chance cog to engage in."[18] Nevertheless, Strindberg could not resist giving his characters a few long monologues, for which he felt obliged to defend himself: "It is, surely, natural for a public speaker to walk up and down the room practicing his speech, natural for an actor to read his part aloud, for a servant girl to talk to her cat, a mother to prattle to her child, an old maid to chatter to her parrot, and a sleeper to talk in his sleep."[19] Natural or not, however, the tendency of modern psychological playwrights has been to avoid monologues, or at least, like Strindberg in this play, to minimize them. Actors no longer think of a role as a set of speeches. Nor, with realistic dialogue, do they think of language as something to manipulate the way Bottom wants to do in *Pyramus and Thisby*. The traditional link between acting and oratory has been broken; actors no longer orate. Instead, they simply try to talk as they would in real life, quietly and casually. The fact that theatres have become relatively small—Strindberg himself eventually wrote "chamber plays" for a tiny playhouse called The Intimate Theatre—enables this, as does the practice of using microphones on stage. Film, with sound amplification and the closeup, enables an actor to speak even *more* quietly and casually than he would in everyday life.

Finally, as already noted, actors have to rehearse much more than they did in the prerealistic period, rehearsing *together* so that "one mind finds in another a chance cog to engage in." Speeches have become short, with much give and take, including interruptions, so that a performance becomes a completely shared experience.

In sum, approaches to acting over the centuries have reflected approaches to the arts generally, and behind them, shifting cultural attitudes about human beings. The romantic era was pivotal. Romantic acting stressed uniqueness and an internal, emotional, organic approach to a role. Realism, though anti-romantic in emphasis, still called for unique characterizations rather than stereotypes, and accepted the internal approach, giving it a new, scientific, psychological basis. In its anti-rhetorical stance, however, realism was a complete break with the past. Although a romantic actor like Kean might have had slovenly diction, he still thought of himself as making speeches, whose purpose was to move the audience rather than to provide an accurate illusion of everyday talk.

Although acting over the past four centuries has evolved, in the sense of developing in response to a changing cultural environment, it is important not to see this evolution as a form of cultural Darwinism, with acting getting better and better. Cultural changes are not improvements; we do not think of the French language as being better than Latin, even though it evolved from it. The approach to acting at a given time is simply the one that is appropriate to it, rather than one that is inherently best for all times. Our own internal, organic, anti-rhetorical approach to acting is appropriate for the predominant kind of plays that have been written over the past century, but it cannot be applied indiscriminately to plays from the past. To approach a role in Shakespeare, for example, by avoiding stereotypes, inventing a character biography like the one that Strindberg gave to Miss Julie, drawing on personal emotion, and speaking in a casual, everyday manner leads to disaster. Shakespeare did not write plays with that approach to acting in mind. It is the height of arrogance to assume that our approach is automatically better than his.

Nor should we think of the evolution of acting as having reached perfection and stopped. Acting continues to evolve. In the past, changes took place because actors felt that the prevalent approach was too limiting or artificial. Similarly, the best American acting conservatories today, and our best actors, sense the limitations of the romantic-realistic style of acting, and are seeking ways of going beyond it. Actors like Dustin Hoffman or Meryl Streep, for example, employ a traditionally internal, organic approach, but they also apply techniques—like speaking with an accent, making themselves physically unattractive, or even playing the opposite sex!—that no member of the Actors Studio of forty years ago would have ever dared to try. Actors, like all artists, look upon tradition as a challenge, rather than something to be slavishly followed or mindlessly rejected; it is energy rather than rule. Our acting will both incorporate the past and break with it, as it evolves to meet the aesthetic needs of the future.

ELEVEN

STANISLAVSKI'S BASIC THEORIES

Stanislavski is one of the few writers in history to offer a comprehensive theory of acting. Most writers on the subject are concerned with what acting *should* or *should not* be; they describe their own personal approach or promote a particular acting style. If, like Diderot or Coquelin, they base their ideas on certain principles, they tend to defend those principles with lengthy appeals to reason rather than elaborate them in practical terms. Stanislavski, however, is concerned with what acting is. His theories, rightly or wrongly, are supposed to accommodate all styles of acting, rather than just his own. (Stanislavski came of age as an artist in the age of realism, so that the rhetoric of realism colors all his writings, but he actually worked in everything from Shakespeare to vaudeville to opera.) He is not calling for a new approach to acting, but instead attempts to codify what actors have always done and, by implication, always will do. Moreover, he does not debate or even defend his principles, but instead, like Darwin with his theory of evolution or Freud with his theory of the unconscious mind, just sets them forth and expands on them. The reader can judge them for himself, and indeed, elaborate on them himself, as I shall try to do.

Stanislavski's ideas can be difficult to understand in the abstract. Students who learn his theories by rote, and who try to apply them like formulas, typically find them of little use. It is not a good idea for beginning students to use his books as texts; they take on meaning only after someone has acted for a while and can relate them to his stage or film experience. In this chapter, I shall try to relate the theories to specific examples using well-known film actors, but even this is a limited approach. Stanislavski's theories are few in number and simple in conception, but they have to be learned over and over. They take on more meaning the more they are lived.

Stanislavski's ideas on acting evolved over many decades. One of the problems in understanding his theories in this country arises from the fact that Richard Boleslavsky and Maria Ouspenskaya, who taught his system at the American Laboratory Theatre in the 1920s, were drawing on concepts that Stanislavski was already apparently moving away from. When he finally set down his system in the last years of his life, in the 1930s, it was notably different from what they taught, and even more different from what Lee Strasberg was to make of their teachings.

Furthermore, Stanislavski's books are notorious for being badly written. They are very disorganized; he will take up an idea, drop it, and come back to it again much later, if ever. The device of pretending that the book is a student diary is awkward, and the way that know-it-all Tortsov repeatedly puts down his students can be infuriating. To complicate the problem of understanding Stanislavski's writings, the only translations available in English, by Elizabeth Reynolds Hapgood, are not accurate. Stanislavski set forth his theories in one large, haphazard, incomplete work in three volumes, the first two entiled *Rabota aktera nad soboi*, meaning "an actor's work on himself," and the third entitled *Rabota aktera nad roliù*, "an actor's work on a role." Hapgood translated these as three *separate* books, published over a twenty-five-year period, which she entitled *An Actor Prepares, Building a Character,* and *Creating a Role.*[1] Many actors have read only the first volume, which carries no announcement that it is part of a larger work, so that the second volume, with its stress on character acting, and the third, with its Method of Physical Action, have gone relatively unnoticed.

In this chapter, I shall try to explicate what I see as Stanislavski's basic ideas as put forth in his first volume. They are not the whole of his system, however. It should always be remembered that he valued character transformation highly, actually maintaining that all good acting was character acting, and also that the Method of Physical Action is an important elaboration of his basic theory. I have discussed character acting throughout this book and have mentioned the Method of Physical Action; I shall discuss the latter again in Chapter 13. The basic work, as put forth in *An Actor Prepares,* is not so much about the art of acting as it is about the *craft* of acting, the fundamental skills that an actor needs in order to achieve an effective performance.

Training in these basic skills will not in itself make an actor into a great artist. They do not even guarantee that every role will be a success—in fact, nothing can do that, since acting is an art form, which means that it can never be reduced to formula. Every actor, no matter how great, has failures, as does every painter, every poet, and every composer. (It is easier for other artists to hide their failures, however!) Nevertheless, the skills that Stanislavski promotes will increase the *likelihood* of an actor's success, and will prevent total disasters. Just as a painter, if well trained, will always be able to produce a recognizable likeness, though the painting may be bad otherwise, so a well trained actor will always be able to give a performance that is entertaining, even though it may be misconceived or outside his range. I recently saw a noted American actor play Hamlet at the New York Shakespeare Festival; his performance lacked emotional expanse, rhetorical power, and sensitivity to rhythm, but it was at least easy to watch. His failure was considerably better than a strained, awkward, amateurish failure one might see in a college production, which could make you run screaming from the auditorium. Stanislavski's basic ideas can be reduced to three key terms: *relaxation, relating,* and *objectives.* They are based on techniques that good actors actually use (wittingly or unwittingly), and can be applied to all possible acting situations. Since the terms operate in tandem, each should only be considered in the context of the others; in fact, any acting precept that is exaggerated and applied in isolation can soon become a grotesque parody of itself. I shall deal with a fourth term, *emotion memory,* in the next chapter, on Lee Strasberg. It is certainly part of Stanislavski's system—*An Actor Prepares* has a whole chapter devoted to it—but it does not deserve the central position that Strasberg gave to it. Nor did emotion memory mean quite the same thing to Stanislavski that it did to Strasberg.

Relaxation

The actual title of Stanislavski's chapter is "Relaxation of Muscles." He is concerned with specific, detailed, *physical* relaxation, rather than an inner lassitude, though, as always, the outer, physical attitude has inner consequences. These consequences are not a feeling of laziness or dullness, however, but instead one of heightened awareness and increased power.

Practically every acting sin can be traced to some kind of tension, a rigidity of muscles that simply prevents the actor from performing effectively. Forgetting lines, stumbling over words, overacting, or any other kind of artificiality can usually be traced to specific muscles that the actor is tensing involuntarily. Even the wooden, lifeless acting of the sort often seen on the amateur stage can be traced to this same root cause. Although a naive observer might assume that the actor giving a lifeless performance has too *little* tension, that he ought to tense himself up to generate more excitement, what in fact has happened is that the actor is so bottled up with tension all over his face and body that the performance cannot get out.

Acting teachers, critics, knowledgeable audience members, and actors themselves should recognize physical relaxation when they see it in an actor and, conversely, should recognize specific points of physical tension when they occur and are vitiating a performance. It is possible to refer to the particular parts of the body where tension is doing its damage. In the face, the most common tension points are in the forehead, in the areas surrounding the eyes (particularly in the temples), in the ring of muscles around the mouth, and in the jaw. In the body, the common tension places are in the shoulders, from which the tension often radiates into the arms and hands, affecting gestures; and in the hips, from which it often radiates into the legs and feet, affecting stance and movement. In the voice, the usual tension spot is right in the larynx, where tension chokes off the flow of air from the lungs; the vocal cords, instead of forming a flexible, resonant instrument, emit limited, harsh sounds.

Facial relaxation is particularly important in film and television acting, where the closeup reproduces the slightest facial nuance. The great film actors all present a smooth mask to the camera, so that, to persons on the film set, the actor often seems not to be acting at all. (Practically every biography of a film actor contains a quotation from an observer that goes something like, "When the cameras were rolling, he didn't seem to be doing much of anything, but then, when I saw the movie....") Figure 1 is a picture of an actual mask from the Japanese Noh Theatre. Note that it is carved and polished to utter smoothness, giving it, on first impression, an expression of bland neutrality and symmetry. We might wonder why an actor would choose to put on such a blank face. But as we stare at the mask, we notice that, as in a real human face, the symmetry is far from exact. The left nostril[2] is slightly larger than the right. The left eye is slightly wider, longer, and lower than the right. The nose slants infinitesimally to the right. The right cheek is less rounded and full than the left. These minute variations make the mask seem *on the verge* of all sorts of expressions. As we continue looking at it, the mask loses its blankness and becomes ever more mysterious and evocative. Is the mouth smiling or grimacing in pain? The eyes seem at times soft and loving, at other times alert with horror. All human emotions are potential in this mask. When the actor wears it, his voice, gestures, and bodily positions will compete a total *Gestalt*, an integrated whole that conveys a particular emotion.

Figure 2 is a photograph of Greta Garbo. The French critic Roland Barthes once described her face as masklike, which is certainly true here; her face forms a smooth, white mask without the slightest trace of tension. Except for the obvious differences between occidental and oriental features, her "mask" is surprisingly similar to the previous one. Again, the left eye is larger than the right, the nose is slanted slightly right, the left cheek is fuller and rounder than the other. The mask is symmetrical yet asymmetrical, abstracted yet human. Is her mouth smiling or pouting? Are those eyes flashing love or hate? When the facial relaxation is this complete, its emotional potential is inexhaustible.

Figure 3 is a photograph of another great film actor, Marlon Brando. Here the costume, pose, and lighting make the emotion more precise than in the Garbo picture. This Brando picture radiates great feelings of power, danger, anger. Yet, despite this emotional intensity, the face is again a relaxed mask. Not a muscle is being tensed.

The fact that a good actor's face is kept relaxed does not mean that it remains immobile. On the contrary, the relaxed face is flexibly responsive to the actor's unconscious play of emotion, "gesturing" in extremely specific and distinctive ways. In Figure 4, Brando's slight raising of the left eyebrow is devastating, but note that it is also isolated. The rest of the face remains in a state of repose. Its basic neutralness sets off the tiny muscle flexing over the eye, magnifying its effect.

A contrast to these first three faces is the face of a weak actor, Richard Powell, in Figure 5. Here the face is shot through with tension at the typical spots: forehead (both eyebrows are raised, unlike Brando's single one), temples, upper and lower lips, nasal-labial creases, jaw. Although the actor is trying to show us lots of emotion, the impression generated is one of tightness, awkwardness, inhibition. The previous faces were mirrors in which we could view all our own emotions; this face is a shield, repelling our efforts to make emotional connection. Most persons viewing this picture find it hard to look at the face for very long; instead of becoming ever more mysterious, it becomes ever more repulsive.

As with the face, so too with the voice and body. The need for relaxation is the reason that good teachers of speech and voice speak not of developing a stage voice, but of freeing an actor's natural voice. Poor speakers employ a tight monotone, as much as a full octave above their natural voice. There is little modulation or other vocal variety; every line is delivered in the same way, which can be particularly irritating to the audience in strongly emotional scenes. Thrusting his chin forward, which has the effect of a vise on the larynx, the actor will attempt to "emote" to the point of frenzy, but to the audience he will merely seem to be shouting endlessly. All meaning will be blurred, and the ebb and flow that occur with genuine emotion will get lost.

A good actor, in delivering the same passionate speech, will actually shout very little. Just as the raised eyebrow in the picture of Brando in Figure 4 is in counterpoint to the relaxed remainder of the face, so too the few loud moments will be in counterpoint to the bulk of the speech, which will be delivered surprisingly softly on average. Both the meaning of the lines and the quality of the emotion will be crystal clear. The good speaker will vary continuously in pitch, volume, and tone. He will be able to "shift gears" quickly and smoothly, laughing one moment, weeping the next, tossing off a line casually the next. Furthermore, no matter how long the role, no two lines in the same performance will be delivered in exactly the same way.

With regard to the body, critics will often write that an actor's gestures seem overdone and unnatural, without recognizing that the source of the problem is tension in the shoulders. A good example of this could be seen in the public speeches of Richard Nixon. Political commentators mocked his awkward arm-flapping, and Nixon's own advisors tried to get him to stop, but they were unsuccessful because they did not identify the root cause—his tense, hunched shoulders. (The comedian Rich Little made this defect clear by exaggerating it.) When the shoulders are hunched that way, it is impossible for the arms and hands to move in an easy, expressive way. The arms are thrust forward and hang like those of a gorilla; the muscles work against each other, causing the gestures to be jerky and difficult to make.

By contrast, when the shoulders are held back and relaxed, the arms will hang naturally at the sides. Most of the time, they will simply remain in this neutral position; gestures moving from this position will be smooth and forceful. Again, these gestures will be relatively few and will gain effectiveness by their counterpoint to the neutral position.

Tension in the hips is common in our society because of our tradition of sexual repressiveness. Thus an actor will often unconsciously keep this "nasty" part of the body under tight overcontrol; when he walks, very little of his stride will involve the hips, which he will not allow to swivel. He will walk mostly from the knee, making his movement stiff and arhythmic. John Wayne, who was famous for his smooth, loping walk, was very free in the hips. There was a homophobic joke around Hollywood that Wayne had a "fag's walk," and there was a grain of truth in it—not that Wayne was himself a homosexual, but in the fact that the flamboyant homosexual, in blatantly advertising his sexuality, moves freely and easily in the hips, allowing them to swivel naturally. The good actor moves the same way (although perhaps less blatantly) because he, too, is unashamed of his lower body and allows it to move freely.

Tension in the hips will also affect an actor's stance. An actor who is tense here will shift his weight forward on his toes, to the point where beginning actors often seem about to pitch forward on their faces. (This posture will also exaggerate the problem of "gorilla arms" discussed above.) The good actor will inevitably have his weight back on his heels, directly under his spine, so that all the body muscles are in easy harmony. From this position, it is very easy to start to walk smoothly, while from the position with the weight on the toes movements start with an awkward lurch.

To sum up the principle of relaxation, when an actor is tense, he is in one way or another working against himself. His acting will seem forced, unvaried, and unemotional. (This last is a paradox, because he will often be thrashing himself into a state of emotional frenzy.) He will be uncomfortable to watch. When an actor is relaxed, he will seem natural, varied, and emotionally powerful. He will be easy to watch. It is possible to cite specific parts of the body by name, and even specific muscles, in describing the tension and relaxation points that are affecting an actor's performance. Working in such a detailed way is much more likely to produce good results than through generalized impressions. If a director or an acting teacher can spot an actor's tension points and help him to relax them, there will usually be immediate, noticeable improvement, while pep talks demanding energy and emotional turmoil are only likely to accelerate a vicious cycle of more tension and more generalization.

Relating

Although relaxation is necessary for the actor to enter into a creative state, it is not sufficient by itself. If a performance is to have an organic vitality, the actor must become involved in the world of the play. His unconscious mind must respond to the real and imaginary stimuli around him.

This is what is meant by Stanislavski's famous phrase, "Live the part." It is not that the actor should believe that the events of the play are truly happening or that he is actually the character he is portraying. Such an approach would be insane. Instead, the actor must become *involved* in the world of the play. It must engage his imagination in the same way that a good play engages the audience or a good novel its reader. When we read a good novel, we may become so caught up in it that we are moved to laughter or tears, but we are not hallucinating. We can put down the novel—albeit reluctantly—and go to dinner.

Thus, "live the part" might better be rendered as "be *alive* in the part." An actor should at all times be awake and alert on stage or on camera, responsive to the potential of the character's world. Rather than planning out moves and speeches in a conscious, plodding fashion, the good actor lets that world work on him, searching for things that will become stimuli for interesting, apt behavior.

Relating[3] can be divided into two broad types: relating to real circumstances and relating to imaginary circumstances. Both are important in every kind of acting situation. Real circumstances include the physicality of the actor's own body with its costume; the sight, sound, and touch of other actors; the sound of sound effects; the sight and feel of properties and the setting. Imaginary circumstances include necessary artifices, such as the glass of tea that must be drunk as if it were whiskey, the doll wrapped in blankets that must be handled like a live baby, the broiling film set on a July day in Hollywood that must be acted on as if it were an ice field at the North Pole. They also include offstage or off-camera circumstances that affect the action, such as the burning orphanage in Ibsen's *Ghosts*, the duel in Chekhov's *Three Sisters*, or the murder of Duncan in *Macbeth*. Although these things of course do not actually happen during a performance, they must be so vivid in the actor's imagination that the audience never questions them.

Relating to other actors is of prime importance. The actor must really look at his partners, rather than just stare in their direction, and really listen to them, always pondering the significance of what they are saying, rather than just wait for his cue. He must make genuine eye contact and physical contact with other actors. Beginning actors find this especially difficult. To look into another actor's eyes or to touch his body so that you can feel the warmth of it

160

Figure 1
Japanese Mask

Figure 2
Greta Garbo

Figure 3
Marlon Brando

Figure 4
Marlon Brando

Figure 5
Ellen Drew and Richard Powell

Figure 6
John Wayne

Figure 7
W. C. Fields

Figure 8
W. C. Fields

Figure 9
Frank McHugh, James Cagney, and Humphrey Bogart

means that you must come out of your shell, giving yourself up to the situation rather than consciously trying to manipulate it.

Such relating is the whole key to *timing*. When an actor's timing is off so that he is always responding a hairbreadth too soon or too late, the performance goes flat. Similarly, a deadness covers the stage when the actor's responses are a touch overplayed or underplayed. In such cases, audience members will be vaguely aware that something is wrong. Their attention will wander from the play, but it will be hard to say why, because the performances may be running quite smoothly, with nothing obviously amiss. A critic in his review will be likely to take refuge in meaningless metaphors, saying that the performances lacked "spark," or to start quibbling about the director's interpretation. In ninety percent of such cases, what was actually wrong was that the actors were not listening to one another.

The actor must similarly be alive to the props and setting around him. The question is how well the actor *uses* the setting and props. The good actor will handle things more than the bad actor does, and will make acting "bits" out of them. He will never forget to pick up fallen objects or to close doors. He will allow his costume to affect him in interesting ways, rather than move about stiffly as if forced to attend a costume party that was beneath his dignity. In sum, the good actor will *notice* things. When Stanislavski faulted the actor playing Khlestakov for not seeing the unmade bed, he was not nit-picking. The bed was the emotional key to the scene; the actor should not only have looked at it, but have let it affect him, rather than just drawing on his generalized inner emotions.

With imaginary circumstances, one can compare the supposed details given by the script with how the actors actually play them. The script says that it is cold; do the actors shiver? They are discussing confidential matters in a public place; do they speak softly? A character is supposed to have run a mile just before entering; is the actor panting? An actor looks out a window and describes the street three floors below (although he is actually looking at the stage floor, on the same level as he is); do his eyes seem focus in the distance? Do they move from place to place as he describes different parts of the offstage or off-camera scene? When another actor describes the same scene, does he seem to look at those same places? To fail in such matters is not just destructive of verisimilitude; it is destructive of the performance's variety and force. Even in a non-realistic play, the actor must relate to the given circumstances with full attention to their details; if he is supposed to look out the window at people turning into rhinoceroses, he must see and describe them as unique, individualized rhinoceroses.

A common acting problem involves imaginary circumstances when the actor must describe past events. When this is well done, the actor will be creating the offstage or off-camera scenes for himself, seeing them in his imagination. As he describes the past events, his emotional reaction to each will be unique. The audience will receive a very specific, vivid picture via the actor's description. When the actor fails to deliver a vivid picture, it is again usually because he is trying to stir himself up emotionally, in vain hopes of impressing the audience with his mighty performance. Since he is not relating to the imaginary circumstances, his emotional reaction remains the same to all the events that he is supposedly describing. He is generalizing, making his description into a blur, which soon bores the audience, no matter how frenzied the actor.

Relating to imaginary circumstances is essential in film acting, where shots and scenes are filmed completely out of order. One actor may converse with another actor who is not even on the set, whose part in the scene will be filmed months later; the former must appear to be excitedly involved, even though the latter's speeches are being read for the moment in a monotone by a director's assistant. The actor must look past the camera at an assortment of wires, lights, script girls, cameramen, grips, and hangers-on and convince us that he is watching a fire or a murder. A decade ago there was a popular television series called *Quincy*, which presented an extraordinary challenge of this sort for Jack Klugman, the actor in the title role. Each script was written to focus on a corpse that Quincy, a forensic pathologist, had to dissect. Since a real dissection of a real corpse could not be shown on television, we could respond to the central plot element of each episode only through Quincy's reaction to it. We saw Quincy bending over and working on a "corpse" that was supposed to be just below the frame of the camera shot, but which was actually just an empty table. The success of the show was a tribute to Klugman's skill in making us believe that the empty table actually supported a dead body that was the source of fascinating criminal evidence.

Figure 7 shows W. C. Fields, a master at relating, looking at someone in the distance. He is carrying all sorts of bizarre, ridiculously oversized equipment, but he relates to it simply and unaffectedly. In no way is he saying to us, "Just look at all this funny stuff I'm carrying." The funniness is our inference, not his. He accepts this ridiculous junk as a tangible, real set of circumstances. Furthermore, he is actually looking through a cluster of cameramen at nothing in particular. But every ounce of his energy appears to be focusing on something that is desperately important to him. It is essential to him that he figure it out. A weak actor would be thinking only of himself, of projecting some attitude on the audience. Fields instead is thinking only of that distant person who means so much to him—and who is not there.

Objectives

Figure 8 shows Fields again, this time pursuing an elusive mouthful of ice-cream soda. There is no doubt in the audience's mind that he *wants* it. This is an example of what Stanislavski meant by *the objective*. It is a goal, whether tangible or abstract, that the actor must pursue. For the great comic actors in particular, this pursuit can become monomaniacal. Whether Fields's objectives were blunt physical needs like booze, food, money, and sex, or emotional needs like maintaining dignity or defeating an infant enemy, he always sought them with his whole being. (In one film, when a bottle of whiskey drops out the window of an airplane, he leaps out after it!) In Figure 8 he is again not trying to impress us or to be funny; he is trying to get his mouth around the elusive morsel on the end of the spoon. His eyes are focused on it, and his mouth twists to the side in a desperate attempt to catch it. The humor arises from the disproportion between the urgency of his desire and the relative paltriness of the goal. In noncomic drama, such a disproportion would not exist. Macbeth's objective of becoming king, for example, is a far from paltry goal, but the actor playing Macbeth must pursue it with an intensity equal to that of Fields.

The objective is the *organizing* principle of the performance of a role. Relating is a neutral, reactive kind of behavior, while relaxation is outright negative behavior, the stripping away of tension so that the face, body, and voice can come under the influence of the unconscious mind. The pursuit of an objective, however, is active behavior, the thing that connects the actor with his role. The actor who is relaxed and relating will always be easy to watch. If he is pursuing the wrong objectives, however, he will not be fulfilling the demands of the play, while if he is pursuing no objective at all, he will seem diffuse and tame. The American stereotype of the "Method Actor" as one who just stands around mumbling and scratching arose because some actors concentrated on the passive side of Stanislavski's theory—relaxation and relating—but ignored the active side of the pursuit of a single, clear objective.

Stanislavski urged the actor to pursue a series of such objectives. These objectives must be in terms of the character and the play rather than in terms of the audience (except in those plays where the audience's presence is acknowledged); they must be expressed in terms of an active verb—to seduce, to humiliate, to convince, to flee. Each objective forms a separate unit of the performance; during that unit, the actor focuses on trying to achieve that objective and on nothing else. Of course, he will be *doing* a lot more; in Figure 8, Fields is elegantly raising his pinkie, a hilarious bit of overrefinement for the nature of the scene, but such bits arise of themselves, unconsciously. He is thinking only of that ice-cream soda. The objective is the conscious channel for the mass of unconscious creative energy that is available when the actor is relaxed and relating. It gives this creative energy coherence. The series of objectives form a kind of score for the role; indeed, the objective in acting is analogous to melody in music. Although as music becomes more complex and dissonant, melody becomes more elusive and difficult to define, ultimately melody is what distinguishes music from mere random sounds. Similarly, as drama becomes more complex and abstract compared to simple forms like the broad farce of Fields's movie, the actor's objectives also become more complicated and more difficult to determine, but ultimately they are essential if the performance is to be intelligible and affecting.

A common flaw is to play attitudes or emotions rather than objectives. An actor playing a sorrowful scene, for example, may churn himself up into an emotional frenzy, thereby hoping to impress us. But, of course, the *character's* objective is not "to impress the audience." Instead, he will want something in the play; in fact, the character may very well want not to show emotion. Similarly, an actor in a drawing room comedy may want to impress the audience by being witty or handsome or scintillating, rather than pursue what the character wants, which in a play of this sort is usually sex or money, although in a play by Shaw it is likely to be the need to convince the other characters of some very urgent ideas. Playing objectives leads to emotions that are varied and *precise*; starting with emotions first leads instead to heaviness and vagueness.

Stanislavski believed that all of an actor's individual objectives in a role could be subsumed under a single superobjective. Francis Fergusson has seen similarities between this concept and Aristotle's concept of action (*praxis*). The superobjective or action defines the entire role and, ultimately, the entire play. Thus, according to Fergusson, in Sophocles's *Oedipus Rex*, the superobjective is "to find the slayer,"[4] in *Hamlet* it is "to find and destroy the hidden 'impostume,'"[5] and in Chekhov's *Three Sisters* it is "to get to Moscow,"[6] with all that Moscow implies in that play in terms of escapism. Fergusson's perceptions are a rare example of critical theory and acting theory actually enriching each other. Nevertheless, the actor should not press the notion of superobjective too hard. The superobjective provides a valuable way of organizing a role, but it is not what an actor plays, moment by moment. Oedipus's superobjective might be "to find the slayer," but at a particular moment, what the actor specifically plays is "to humiliate Teiresias," or "to examine the evidence." The superobjective is helpful in cases when, as sometimes happens, you are doing your best, moment by moment, but the role is not working overall. A new superobjective helps you to re-examine and redefine all the individual objectives that you have been playing.

It is important to distinguish objective from motive. *Motivation* is a word tossed about far too casually in the theatre. It differs crucially from objective in that it looks backward, not forward, and is likely to be hidden and psychological rather than conscious and clear. Motivation is, of course, quite important in modern psychological drama. Miss Julie, as Strindberg informs us, is motivated by her upbringing, her menstrual period, the atmosphere of Midsummer Eve, and a host of other things. But in plays written before the realistic era and in many modern antirealistic plays as well, it is quite possible for characters to have no motives at all in any deep sense, and modern actors are wrong when they try to invent some, like deciding that Iago is motivated by an unconscious homosexual passion for Othello. But whether characters have motives or not, they always have conscious objectives if the play is any good at all. Assuming that Iago has "motiveless malignity" (Coleridge's theory), he does not have "objectiveless malignity." There is no doubt that he wants to destroy Othello. Similarly, we may argue forever about whether Hamlet has any motive for delaying, but there is no doubt that he wants to delay, and, in the process, he wants to put on a play to catch the conscience of the king, to put down Rosencrantz and Guildenstern, to talk his mother out of sleeping with Claudius, to stab the person behind the arras, to go to England, to return and challenge Claudius, to fight Laertes in Ophelia's open grave, to fight a duel, to kill Claudius (at last), and, dying, to have Horatio tell his story.

All three principal concepts of acting can be summed up by using the final photograph, Figure 9. (Study it for a few moments before reading any further.) Most people, in looking at this picture, find their attention immediately taken by James Cagney because of his strong, front-and-center position. Gradually and inexorably, however, their attention is drawn to Humphrey Bogart, at our right. This attraction cannot be attributed to a mystical "star quality" of Bogart's, since Cagney was just as big a star as he. Nor can it have anything to do with Bogart's looks; the man was homely. Nor can it be attributed to positioning; Cagney has the central position and is slightly "upstage" of Bogart. Indeed, Bogart, at our right, is in what is theoretically the weakest position of all three actors; since we read from left to right, our eye is believed to go first, by habit, to the left, all else being equal. The reason for Bogart's attraction is simply that he is relaxing, relating, and pursuing his objective better than the other two actors.

Note first the three actors' faces. Frank McHugh, the actor at Cagney's right, shows tension in his slightly raised eyebrows and in his slightly closed eyelids; this gives him a vacuous, dead expression that cannot attract us. Cagney's eyes are more relaxed and open, but there are strong tension lines between his brows; tension in his upper lip, causing it to curl slightly open; and tension in his jaw (a common problem for Cagney) as evidenced by the tensed muscles in his left cheek. The relaxed eyes give him a powerful expression that catches our attention initially, but the tension elsewhere makes the expression frozen and lacking in mystery. We tire of looking at him. Bogart, in contrast to the other two, shows no tension in his face at all; it is utterly composed and relaxed.

Next, look at the actors' bodies. Cagney's weight is on his toes, and there is tension in his shoulders, causing a slight case of "gorilla arms"; they should be back at his sides. His body is four-square to the camera, showing no resilience. The actor at his right is doing somewhat better; his weight is back on his heels, and he shows no tension in his shoulders, so that the hand not holding the gun hangs easily at his side. His body is turned slightly from the camera, but like Cagney's is set very squarely in terms of this orientation. He thus exhibits a fair degree of bodily relaxation, but it is less than Bogart's. Bogart too has his weight back on his heels and is very loose in the shoulders. His free arm hangs loosely at his side, where it belongs. But most important, note that, unlike the others, he has his torso slightly twisted in a classic *contrapposto* pose. Classical sculptors used this pose for the standing human figure, because it seemed to them to be the most graceful and natural, as indeed it is. It is possible to stand this way only when the body is relaxed and supple. The pose gives an impression of ease and of a potential for quick movement. If someone could tell all three actors here to walk forward, Bogart would be the first to move and would make the movement with fluidity. This potential for action helps to make him seem the most menacing of the three actors.

The director of this film has chosen here to identify the person who is ostensibly the object of these three characters' attention with the camera itself. (This is a standard cinematic device for heightening the audience's excitement; it seems that we ourselves are confronting these three men.) With regard to relating, Cagney and Bogart are both focusing very strongly on the camera, but the third actor is focusing above and slightly to the side, if he can be said to be focusing at all. Unlike Cagney and Bogart, he seems to be in the scene but not of it, which is why it is an effort even to notice him.

Finally, of the three actors, only Bogart is pursuing a clear objective—to intimidate his challenger. Cagney, though tense, is passive; who knows what he wants? McHugh is pointing his gun down and to his left, as if he does not believe it is really a weapon. It is a mere prop for him, an emblem that is supposed to say, "This man is a crook." It is not something that he *wants to use.* Only Bogart's gun is actually aimed at the imaginary adversary. This prop really is a weapon for Bogart, and we have no doubt that he might actually want to shoot it. Knowing what he wants, we find his pose the most coherent of the three. In sum, then, Bogart, by employing all three principles of acting—relaxing, relating, and the pursuit of an objective—is able to steal the scene, despite a weak position in the pictorial composition and despite the fact that he is sharing the scene with another charismatic star.

In my discussions above, I have purposefully blurred distinctions between stage and film acting, realism and style, tragedy and comedy. Different types of acting obviously require differing techniques. Stanislavski's concepts, however, provide a fundamental way of dealing with all types. Despite Stanislavski's reputation in America, his ideas are certainly not limited to psychological, realistic, "serious" acting; in fact, in some instances comic acting provides the best examples of what Stanislavski is driving at.

To understand the range of Stanislavski's theories, consider, for example, an obvious unreality like blank verse. To Stanislavski, this is simply a given circumstance of a play to which an actor must *relate.* The actor must be sensitive to the sound of his and the other actors' voices, the rhythms and imagery that are an essential part of the experience of the particular play. In a realistic play, the warmth of a coffee cup is important as a stimulus to the actor; in *A Midsummer Night's Dream*, the sensuous, hissing alliteration in the line "There sleeps Titania sometime of the night" is similarly important.

Note, then, that relating means *reacting to the given circumstances of the play,* rather than reacting to remembered everyday life. Playing a role in Shakespeare (or any other play, even a realistic one) does not involve reducing everything to your personal real-life experience, "substituting" your own memories for the character's emotions. Your personal life simply does not come into play with relaxation, relating, and objectives, the purpose of which is to plunge you into the world of the play, rather than to take you away from it and get you thinking about the time your pet dog died.

Recently, I played the role of Brabantio, Desdemona's father, in a production of *Othello*. I happen to have a daughter about Desdemona's age, who, by coincidence, was just about to be married. By the conventional wisdom, I ought to have been spending all my time on stage thinking about my daughter Sarah, relating my feelings about her and her fiancé to Desdemona and Othello. But *Othello* is a play that moved me deeply the first time I read it, long before my daughter was born, and continues to move me every time I see it, read it, or teach it; was I supposed to ignore *those* feelings? Furthermore, the actress playing Desdemona in this production gave a consistently strong performance that brought tears to my eyes every single night; was I supposed to ignore her exciting acting and think about my own daughter instead? The play itself was my source of inspiration, not my own life; relaxing, relating to my fellow actors and to the given circumstances of the script (including the immensely potent language, which felt like a jet engine at my disposal), and pursuing the objective of trying to save Desdemona from the "foul thief" Othello, helped turn me into Shakespeare's wealthy, powerful, raging, poetic Brabantio, rather than reducing Brabantio to my impoverished, tame, professorial, prosaic self.

Stanislavski's theories are active. They are not abstract truths about acting, but stimuli for action. Different people will make differing things of them. My explications of Stanislavski above are very much my own personal ones; the important thing is not whether they are "correct" (though I hope they are), but rather how Stanislavski's ideas have stimulated me, as a critic and as an actor. They have helped me to see things that I would not otherwise have seen, and to do things that I would not otherwise have been able to do.

This is Stanislavski's ultimate legacy, as an enabler. As already noted, his system does not guarantee success; it cannot *cause* a good performance, but can only *enable* one. Relaxation, relating, and the pursuit of objectives are means to an end, skills rather than art itself, and like all artistic skills must be learned to the point of becoming second nature. Only then does acting begin.

TWELVE

STRASBERG AND "AFFECTIVE MEMORY"

L ee Strasberg provides a good example of the tendency to take personal meanings from Stanislavski's theories. Strasberg's teaching was a radical adaptation of Stanislavski's ideas, in a manner suited to Strasberg's own background and personality, and to what he perceived as the needs of the American actor.

Strasberg never met Stanislavski, never studied his works systematically, never learned Russian. As a youth in the 1920s, he came in contact with Stanislavski's ideas at the American Laboratory Theatre in New York, where he studied acting with two Russian emigrés from the Moscow Art Theatre, Richard Boleslavsky and Maria Ouspenskaya. After that, Strasberg appears never to have had contact with the Moscow Art Theatre[1] or its members again, though there were plenty of them in the United States.

Unlike Stanislavski, one of the great actors of history with a wide range of roles, Strasberg did little acting himself. He did not act with the Group Theatre, nor at the Actors Studio. Late in life, he appeared in a few films, starting with *The Godfather, Part II*. His performances are unrevealing. They certainly lack the emotional explosiveness of his finest students, but they also lack the introspection and self-indulgence of his worst. Straightforward, workmanlike, his acting has little to distinguish it from that of thousands of other Hollywood character actors.

Also unlike Stanislavski, a great director who staged some of the landmark productions of the Russian theatre, Strasberg directed very little. His best work was in realistic dramas with the Group Theatre, most notably Sidney Kingsley's *Men in White* (1933), which attracted attention for its long, silent pantomime scene of a surgical operation. After the thirties, he directed only sporadically; in fact, one reason he became the dominant figure at the Actors Studio in the forties was that he was far less busy professionally than its founders, Cheryl Crawford, Elia Kazan, and Robert Lewis. Strasberg had particular trouble directing nonrealistic material; his *Peer Gynt* (1951), starring John Garfield, and his *Three Sisters* (1965), with several excellent Studio actors, were critical and box office failures.

One characteristic Strasberg shared with Stanislavski was an insensitivity to dramatic literature. Stanislavski did not like Chekhov's plays at first; could not fathom Symbolism, a major literary and artistic movement of the 1890s; and, as Chekhov charged, did not understand Ibsen. Stanislavski's literary tastes—for all his interest in realism on stage—tended toward the romantic and overblown. His salvation was his co-founder of the Moscow Art Theatre, Vladimir Nemirovich-Danchenko, a sensitive playwright and teacher who became Stanislavski's literary advisor. It was Nemirovich-Danchenko who first recognized Chekhov's worth as a playwright and who talked Stanislavski into doing his plays. Despite many differences of opinion, the two co-founders continued to work together at the Moscow Art Theatre for over forty years, until Stanislavski's death.

Strasberg's problem may have been that he had no Nemirovich-Danchenko. There were dramatic critics at the American

Laboratory Theatre, including John Mason Brown and the superb Francis Fergusson, but they did not come over into the Group Theatre and seem to have had no influence at all on Strasberg. Harold Clurman, a well-read man with a good literary education, was one of the co-founders of the Group Theatre; when Strasberg resisted doing the plays of Clifford Odets there (recapitulating Stanislavski's initial attitude toward Chekhov!), it was primarily Clurman's influence that brought him around. But after the break-up of the Group Theatre in 1941, the two did not collaborate again. Perhaps as a result, the curriculum at the Actors Studio and at the Strasberg Institute never involved serious literary study; had Clurman been involved, the syllabus would have been different.

Strasberg's literary naivete, however, went beyond Stanislavski's to an outright antiliterary bias. Strasberg was forever making statements like the following: "One can have brilliant theoretic, literary, critical, or philosophical concepts of a play and not be able to create reality on stage."[2] That the opposite might be true, that one can "create reality on stage" as an actor, and yet botch a performance because of not understanding the play, never occurred to him. The subliminal message to his students was clear: Don't study literature. It only distracts you from your job of creating emotional intensity on stage. He followed through this attitude in his classroom teaching, where not only was there no discussion of literature in the highbrow sense of "theoretic, literary, critical, or philosophical concepts," but in the more immediate sense of what was going on in the play being worked on. Stanislavski, for all his literary weaknesses, had great respect for the play *in performance*. For Strasberg, as we shall see, the stress was instead on creating the illusion of reality. He even maintained it was better for students to perform short stories than plays, because the dialogue in a short story is "more representative of what a character would really say."[3]

This perverse avoidance of plays was a habit of mind for Strasberg, both in his directing and in his teaching. He describes in his memoirs how he directed the actors in Group Theatre productions by giving them "adjustments," which involved imagining something not in the script, which could even be false to it. To get an "ethereal" quality from Stella Adler, for example, he had her imagine a scene from John Howard Lawson's *Success Story* taking place on a ship, though in fact it was supposed to be on dry land. "The purpose," Strasberg wrote, "was to find a way of creating the emotional reaction demanded of the character by the text."[4] But why was the text itself insufficient? Why not try to make the *play* more vivid for Adler, through verbal descriptions, or a costume, a prop, the scenery, the lighting? He gives several examples of such "adjustments," but, as in all his writings, interviews, and transcribed teaching, he never discusses the play itself except in brief, general terms. The transcriptions of the tapes of his classes at the Actors Studio often show him commenting on a student's work in a scene for many pages without ever mentioning the play at all.

Strasberg considered himself an ardent disciple of Stanislavski, using the Russian's name to describe his approach to teaching acting rather than presenting it as something original. *Strasberg at the Actors Studio*, a book of tape-recorded sessions, lists fifty-one references to Stanislavski in its index.[5] It is always "Stanislavski discovered," "Stanislavski's basic point is," "Stanislavski posited," "Stanislavski stressed," not "I discovered," "My basic point is," etc. Strasberg also sometimes cited the late nineteenth-century French psychologist Théodule Ribot, who studied imaginary emotions, but, typically, stressed Ribot's influence on Stanislavski: "Ribot's discoveries obviously played a great role in Stanislavsky's growing awareness of the actor's unconscious procedures during the creative process."[6]

Strasberg, then, was like St. Paul, who never met Jesus in the flesh but who felt he knew him better than anyone because of a mystical communion, and who felt the need to spread the Gospel in Jesus's name rather than his own. The American Laboratory Theatre was Strasberg's road to Damascus. The flash of insight he received there changed his life. After that, he never changed again;

his own students remarked proudly on how he still was using his notes from the Lab Theatre fifty years later. Stanislavski himself was constantly questioning and altering his system, at one point radically; the American "Method," as Strasberg taught it at the Group Theatre, the Actors Studio, and in his own Lee Strasberg Theatre Institute (which has branches in New York, Los Angeles, and London), has evolved very little.

Nevertheless, the Strasberg Method deserves to be judged on its own merits. There can be no doubt that it has had enormous influence on acting in our theatre, and even more on acting in film. Strasberg was criticized early on for not being "true" to Stanislavski; in fact, when Stella Adler came back from meeting with Stanislavski in the 1930s to challenge Strasberg with words from the master himself, Strasberg accused *Stanislavski* with not being true to his own system. (He was partially correct, since Stanislavski's ideas, as noted, were evolving.) But true or false, the proof of the pudding is in the eating. In the theatre, the important thing is not the purity of the Method, but its results.

And the Method does work. At times, the results can seem miraculous. The actual techniques involved, however, are more subtle and complex than popularly believed. Despite the widespread view of the Method as pushing realism to its wildest extreme, Strasberg did *not* call for real emotion, did *not* maintain that the actor should literally believe that he was the character, did *not* want actors to hallucinate that the play was actually happening. Strasberg's approach was emotion-based, which is the source of both its strengths and its weaknesses, but he made it abundantly clear that the actor was not to use "real, honest emotion," but *remembered* emotion:

> In acting we never use literal emotion. You've heard actors say, "Hit me, hit me—if you won't hit me, I won't get it." Well, that's not acting.... The basic idea of affective memory is not emotional recall but that the actor's emotion on the stage

should never be really real. It should always be only *remembered* emotion.[7]

Furthermore, the remembered emotion is not even recalled *directly*. The actor playing Hamlet, for example, is not supposed to think about how he felt when his own father died. Instead, the technique of "affective memory" requires the actor to recall the *events surrounding the emotion* as vividly as possible:

> You do not start to remember the emotion, you start to remember the place, the taste of something, the touch of something, the sound of something, and you remember that as simply and as clearly as you can. You touch the things, in your mind, but with the senses alive.[8]

Thus, if you decided to draw upon the experience of the death of your father (and Strasberg stressed that it was *not* good to use such extreme, painful events unless they were well back in the past), you would not try to relive the emotion directly, but instead would try to recall such background sensations as the smell of the medications, the murmur of the nurses in the hall of the hospital, the hiss of the oxygen equipment, the sight of a fly on the wall.

In other words, affective memory takes Stanislavski's notion of relating and applies it to remembered real-life experiences. When applied in this specific way, the memories undoubtedly "affect" the actor. In response to the recalled surrounding events, the remembered feelings come welling up, and can be used to give the required emotional punch to an actor's performance. Acting classes that use affective memory can be spectacular performances in themselves, with students weeping or laughing hysterically. Yet, because emotion remembered this way is imaginary emotion, their performances can be shaped and controlled. If not, it means that the recalled experiences are too recent and raw. Others should be substituted.

178

Remembered emotions tend to weaken or fade over time. A recalled experience that has you racked with weeping when you first use it may barely produce a snivel after you have repeated the exercise frequently. This is obviously a problem in the theatre, where you may have to give hundreds of performances of the same emotion; it is less a problem in film, where one good "take" will suffice. (Even there multiple takes may be necessary for reasons that have nothing to do with your acting, and you are expected to give your best each time.) The trick, as with any relating exercise, is always to find new details—the tick of a clock, a fold in the blanket, the dust on the floor. The details that worked in the past tend to become cut and dried, categorized, and thus lose their punch. It is necessary continually to find new ones, but this is no great difficulty in most instances. Strasberg thus placed affective memory at the center of his system, maintaining that an actor could have a dozen or so emotions to recapture in this manner, which could be used in all possible acting situations. Ribot had pointed out the slowness with which imaginary emotions arise, but Strasberg demonstrated that with training, the actor could summon an emotion in about one minute.

Strasberg's total system stressed relaxation as an essential preparation for affective memory. He would do extensive, specific work with an actor on facial and bodily relaxation, before moving on to *sense memory*, in which past physical sensations are recalled, and which was in turn the basis for emotion memory. His system also involved peripheral experiences like imitating animals, which he felt was useful in learning characterization (again, he did not insist that the actor play only himself), song and dance exercises, and a controversial exercise called "the Private Moment," which required the actor to perform in class something that he ordinarily would do only when alone.[9] Finally, as with most American acting teachers, the bulk of Strasberg's teaching consisted of observing and commenting on actors in scenes, usually excerpted from realistic American drama, and usually involving only two characters.

179

Sometimes students would perform entire plays, which were not limited to realism. Strasberg himself would not usually direct these, however.

How much does Strasberg's system really owe to Stanislavski? At one extreme, the stress on relaxation is certainly Stanislavskian; at the other, the Private Moment is Strasberg's own invention. Affective memory itself, however, is in a more complex position. Stanislavski does devote a chapter in *An Actor Prepares* to "Emotion Memory,"[10] but he (as Tortsov) does not provide specific exercises for students to recall their personal emotions. He first cites Ribot, and discusses briefly how emotion memory can bring back feelings already experienced. Then Kostya sees a horrible accident on the street, and notices how his feelings about it change with the passage of time. Tortsov then provides a rhapsodic commentary on remembered emotions: "Time is a splendid filter for our remembered feelings—besides it is a great artist. It not only purifies, it also transmutes even painfully realistic emotions into poetry."[11] Tortsov does not suggest that Kostya should use the memory of the accident in a scene or a play, however; the stress instead is on the *nature* of remembered emotions, which are transmuted by time into poetry.

Stanislavski/Tortsov comes closest to emotion memory in the Strasbergian sense when he proposes that the actor "chooses very carefully from among his memories and culls out of his living experiences the ones that are most enticing."[12] Even here, Stanislavski is talking about a much more general process than the specialized techniques perfected at the Actors Studio—a refinement of sensibility rather than the imaginary reliving of *individual* personal events.

The only exercise in the chapter has the students on stage, noting how different arrangements of furniture, and changing sound and lighting effects, affect their moods. There is much discussion of how particular stimuli, both inner and outer, can bring on emotion memory. Stanislavski stresses the importance of sets, lighting, and sound effects not so much as stimuli for the audience as for the actors. In addition to such "outer" stimuli, he also mentions "inner" ones, which turn out *not* to come from the actors' personal lives, but from the objectives of the play: "As time goes on you will become acquainted with many new inner sources of stimulation. The most powerful of them lies in the text of the play, the implications of thought and feeling that underlie it and affect the interrelationship of the actors."[13]

Ivan Petrovich Pavlov, the psychologist who influenced all Russian theorists of acting from Stanislavski onward, was important for this concept of emotion memory. In a famous experiment, Pavlov would ring a bell whenever he fed a dog. After a while, the dog would salivate merely at the sound of the bell, without any food being present. Pavlov called this a *conditioned response*; the dog was conditioned by repeated experiences to associate the bell with food, and thus respond to it. For Stanislavski, the internal and external stage conditions are like Pavlov's bell, stimulating conditioned responses by the associations they evoke. They do not bring back *individual* emotional experiences, but a lifetime of them. According to Jean Benedetti, Stanislavski's biographer, this is what Ribot meant by affective memory as well: "A touch, a sound, a smell may enable a patient to relive *not just one experience but a grouping of similar experiences* which merge to create a single emotional state."[14]

Emotion memory, then, for Stanislavski is simply the imaginary emotion that the actor feels on stage, regardless of how it is achieved. It relies on the actor's past emotional life *as a whole*, rather than the recall of specific instances; past emotional life is "filtered," or poeticized, but you do not run through it seeking individual events for direct use in performance. Finally, the immediate stimuli for Stanislavski's emotion memory are found *in the play itself*—either "outer" elements like sets and lighting or "inner" ones like the objectives and character relationships —rather than in recalled personal experiences. If the imaginary stimuli are vivid enough, we respond to them emotionally, because we have been conditioned throughout our lives to respond to similar ones many times.[15]

How did Strasberg get from this view of emotion memory to his own? The key figure was Richard Boleslavsky, his teacher and main link with Stanislavski. At the American Laboratory Theatre, Boleslavsky stressed "living the part," concentration, and emotion memory. Boleslavsky's lecture notes contain an example of the last that is closer to Strasberg's concept than to the one found in Stanislavski's *An Actor Prepares*: An actor playing Othello searches in his memory for examples of jealousy. He recalls a newspaper review praising another actor, which made him feel envious; he remembers his wife receiving a letter addressed in a strange handwriting; he recalls coming to the theatre and finding his regular seat occupied by another person. All these recollections help him to find the required jealous feelings.[16] Strasberg no doubt responded to lectures like this by codifying the described process. Emotion memory was not so *central* to Boleslavsky, however; his book, *Acting: The First Six Lessons*,[17] lists it as only one of the six lessons, the other five being Concentration, Dramatic Action, Characterization, Observation, and Rhythm.

Thus, although Strasberg's affective memory techniques can be traced to Stanislavski, they had radically changed. There was a shift in emphasis from the play (whether as written or on the stage) to the actor's personal life, with a zeroing in on specific incidents. This shift may be related to Strasberg's lack of experience in the theatre itself. For decades, the bulk of his work was confined to the classroom. There, his emotion memory exercises drew stunning results. (His memoirs contain a page of photographs of him conducting his wife in a demonstration of emotion memory in Germany; even though the photos are small and of poor quality, the intensity of her writhing, screaming, and laughing is evident.)[18] Adapting such results to the stage, however, remained problematic. There is the difficulty of repeating an exercise over and over that tends to fade with time, though Strasberg did recognize the problem and develop strategies for dealing with it. More fundamental is the fact that a Strasberg emotion memory exercise takes the actor away from the here and now of performance to an imaginary world of memories. Relating to the events surrounding the death of your father keeps you from relating to the set, properties, lighting, and, most important, your fellow actors. An actor doing emotion memory will often seem to be in a daze. The other actors find him hard to deal with, when there should be an easy camaraderie on stage at all times, a give and take that are essential to bringing performances to life. To the audience, the traditional Method actor can seem powerful but detached, not part of the play somehow.

There is also a problem with timing. "Take a minute" was a catch phrase for Method actors from the days of the Group Theatre, but one minute is actually a rather long time on stage. The actor using emotion memory tends to lag behind the play, where a quick, drastic ebb and flow of action is common. Finally, there is the problem of dealing with unreal elements of a play. You cannot use emotion memory to recall blank verse, because you never speak it in real life. The Method is notorious for its failures in nonrealistic drama. Strasberg himself, as noted, had no success in directing the classics, and appears never to have acted in them.

There are occasions, however, when Strasberg's emotion memory is useful. Sometimes it is simply impossible to use the given circumstances of a play as an emotional stimulus, as when a scene starts at an emotional peak. An actor called upon to enter weeping might very well find emotion memory the key to doing it effectively, though once he gets on stage he ought to shift his attention from whatever is causing the tears to his surroundings and his fellow actors.

But it is in film that Strasberg's technique really comes into its own. Shooting a film involves sitting around for long periods, and then from time to time doing shots in isolation, which may be as brief as a few seconds. In place of the flow of action that carries you along emotionally in a play, there is endless starting and stopping. It may not be possible to use your surroundings as a stimulus—in a process shot, the setting is not even there, but is instead added on the film later. As for using your fellow actors, they may not be there either—a scene between two actors may actually be shot at two different times in two different cities, with each actor by himself. Even the script may be of little help—it is common in filmmaking for the script to be revised as you go along, so that the actors may have little sense of the whole film while they make parts of it. There have even been films that were substantially revised in the editing room, after all the scenes were shot. Thus, emotion memory may be the only way an actor can give an effective performance on film, where, after all, each scene requires only one good take. It is no accident that American Method actors have gone on to achieve their greatest successes in the movies. Some have never come back to the stage again.

Strasberg's emotion memory, then, can be seen partly as a cause, but even more as a result, of the decline of the American theatre. The Method never caught on in other countries, because there actors have tended to work in both film and theatre; even today, live theatre in most advanced countries continues to thrive, so that actors can play many stage roles per year. In the United States, however, the only place most actors can do much stage work is in a classroom. Not many plays are done here professionally anymore, even in New York, and professional repertory companies offering long-term employment on a steady salary are almost nonexistent. The stage experience that a German or French or British actor gets in actual plays, in a wide range of styles, for paying audiences, is attained here instead in excerpted scenes, mostly modern and realistic, for an audience consisting of fellow students and a teacher.

The Method would never have been possible without a classroom approach to teaching acting. The American Laboratory Theatre was more school than theatre. Even in the Group Theatre, a producing organization, summers were spent in the country doing workshops, run by Strasberg. When the Actors Studio began in the 1940s, it was only a school; it produced no plays until the early sixties, when its attempt to become a producing repertory company failed. (Strasberg's *Three Sisters* was central to this failed effort.) For thousands of years, actors had learned their art through an apprentice system, acting in hundreds of plays, working their way up from small roles to larger ones, to leading roles if they were good enough. American actors now learn by getting in touch with their emotions in a classroom, rarely performing in full plays for an audience. Even in university theatre departments, the classroom rather than the stage has become the center of the students' learning; some acting teachers even forbid their students to perform in plays until they are "ready," an attitude that would have amazed actors in the days of Sophocles, Shakespeare, or Molière. The *specialized* audience of students and teacher come to the classroom to analyze rather than to enjoy. Instead of responding to a play as a whole, they home in on the individual actors, picking apart their performances for "honesty," "truth," "reality," and emotional intensity. The resultant style of acting is therefore inevitably individualistic, to the point of being detached and self-absorbed.

Most of the actors who came to Strasberg's classes at the Group Theatre already had a great deal of stage experience. Not all of them liked what was being taught in the classes; Stella Adler, for one, strongly rebelled. Nevertheless, the Method enriched their acting because it could be taken in context; the Group did produce plays, and there was also plenty of other stage work still available in New York at the time. Even in the forties and early fifties, in the heyday of the Actors Studio, there was still a substantial professional theatre in New York, plus live television (which resembles theatre more than it does film) and radio drama. Today, it is just about impossible to make a living doing stage work. You try to make one from television commercials and films, do an occasional play—and take classes. It is like being on a football team that hardly ever plays a game. No matter how talented you are, and no matter how good your coaching, it is hard to improve.

Strasberg's emotion memory is a worthwhile innovation in acting. The fact that he applied Stanislavski's name to what was really his own technique in no way detracts from its validity. Every actor should learn Strasberg's emotion memory and be prepared to use it in the proper circumstances. The actor should recognize, however, that it is a specialized technique, which you would no more use for every acting situation than you would play every role in a gray wig. The central ideas from Stanislavski—relaxation, relating, objectives—are far more important, and are universal in their usefulness.

THIRTEEN

OTHER TWENTIETH-CENTURY ACTING THEORIES

A cting theory in the twentieth century has been influenced by the same aesthetic movements that have influenced the theatre and the arts generally, especially realism, Symbolism, Formalism, Surrealism, and Epic Theatre. There has also been a considerable influence from the science of psychology, though usually from behavioralists and experimentalists like Ribot, James, Lange, and Pavlov rather than from psychoanalysts like Freud or Lacan. (Categorizing the American Method school as Freudian is, as we have already seen, erroneous.) There has also been occasional influence from the social sciences, including anthropology and Marxism.

There is a tendency to polarize twentieth-century acting theorists into internalists and externalists, perpetuating the Cartesian dualism that began with Diderot. Nevertheless, the best theorists are much subtler in their arguments; they often aim at overcoming dualism rather than promoting a purely internal or external view.

The following is a discussion of a half-dozen major twentieth-century acting theorists in light of the ideas already developed in this book. Many others have written on acting in the past hundred years. For information on them, see Toby Cole's and Helen Chinoy's *Actors on Acting*; Marvin Carlson's *Theories of the Theatre*; and Bernard Dukore's *Dramatic Theory and Criticism: Greeks to Grotowski*, all cited in the bibliography at the end of this book, where I also provide brief reviews of a number of acting texts. In Chapter 7, I have already discussed in detail Michael Chekhov's important theory of the Psychological Gesture, which I cite again below with regard to Stanislavski's Method of Physical Action.

GORDON CRAIG (1872–1966)

Gordon Craig, son of the great English actress Ellen Terry, began his career in the theatre as an actor in London, but switched to directing and, especially, design. Few of his designs were ever actually realized on stage, but his influence on twentieth-century scene design has been enormous. His designs for a production of *Hamlet* at the Moscow Art Theatre in 1912 were too ambitious to function properly, but as a result of the experience, he influenced Stanislavski, Vakhtangov, and Meyerhold. Craig wrote extensively on theatre, in books and in his own magazine, *The Mask*. His woodcuts, drawings, and theatrical designs are beautiful works of art in their own right.

No theorist of acting has been more misunderstood than Craig. There is a mythology about him being vehemently anti-actor, which is surprisingly widespread. The misconception goes something like this: Gordon Craig hated actors. He was jealous of his mother's stardom. He felt that she got too much recognition and that his own theatrical art, design, was being slighted. He therefore wanted to turn the actor into something he called the *Ueber-Marionette*. Reduced to a mere puppet, the actor would at last come under the dominance of the masterful stage designer.

Every one of these statements is false. Craig loved actors. As noted, he had a successful acting career himself. If he was jealous of his mother, there is no documented evidence of it. His correspondence with her, now in the library of the University of Texas at Austin, is cordial in tone and is all about acting rather than about design.[1] The notion of the Ueber-Marionette, whether valid or not, was never intended to reduce the actor, but rather to *enhance* him. And the puppet master for this marionette was not to be the director, and certainly not the designer, but rather the actor himself.

Craig's ideas were inspired by Symbolism. This late nineteenth-century French movement, although rarely acknowledged, has had a profound influence on theories of the theatre ever since. The Symbolists rejected realism, which they saw as cluttered, petty, and narrowly psychological, focusing on the personal difficulties of particularized individuals rather than on universal ideas. In its place, they wanted simplicity, suggestiveness, and the depiction of archetypal characters. Instead of stories of contemporary life, the Symbolists preferred myths and fairy tales. Instead of settings that looked like real places, they called for generalized locales that gave an emotional impression. Camille Mauclair, for example, wrote that "a simple shade of green will perhaps give a better impression of a forest than a cardboard cutout, imitating nature leaf by leaf. An intense purple background will perhaps inspire the joy of a triumphant dawn."[2] Symbolism, then, was not meant in the simple sense of one thing standing for another, but in the more profound sense of something suggesting a range of things and feelings, an emotional resonator. Vagueness, generalness, ambiguity, mysticism, were not flaws but signs of greatness.

Just as the symbolists were drawn to myths and fairy tales because of their simplicity, abstractness, and universality, so too were they interested in masks and puppets for the same reasons. Craig's calling for an Ueber-Marionette, in a book published in 1911,[3] is in this tradition. He first insists that acting, at least as practiced in the early twentieth century, is not an art, because it is too much subject to accident: "There never has been an actor who reached such a state of mechanical perfection that his body was *absolutely* the slave of his mind," while the artist or architect has total control of his materials.[4] It is not a particularly appealing argument, which is probably the reason for Craig's reputation as being anti-actor. The artist's paint and canvas are, it is true, inanimate, but why is the hand that wields the brush any less subject to accident than the hand that gestures on stage? Besides, imposing the conscious will on materials is not how an artist creates; as Dufrenne later pointed out, the artist does not take a full-blown concept and merely realize it in material form, but undergoes a dialogue with the art work as it evolves. Craig insists that art "can admit of no accidents,"[5] but in fact, accident, or at least serendipity, is always *part* of successful artistic creation.

The attack on "accidents," however, is actually part of a larger attack on realistic acting, which Craig, following the Symbolists, feels merely imitates the randomness of everyday life. He attacks the realistic actor in no uncertain terms: "He tries to reproduce nature; he seldom thinks to invent with the aid of nature, and he never dreams of *creating*.... Is it not a poor art and a poor cleverness, which cannot convey the spirit and essence of an idea to an audience, but can only show an artless copy, a facsimile of the thing itself. This is to be an Imitator not an Artist."[6] Just as Mauclair had called for a simple shade of green in a theatrical setting rather than "imitating nature leaf by leaf," so is Craig calling for something simple and essential in acting—the Ueber-Marionette—rather than "a facsimile of the thing itself."

Far from being a reduction, a puppet is "a descendent of the stone images of the old Temples." Although known in modern society only in degenerate, trivialized form, puppets are actually "the descendants of a great and noble family of Images."[7] While Craig initially seemed to call for *replacing* the actor by an inanimate figure, he later made it clear that the Ueber-Marionette concept can be applied to the living performer. The ultimate reason for Craig's diatribe against "accident" in acting was so that the actor would develop physically, to the point where he could manipulate his voice and body to produce the simplicity, mystery, and grandeur characteristic of the "Divine Puppet." The actor is not *literally* to become a marionette (we should not forget the "Ueber" prefix),[8] but instead is to become *like* one, in order to become more an artist.

Later, in this vein, Craig wrote, "I ask only for the liberation of the actor that he may develop his own powers and cease from being the marionette of the playwright."[9] There is clearly no reduction of the actor here, nor jealousy of his acclaim, but instead a desire to enlarge him. The idea of the Ueber-Marionette is to develop the actor to his full potential. At the same time, there is in this passage, and elsewhere in Craig's writings, a denigration of the playwright that recurs in many subsequent theories of acting. Actually, the context of the passage here is only a call for playwrights to create roles that give freedom to actors, leaving them room to create rather than prescribing detailed, realistic characterizations. Nevertheless, an antiliterary bias is often a problem with twentieth-century acting theory, which has had deleterious effects on our theatre.

In America today, acting has developed even further along the realistic lines that Craig despised. When actors are trained merely to imitate what they do in everyday life, the results are inevitably cluttered, busy, and insipid. The lesson of the Ueber-Marionette is that the actor can achieve vastly more. When acting is seen as self-transformation, with the purpose of affecting an audience, the actor changes, in Craig's terms, from Imitator to Artist.

VSEVOLOD MEYERHOLD (1874–1940)

Meyerhold was another opponent of realism in acting. He too began as an actor himself, spending four years performing at the Moscow Art Theatre in its early days. He actually played the role of Treplev, the Symbolist writer, in Stanislavski's production of Anton Chekhov's *The Seagull*, with Stanislavski playing Trigorin, the realist. (The terms *Symbolist* and *realist* are not found in the play, but the two writers are clearly opposed on these terms. Nina's famous speech in the play-within-the-play in Act I, dealing with no less than "all living creatures," and containing the grandiose phrase "That great world soul is—I.... I...., " is a classic parody of Symbolism.) It is common to describe Meyerhold and Stanislavski as opposed artistically on more or less the same terms. They certainly had their differences, but in fact the two also respected and learned from each other. It was largely through Stanislavski's protection that Meyerhold survived his political difficulties in the 1930s, though he died soon after Stanislavski, apparently murdered by the secret police.

In the early twentieth century, Meyerhold became interested in Symbolist drama, and began directing it, originally under Stanislavski's auspices. They differed over Meyerhold's production of a Hauptmann play, however; from that time (1906), Meyerhold worked independently as artistic director of various theatres, including his own. Meyerhold experimented with stylized acting methods, continuing always to do Symbolist or other nonrealistic plays. His experiments with *Commedia dell'Arte*, the improvisatory theatre of the Italian Renaissance, led to his theory of the actor-*cabotin*, a mummer who would combine acting with singing, dancing, juggling, and tumbling.

By the 1920s, Meyerhold had developed an approach to acting he called *Biomechanics*. Drawing on sports, acrobatics, and time-and-motion studies, Biomechanics can be seen as a practical application of Craig's theoretical Ueber-Marionette; Meyerhold even used puppets to demonstrate his ideas. Actors were given rigorous physical training, including acting exercises that were inherently physical:

> In a particular manner [the actor] grabs the body of his partner, who is lying on the floor, throws it over his shoulder and carries it off. He lets the body fall to the floor. He throws an imaginary disc and draws an imaginary bow. He slaps his partner (in a certain manner) and gets slapped. He jumps on his partner's chest and gets jumped on in return. He jumps on his

partner's shoulders, and his partner runs around with him, etc. There were simpler exercises: take the partner's hand and pull him to the side, push the partner away, grab him by the throat, etc.[10]

Note that the movements, though extreme, are generally rational and natural; Biomechanics was not supposed to involve stylization for its own sake, or abstract, dancelike movements. The activities described here could all be found in actual plays, including realistic ones.

Meyerhold himself directed plays that were often highly stylized, including a "constructivist" production of Crommelynck's *The Magnanimous Cuckold* (1922), which used an arrangement of platforms, ramps, wheels, stairs, and trapezes to create "a machine for acting." He would also score a play physically, prescribing movements for the actors so that he became their puppet master; his theatre was much more director-centered than the one called for by Craig, who had stressed the actor's freedom to create. Nevertheless, Biomechanics was supposed to be a method for learning and doing *all* types of acting. "Biomechanics teaches the actor to use the space about him on the stage three-dimensionally," wrote a British observer. "Through exercises he is taught to achieve the feeling of the place of the actor in space, time and rhythm. But more important still, he is taught how to co-ordinate his own body with other people on the stage, with the properties he handles and the scenery he is acting against so that he becomes a plastic part of a harmonious whole."[11]

The psychological basis for Biomechanics came from Pavlov, with the notion of the conditioned response, and from the James-Lange theory. "The physical position of an actor's body determines his emotions and the expressions in his voice,"[12] wrote Meyerhold's leading actor. In his demonstrations with a puppet, Meyerhold would show how different positions expressed a wide range of emotions: widely extended arms expressed joy, a hanging head grief, the head thrown backward pride. The actor, in duplicating the positions, would feel the emotions himself, a quality Meyerhold called the "self-mirror."[13]

Meyerhold, like Craig, showed an antiliterary bias in his work, often radically adapting classical texts. His famous 1926 production of Gogol's *The Inspector General* (originally produced in Russia ninety years earlier), for example, transferred the action to a large city, reshaped all the characters, and added new ones. In one scene, Meyerhold arranged fifteen doors around the stage, so that an official could emerge from each one to offer the hero a bribe.[14] Nevertheless, we should not think of Biomechanics as being limited to such avant-garde work. The emphasis on acting with the whole body, the importance of physical dexterity and simplicity, and the reminder that physical positioning and gesture affect the actor as well as the audience, are all valuable ideas that apply to all acting in all kinds of plays and films.

EUGENE VAKHTANGOV (1883–1923)

Vakhtangov was perhaps the most talented of Stanislavski's pupils. His production of Gozzi's *Turandot* (1922), created in Moscow under desperate conditions of civil war, while Vakhtangov himself was dying of cancer, was one of the loveliest works of the twentieth-century stage, combining stylization with delightful spontaneity.

Stanislavski's relation to his disciples was admirable. Far from requiring them to follow his methods slavishly, he created studios for them, in which they were not only allowed artistic freedom, but encouraged to experiment with the latest theatrical styles. Vakhtangov, Michael Chekhov, and Richard Boleslavsky were all members of Stanislavski's First Studio. Although Vakhtangov died young, he has had the most lasting influence because of the quality of his productions and the outstanding young actors he worked with.

Vakhtangov's theory of stage production was based on what he called *Fantastic Realism*. This involved heightened, often grotesque use of movement and design to maximize meaning and emotional impact. In his production of Strindberg's *Erik XIV*, for example, given at the First Studio in 1921, the courtiers and bureaucrats were played as automatons in stylized makeup, while the common people were played realistically. Vakhtangov insisted, however, that Stanislavski's methods, properly understood, were not only adaptable to stylized acting, but essential to its effectiveness. Vakhtangov stressed *action* in acting, writing that "an actor must not simply stand upon the stage, but act." Applying Stanislavski's concept of the *objective*, however, Vakhtangov went on to stress that the action must express an element of will:

> Every action differs from feeling by the presence of the will element. To persuade, to comfort, to ask, to reproach, to forgive, to wait, to chase away—these are verbs expressing *will action*. These verbs denote the task which the actor places before himself when working upon a character, while the verbs to become irritated, to pity, to weep, to laugh, to be impatient, to hate, to love—express feeling, and therefore cannot and must not figure as a task in the analysis of a role.[15]

The primacy of action, which Vakhtangov insisted should be the basis for emotion, and not the reverse, shows an influence of the James-Lange theory, and an affinity with Biomechanics. Vakhtangov's productions were very physicalized, yet were more spontaneous than Meyerhold's.

STANISLAVSKI AND THE METHOD OF PHYSICAL ACTION

Stanislavski presents his Method of Physical Action in the very last section of his three-volume acting text, at the end of the volume translated into English as *Creating a Role*. Still using the persona of Tortsov, he announces that under this approach, it is possible for actors to come to a rehearsal of a play without having had any conferences or readings of it. When his students seem bewildered, he goes on to insist that they can even "act a play not yet written."[16] The antiliterary bias surfaces again, to "free" the actor from the playwright. It may have had something to do with the political situation in Russia in the thirties, when new plays of any kind were always dangerous. Turning the actor into a "pure" performer, like a musician, was politically safe.

Tortsov then goes on to evaluate the scene from Gogol's *Inspector General* that I have already described in Chapter 7. The play was a standard Russian classic, nearly a century old, strongly critical of the czarist bureaucracy and therefore politically safe as well. It had also been done fairly recently in Meyerhold's avant-garde production; Stanislavski may have been trying to show how an "action" approach to the play need not be so radical and disturbing. Tortsov describes his new approach to a role: "Call to mind each episode in the act; realize what actions each one consists of; follow through the logic and consecutiveness of all these actions."[17] They work on the scene for some time, dealing with the physical actions in detail. Tortsov himself even plays Khlestakov for a while and, in a rare moment of humility, actually criticizes his own performance: "I overdid it! ... It should be done more simply. Besides, would that be right for Khlestakov? After all he, as a resident of St. Petersburg, felt himself superior to anyone in the provinces."[18] Note how, as usual, the criticism is in terms of the play and the character, rather than in terms of Tortsov's personal life, about which we never learn anything.

After more work on the scene in this vein, there is an interesting little interlude in which Tortsov and the students meet in the green room with some older, experienced actors who do not accept the new Method of Physical Action. The traditional approach, it seems, was to discuss the play and the characters with the director at great length before doing any blocking, developing a string of objectives which were then translated into action. Were these actions "difficult, complex, intangible?" asks Tortsov. "They used to be," replies one of the senior actors, "but finally they were resolved into about ten very clear, realistic, comprehensible, accessible actions, what you might call the marked channel of the play and part." Tortsov points out that, in other words, what the actor ends up with is "simple physical action," which is what the new method *starts* with. "So why not coax it out from the very start, when you take your first steps? Why sit at a table for months to try to force out your dormant feelings?"[19] Alluding to months is no hyperbole; rehearsal periods in Russia, as in continental Europe generally, can last a year or longer, even today. The Method of Physical Action presented a new model of actor creation; in place of the traditional approach of talking out the roles first, at great length, and then going on to realize them on stage, Stanislavski now recognized the ongoing, dialectical nature of developing a role. There would still be a long rehearsal period, but instead of conception first, followed by action, conception and action would work in tandem from the beginning.

The Method of Physical Action, then, is a rejection of the mind-body polarity. "In every *physical action*, unless it is purely mechanical, there is concealed some *inner action*, some feelings," Stanislavski/Tortsov insists. "This is how the two levels of life in a part are created, the inner and the outer. They are intertwined."[20] Otherwise, the Method of Physical Action represents nothing new. There is still a stress on objectives and on relating to given circumstances, but instead of talking about these things, using isolated, secondary-process thinking, the actor now works on them in action, using *both* primary and secondary processes. The actor tries something, then analyzes it ("Would that be right for Khlestakov?"), then tries again, and so on until the unit works. It is not that Stanislavski, after years of working from the inside, suddenly reversed himself and decided to work from the outside in some cold, mechanical way; instead, he recognized that inner and outer work together, feeding off each other.

Thus, although the Method of Physical Action represented a revision of rehearsal technique, it was by no means a rejection of

Stanislavski's basic theories. If anything, it takes his notions of relaxation, objectives, and relating, and applies them in a manner more logically consistent with their implications, since they all are directed toward actors *in performance on stage* rather than toward actors sitting around a table and talking. Nor was Stanislavski's new method something he cooked up in isolation. It shows the clear influence of Craig's Ueber-Marionette, Meyerhold's Biomechanics, and Vakhtangov's Fantastic Realism, as well as an affinity with Michael Chekhov's Psychological Gesture,[21] all of which were physically oriented, and all of which saw an emotional or spiritual quality coming *from* the physical. Much of twentieth-century acting theory, in fact, consists of rejecting the traditional mind-body polarity of Diderot and his successors; only in America do we still seem to be stuck with it.

Francis Fergusson, the outstanding American critic and scholar who taught at the American Laboratory Theatre in the twenties, when the future Group Theatre founders were students there, once pointed out that Boleslavsky and Ouspenskaya stressed "action" in their teaching. "All action, they would say, aims at some 'objective,' and if you can see what that is, you can understand the action," wrote Fergusson many years later. Boleslavsky and Ouspenskaya "saw the movement of the psyche toward the object of its desire as what the dramatist was imitating in plot, character, and language, and what the actor imitates in the medium of his own feeling and perception."[22] Stanislavski may have been driving at the same point when he maintained that one can rehearse and act a play not yet written. He recognized that a play is ultimately not a set of words or ideas, but a set of *actions*, in this purposeful sense, and that the actor's job is to *find* those implicit actions and make them explicit. It overstates the matter to say that you can act a play "not yet written," since you have to consider what the playwright has written down in order to search for the actions implied by his words, but a case can certainly be made that purposeful actions are what underlie the play and define its essence.

In the Method of Physical Action, the actor is not the slave of the playwright, but neither is he completely divorced from him. Instead, the actor is *collaborating* with the playwright, imitating the "movement of the psyche" in action, which the playwright was implicitly imitating in words. This no more reduces the actor as a creative artist than working with other actors reduces him. It is simply another example of the collective nature of the art of acting, in which the actor always draws inspiration from others, yet also develops his character in his own unique way.

BERTOLT BRECHT (1898–1956)

Bertolt Brecht's theories of acting must be seen in the contexts of his life, his career, and the traditions of the German theatre. His experiences as a medical corpsman amid the horrors of World War I meant that he became part of that group of 1920s writers and artists alienated from traditional culture. He became well known as a radical playwright but, despised by the Nazis for his "decadence," had to flee Germany in the 1930s, spending about a decade as an unsuccessful screenwriter in Hollywood. Investigated as a suspected Communist by the House Un-American Activities Committee in 1947, he left the United States for East Berlin, where he became artistic director of the Berliner Ensemble for the last years of his life. Thus Brecht was always an outsider; even in East Berlin, he managed to obtain an Austrian passport, so as to be ready to flee yet again, if necessary. Brecht's theories of theatre reflect his personal alienation; he was always the iconoclast, always *against* something.

Brecht's theories changed over time, reflecting the strategies he used to deal with the particular problems he saw at any given moment. It is wrong to take his aggressive essays of the 1920s too literally, for example. His theoretical writing became far more subtle when he actually had a theatre to run, at the Berliner Ensemble, than when he had been a polemicist trying to draw attention to himself and his ideas. Furthermore, unlike most other important modern acting theorists, Brecht never acted himself. Nor did he even direct all that much; he had practically no experience as a director before his days with the Berliner Ensemble, and never directed anything but his own works. (When he did classical plays like Sophocles's *Antigone*, he adapted them so heavily as to make them wholly his own.) He was writing about acting primarily as a playwright, interested in having his plays performed in a certain way.

Writing about acting as an outsider can, as with Diderot, lead to eccentric views of it. For example, when Brecht insisted, as he did repeatedly, that an actor must demonstrate the character rather than identify with him, my own reaction as an actor would have been to say, "Why are those the only two alternatives? Acting doesn't feel like either *demonstrating* or *identifying* to me." Nevertheless, Brecht's ideas about acting have a certain coherence if we keep in mind that they are *not* intended to be a comprehensive theory about acting. Unlike Stanislavski, whose concepts were supposed to fit all acting situations, Brecht was calling for a particular *style* of acting. His imaginary "Dialogue about Acting," published in 1929, contains the following interchange:

> The actors always score great successes in your plays. Are you yourself satisfied with them?
> No.
> Because they act badly?
> No. Because they act wrong.[23]

With Stanislavski, you act well or badly or somewhere in between, but you do not act "wrong"; with Brecht, it is possible to be wrong, even when acting perfectly well. By the standards of the German theatre of the time, the actors in his plays were highly successful, but it was not the kind of success that Brecht wanted. He felt that the actors were too emotional, too empathetic:

> They go into a trance and take the audience with them.
> Give an example.
> Suppose they have to act a leave-taking. They put themselves in a leave-taking mood. They want to induce a

leave-taking mood in the audience. If the seance is successful it ends up with nobody seeing anything further, nobody learning any lessons, at best everyone recollecting. In short, everybody feels.
That sounds almost like some erotic process. What ought it to be like, then?
Witty. Ceremonious. Ritual. Spectator and actor ought not to approach one another but to move apart.[24]

For Brecht, then, identifying emotionally with the characters was a very bad thing. When actors did it, the audience did as well—"They go into a trance and take the audience with them." This, he would not deny, was a very potent form of theatre, but it was not a form he wanted. A committed political radical, especially in the thirties when he espoused Communism, Brecht wanted the theatre to raise questions, point out social inequities, stimulate controversy, rather than stimulate emotional identification and release.

The term Brecht came to use for the kind of theatrical experience he wanted was *alienation effect*, the usual translation of his German coinage, *Verfremdungseffekt*. This concept can be traced back to the Russian Formalists and, behind them, the Symbolists. The Formalists were a group of thinkers in the twenties, influenced by Symbolism and by the science of linguistics; they primarily wrote on literature, including folk literature, but occasionally dealt with other art forms as well. In addition, their writings influenced, and were influenced by, the theatrical work of Meyerhold.

A prominent member of the Formalists was Viktor Shklovsky, who saw the function of art to be *ostranenie*, or strangeness:

Art exists that one may recover the sensation of life; it exists to make one feel things, to make the stone *stony*. The purpose of art is to impart the sensation of things as they are perceived and not as they are known. The technique of art is to make objects "unfamiliar," to make forms difficult.[25]

In the 1930s, after his exile from Germany, Brecht met Shklovsky during a brief visit to Moscow. Brecht had already heard of the work of Meyerhold, whom he considered more modern and progressive in approach than Stanislavski, and had already been calling for an acting style that was ceremonious and detached. (The "Dialogue about Acting," quoted above, dates from 1929.) Shklovsky's theories seemed to verify Brecht's ideas, and provided him with his terminology; the *fremd* in *Verfremdungseffekt* means strange.[26] For Brecht, the strangeness was to have a political significance, however; the function of theatre was to highlight the social and economic system under which we live. We usually take this system for granted, as if, for example, the simultaneous existence of wealth and poverty were as natural as the air around us, but Brecht's plays would make us see this contradiction as strange, arbitrary, and capable of being altered.

Thus, the Formalists like Shklovsky took the Symbolists' notion of ambiguity and strangeness, and demystified it. Instead of evoking a mystical, transcendent world, a work of art would make us see strangeness in *this* world, would "make the stone stony." Brecht focused this essentially materialist approach on the political sphere. He would make us see strangeness in our social relationships, with the ultimate goal of improving them. It was not enough to make the stone stony; theatre should make oppression seem oppressive.

This is all very well from the point of view of the playwright and director, but what of the actor? Is he supposed to "alienate" himself on stage, or do something special in order to "alienate" the audience? Is a performance supposed to be a lecture or a political speech? The answer arises again from the fact that Brecht was thinking about the production of particular plays—his own—for a particular audience. His plays have a detached, sardonic quality, and his characters underreact to the most serious matters. When Mother Courage's children die, one by one, her only emotional response is a brief, silent scream; otherwise, she just gets back to business. When the charming scoundrel Azdak has to judge which woman is fit to be the mother of the child in *The Caucasian Chalk Circle*, he shrewdly but casually orders them to try to pull the child out of a circle, endangering its life. For the actress playing Mother Courage, or the actor playing Azdak, to emote heavily in these scenes would be false to the characters' objectives and given circumstances. Alienation is the proper way to play *these characters*, rather than a way to play all characters in all plays ever produced.

Martin Esslin has pointed out that traditionally, German acting was highly bombastic; actors tended to be rated "according to the violence and frenetic intensity of the emotions they portray."[27] The special impact of Brecht's actors—the alienation, or estrangement—came from the fact that they would underplay their roles, in terms of what the audience had come to expect. Brecht also had a major impact on the style of speaking on stage, which in Germany had traditionally been elevated and special; he introduced slang, Anglicisms (there is a lot of English in his plays, whose impact is lost when the plays are translated into English), and low expressions. In other words, the Brechtian actor was more *realistic* than the traditional German tragedian. It is interesting that Lee Strasberg greatly admired the acting of the Berliner Ensemble; in fact, the few plays he discusses at any length in his autobiography are by Brecht. The acting of the Ensemble was, and is, not stylized in the sense of being artificial or bizarre, but in the sense of being simplified, understated, and clear.

In sum, there is no disparity at all between the acting theories of Stanislavski and those of Brecht. Both come down to being true to the character and the play you are acting in. Acting in a Brecht play does not mean chanting mindlessly or lurching about like a robot; it means finding the special ironic, witty style that is characteristic of his imaginary worlds. It is possible to give a good performance in a play by Brecht without ever having read a word of his acting theories. Play the objectives and given circumstances honestly, and you will have all the alienation effect you need. It is worth noting that, when Brecht finally got to direct, as artistic director of the

Berliner Ensemble, he *never* used technical terms like alienation in rehearsals. As with any good director, there was just a careful working out of details, with experimentation, and an openness to suggestions from the actors themselves.

From the actor's point of view, a more important Brechtian concept than alienation is that of *Gestus*. This, explains John Willett, Brecht's editor and translator, "means both gist and gesture; an attitude or a single aspect of an attitude, expressible in words or actions."[28] Like Michael Chekhov, Brecht recognized that physical positioning on stage, vocal intonation, movements, gestures, and so on, are not mere externals, but that *staging carries meaning*. Brecht provides some examples in his "Short Organum for the Theatre," written in 1948, after he had left the United States:

> Each single incident has its basic Gestus: *Richard Gloster* [sic] *courts his victim's widow. The child's true mother is found by means of a chalk circle. God has a bet with the Devil for Dr Faustus's soul. Woyzeck buys a cheap knife in order to do his wife in,* etc. The grouping of the characters on the stage and the movements of the groups must be such that the necessary beauty is attained above all by the elegance with which the material conveying that Gestus is set out and laid bare to the understanding of the audience.[29]

For Brecht, it is not that meaning is conveyed in drama by the dialogue, while action exists only to make the play tangible and lively. Instead, action conveys as much or more than words. The brief scene where Woyzeck buys the knife, for example, has terse dialogue with a Jewish peddler, who knows nothing of Woyzeck's problems. If you were to play the same dialogue out of context, or in another play, it would just seem to be a bit of haggling over a minor purchase. It is Woyzeck's action, his *objective*, which the actor must play with honesty and vigor, that gives the scene its true significance. Woyzeck wants to murder his wife; he is so poor that he must dicker with a peddler to buy a cheap knife as a murder weapon; both he and the peddler are part of a ruthless commercial system in which human values are subordinated to cash transactions. It is the staging of the scene that provides this meaning, which is implicit in the script, but which is not spelled out in dialogue.

This sensitivity to the details of staging, which Brecht shared with all good directors, meant that he laid great importance on such things as groupings, positionings, and movements, which we know under the general term *blocking*. After a play had been blocked, for example, he would have a series of still photographs taken of all the scenes, and check carefully to see if they told the progressing story. He may have got this idea in Hollywood, where the storyboard technique of planning films was common. American actors today could learn a great deal from the concept of Gestus, including a respect for blocking as part of the artistic process, rather than something added on by hacks. Gestus implies a *semiotic* view of theatre, which, I shall argue in the next chapter, is needed to rescue our acting from the ideological traps that realism has left it in. Acting does not consist of orating (the traditional view); nor does it consist of emoting (the traditional German view in Brecht's youth); nor does it consist of reflecting everyday life (the current American view); acting consists of signifying. The audience "reads" a performance, in a manner similar to the way it reads a text. Acting *means*.

ANTONIN ARTAUD (1896–1948)

As with Brecht, Antonin Artaud's theories must be seen in the context of his life, times, and culture. Born in Marseilles, Artaud came to Paris in 1920, where he acted successfully in plays and films. He became a member of André Breton's Surrealist group, but broke with them in 1927 when they became politicized. He felt that *they* were being untrue to their principles by embracing Communism. Artaud remained for the rest of his career more Surrealist than the Surrealists, and can best be understood in those terms.

Surrealism was yet another reaction against realism. All such reactions saw realism as being overly concerned with the surfaces of everyday life; in contrast with this, the Symbolists stressed the mystical, the Formalists the existential, Brecht the political or economic. The French Surrealists, who included the poets Breton and Guillaume Apollinaire, the playwrights Jean Cocteau and Roger Vitrac, and the painter Salvador Dali, in addition to Artaud, stressed the psychoanalytic. Influenced by Freud (at least as they understood him), their writings, paintings, films, and theatrical productions depicted the workings of the unconscious mind, highlighting the erotic, the spontaneous, and the shocking. A common method of composition was automatic writing, related to the free association method of psychoanalysis.

Artaud's reputation rests primarily on his essays from the twenties and thirties, which are often wildly polemical. Unlike Brecht, he did not have the opportunity to moderate his views through actual practice. Artaud's "Theatre of Cruelty" produced only one play, *The Cenci*, which did not realize his views; financial difficulties, war, and illness (both mental and physical) prevented him from accomplishing much afterward, though his writings became influential on others.

"The Theatre and the Plague," written in 1934, is Artaud's challenge to the French theatre, which he saw as having dwindled to a tepid world of boulevard comedies, glib psychological dramas, and traditional classics performed endlessly in the same sterile, oratorical manner. In this essay, Artaud compares theatre (i.e., the *true* theatre that he is trying to recall into existence) to a legendary plague of 1720 in his native Marseilles. This plague, Artaud insists, does not reveal its symptoms. There are no microbes, and "the corpse of the plague victim shows no lesions when opened."[30] Yet it killed thousands and caused all social forms to disintegrate. This plague, then, turns out to be Artaud's elaborate metaphor for explaining the paradoxical nature of theatre: On the one hand, it is unreal and impractical, being "an immediate gratuitousness provoking acts without use or profit."[31] On the other, it is totally transforming, "a formidable call to the forces that impel the mind by example to the source of its conflicts."[32] Artaud does not mention Freud in the essay (although terms like *libido* pop up), but the influence is obvious; theatre is a kind of mass psychoanalysis, putting us in touch with our unconscious drives and becoming a safety valve for them. The disintegration of social forms that Artaud refers to recalls Freud's oceanic feeling, that infantile state in which there were no fixed identities and one's potentials seemed limitless.

In the context of France in the early thirties, this essay is a rebuke to the Surrealists like Breton who were trying to politicize theatre, which Artaud felt only diminished it. Artaud is hearkening back to the Symbolists and the aesthetes of the late nineteenth century, with their doctrine of art for art's sake; art was not a mirror of reality, but a challenge to it. The essay is also the anguished cry of an outsider, who has enormous talent but little influence or opportunity to create the kind of theatre he wants.

A reminder of the importance of theatre is valuable in any period. But we should remember that the problems Artaud saw in the French theatre of sixty years ago are not necessarily those of our theatre today. We certainly have our equivalent of boulevard comedies and psychological dramas. Artaud's scornful descriptions, from the later essay "No More Masterpieces," could fit most commercial and many noncommercial plays done today: "Stories about money, worry about money, social careerism, the pangs of love unspoiled by altruism, sexuality sugar-coated with an eroticism that has lost its mystery have nothing to do with the theater, even if they do belong to psychology."[33] Artaud was influenced by psychoanalysis, but despised "psychology," which removes the mystery from the theatre, which was not supposed to explain what makes characters tick, but instead put us in touch with our essential selves.

The classical drama that Artaud also attacked, however, has no equivalent in our theatre today, nor in most theatres outside France at any time. The "masterpieces" that he wanted no more of were those of the great French playwrights of the seventeenth century,

Corneille, Racine, and Molière, whose texts had become venerated as cultural icons. Taught to French schoolchildren at an early age, memorized as a matter of patriotic duty, cited automatically by politicians, they had lost all theatrical vitality. They were performed at the Comédie Française in a manner that went unchanged for centuries; young actors copied older ones, so that there was an unbroken tradition of playing roles the same way, supposedly going back to Molière himself. An actor was not a creative artist, but merely a transmitter; fine acting was valued, but as a craft, a skill, as one would value fine cabinetwork or *haute cuisine*. The masterpiece was the text, not the performance of it.

Artaud's reaction to this was to insist on the artistic value of performance. Not only did he maintain that there was a "poetry in space," but, echoing antiliterary theorists like Craig, he wanted to "put an end to the subjugation of the theatre to the text."[34] Masterpieces, he felt, should be performed once, and the texts thrown away. He even wanted to abolish dialogue; language would be used only as "incantation."[35]

English-speaking countries like ours have never had a theatrical tradition anything like that of France. Our equivalent to Corneille, Racine, and Molière would be Shakespeare, but we have *not* always performed him the same way; our tradition has been for each age, each theatre company, and even each actor, to perform Shakespeare in a new way. Students do read Shakespeare in the schools, but see him performed much less often than French students see their classics. And when was the last time you heard an American politician quote Shakespeare, or any other poet? Nor do powerful Americans react with fear and outrage if Shakespeare is performed "incorrectly"; rather than seeing great drama as a cornerstone of the established order, our power holders are largely indifferent to it. In America, a contempt for masterpieces merely feeds our traditional philistinism.

Mikel Dufrenne, reacting to the same antitheatrical prejudice in French culture that Artaud did, insisted that the actor, even when faithfully performing a well-known literary text, was nonetheless a full-fledged artist, a creator. Rather than a prescription to be followed blindly, a text can be a source of inspiration, can liberate rather than confine. It would have been far better for the American theatre if this attitude had been as influential as that of Artaud, whose antiliterary bias has aggravated two of the weaknesses in our theatre: First, American actors do not know plays very well. Except for plays they have actually performed in, they have typically read few scripts, and read those only superficially. Most of our actors do not know how to read a play—what a metaphor is, for example, or what motifs are, or how verse operates. This means that their approach to a role is often slapdash, careless of details.

Similarly, American directors of classical plays have been encouraged to take extensive liberties with texts. Updated, altered, adapted classics are now the norm in the American theatre, echoing Artaud's fuzzy notion that "beneath the poetry of the texts, there is the actual poetry, without form and without text."[36] The director is supposed to strip the play of its text, and produce the poetic undertext in a manner relevant to his time. But how can this hidden poetry manifest itself except through the specific details of a play? And if you change those details, how do you avoid changing the supposedly formless, textless poetry underneath? Setting *Julius Caesar* in Nazi Germany or *Hamlet* in East Harlem is not merely a novel way of producing a traditional play, it yields a new play entirely—and a much less interesting one. Artaud's dualism here amounts to a directorial blank check. By his reckoning, it is impossible to be false to a text, since you can always refer to the hidden one "beneath."

Artaud's proposed Theatre of Cruelty, with its elaborate scenic effects and costumes, its extravagant use of lighting, music, and sound effects, and its incantation, was essentially a dance theatre. Unlike other Surrealists with their "spontaneous writing," and unlike many avant-garde theatre artists in America today, he vehemently opposed improvisation, calling instead for highly disciplined actors who would, like Balinese dancers, have a language of gesture. (Like Brecht, Artaud recognized that there could be a semiotics of theatre, but for him it was to be far more formalized.) The Performance Artists of today, like Martha Clarke, Robert Wilson, Richard Foreman, or the Mabou Mines troupe, are frequently cited as being in the Artaud tradition because of their avoidance of literary texts and their use of extravagant spectacle, but they have steered clear of developing the kind of code language that Artaud called for. Perhaps the nearest thing to it would be modern dance; Martha Graham, for example, developed specific positions and movements that could be seen as a "vocabulary" of dance. As with traditional ballet, the choreographer then works by putting together the standardized elements rather than by inventing brand new movements for each piece. But the temper of our times is opposed to using standardized elements in any of the arts, which is probably why this aspect of Artaud's theory has languished.

Artaud's greatest achievement was in recognizing the artistic validity of performance. This was particularly important for France, where the antitheatrical prejudice had been especially strong. (A French ideal for performance, dating from the seventeenth century, based on a misreading of Aristotle's *Poetics*, was to have plays that were totally oratorical, with *no action at all*, aside from minimal walking about and gesturing. Needless to say, such extreme avoidance of action has never caught on in the English-speaking theatre!) In addition, many of the specifics that Artaud called for were visionary. He was one of the first in our culture to call for an open stage for performance, breaking the dominance of the proscenium arch that had been around for centuries: "We abolish the stage and the auditorium and replace them by a single site, without partition or barrier of any kind, which will become the theatre of the action."[37] Even Brecht, an iconoclast in so much else, never abolished the proscenium.

Like Craig, Artaud wanted to elevate the actor, to fulfill his physical potential, and recognize the spiritual elements *within* the

210

physical. In this regard, Artaud called for "an affective athleticism," describing the actor as "an athlete of the heart."[38] He outlined exercises in tempo and rhythm for training the actor, and, drawing on the cabala and yoga, proposed elaborate exercises in breathing. These have had little influence in America (as always, we tend to ignore the physical aspects of the theories that we like!), though some practitioners, like Richard Schechner and Joseph Chaikin, have occasionally experimented with them. Although described in Artaud's typically visionary language, the exercises have a core of practicality that deserves attention. In the long run, Artaud's ideas for the *actor* may prove more important than his ideas for the *theatre*, which are often overblown and antiliterary.

The long tradition in twentieth-century acting theory of trying to liberate the actor from the supposedly oppressive hand of the playwright amounts to an overreaction to the antitheatrical prejudice. It turns that prejudice on its head, becoming an equally narrow and foolish antiliterary bias. Attacking the playscript is one of those concocted, abstract notions that have little to do with acting as it is experienced; in general, actors have not looked upon a script as a nagging, confining set of regulations, but rather as an inspiration, a challenge, an aid. Memorizing the lines of a play is tedious, yet no actor ever says to himself, "If only I could throw away this text and say whatever I want." The main form of theatre without a playscript is *improvisation*, which is not easier or freer than acting with one; if anything, it is harder. Artaud did not want improvisation, however; instead, his unscripted theatre would have to follow the creative ideas of a director in a controlled, structured way. But in that case, why would the director's hand be inherently lighter than a playwright's? Why would the director's mise-en-scène be inherently more liberating than a playscript? Actors often complain about autocratic directors; I have never heard the same complaint about a script.

Theatre is a collaborative art. Actors draw inspiration from the playwright, as they do from the director, their fellow actors, and, for

211

that matter, from the setting, their costumes, and their props. We do not speak of actors being "confined" by the set or costume designer, nor postulate some kind of "pure" theatre where these other artists would not be needed! A theatre without literature is not pure; instead, it is cut off from a good deal of subtlety, complexity, and energy.

FOURTEEN

REALISM AND STYLE:
A SEMIOTIC VIEW

In place of the mimetic view that has dominated the criticism of both dramatic literature and performance for so long, current theory considers theatre as a form of communication. The major question is not how close too, or far from, real life a play is, but rather what—and, more important, *how*—it means. A play is seen as a "system of signification," which the audience "reads" like a "text."

Semiotics, the philosophic theory of the function of signs, has had considerable influence on aesthetics in recent years. It is particularly well suited to study of the theatre, since semioticians study both verbal and nonverbal forms of communication, which are of equal importance in theatrical performance. The question of what and how theatre means is far too large for this book. I propose instead to consider the narrower question of the relationship between realism and what is called, in contrast to it, style. This dichotomy is not often found in literary criticism, whether of drama or of any other literary form, but is commonplace in discussions of acting. Realism in this context means playing yourself, copying your own everyday-life behavior, and reality-testing everything you do on stage against that behavior. Style means artificialities, especially as found in historical plays, blank verse in Shakespeare being an obvious example. Realism is widely believed to be *basic*. It is common in American acting schools to teach realistic acting first, often for years, before going on to other kinds. There is even a popular acting textbook called *Acting in Person and in Style*, which insists that "style should be encountered only when an actor is advancing in development",[1] after completion of the work on the self.

The realism/style dichotomy has had a pernicious influence on American acting. It is obviously based in Cartesian dualism. Realism is supposed to be internal, personal, real, and emotional; style is external, conventional, artificial, and cold. Thinking about acting in this way is a major reason for the difficulty American actors have in performing in nonrealistic plays, but it also has deleterious effects on performing in realistic ones. A semiotic view will help us to see realism for what it is—not stylelessness, nor the basis for other styles, but simply one acting style among many. It is just as conventionalized as any other acting style; conversely, other acting styles, including historical ones, are just as emotional and "real" as realism.

Semiotics is both a reaction against and an expansion of linguistics, the study of human speech. Language is so powerful a means of communication, so important to human beings, that we tend to think of it as the only possible kind of communication, and reduce all other kinds to it. In fact, other forms of signification (including theatre) convey meaning in ways that vary considerably from the way language does. There has been some resistance to semiotic theories of theatre from people who imagine that such theories imply that theatre conveys neat little messages to the audience, operating like a telephone wire or a FAX machine. Or they imagine that semiotic theories maintain that "everything onstage stands for something else," so that understanding theatre comes down to playing shallow guessing games. In fact theatre and the other arts, do not communicate in those ways at all. Theatre is not a language (secret or overt), and cannot be reduced to one. Language does, in fact, sometimes provide helpful analogies as to how theatre communicates, but we must always be wary of going too far with such approaches. The linguistic model is seductive.

In this regard, an unsuccessful attempt at a semiotic approach to acting can be found in the theories of François Delsarte (1811–1871), a nineteenth-century Frenchman who developed an elaborate acting system that was popular for many years. (There were as many Delsarte studios in New York City at the turn of the century as there are Stanislavski studios today.) Gesture, Delsarte maintained, was more important than speech, "which is but a reflected and subordinate expression."[2] He then went on to develop a system of gesturing that sounds all too much *like* speech, complete with a vocabulary. Here are a few examples:

> The mouth plays a part in everything evil which we would express, by a grimace which consists of protruding the lips and lowering the corners ....
> Conscious menace—that of a master to his subordinate—is expressed by a movement of the head carried from above downward. Impotent menace requires the head to be moved from below upward.
> Any interrogation made with crossed arms must partake of the character of a threat.[3]

Delsarte's based his system on actual observation; in fact, it was part of the realistic movement in theatre. Nevertheless, it still seems, as Lee Strasberg succinctly put it, "mechanical and stultifying."[4] In early silent films, you can see a lot of Delsartean acting; it is certainly expressive, but it also seems stagy and obvious. This may be because the actors erroneously believed they had to exaggerate for the camera, since they were denied the use of their voice. Nonetheless, the approach seems in the end unavoidably artificial because of its assumption that acting is *structured* like language, having distinct elements that can be defined the way words can in a dictionary. Certainly grimacing the mouth, with protruding lips and lowered corners, will seem negative, but can we say that it does this for "everything evil which we would express"? Does impotent menace *require* the head to be moved from below upward? Can it not be expressed in many different ways? Must *any* interrogation made with crossed arms imply a threat? Delsarte's methods are oversystematized, because he cannot help thinking of communication in terms of a language. (Artaud's proposed language of gesture, which may have been influenced by Delsarte, suffers from the same problem.) Susanne Langer, the American semiotician, noted that the arts generally are "presentational forms," which simply do not have a discrete vocabulary the way language does. A work of art moves us as a whole, rather than in piecemeal fashion; to catalog gestures and say that specific ones mean this or that is like saying that the color blue in paintings always means sadness.

The science of linguistics is based on the writings of the Swiss professor Ferdinand de Saussure (1857–1913). Language study in his day had been mainly historical, discovering how language has developed over thousands of years; using theories of how speech changes and making careful analyses of dozens of known languages, researchers were even able to reconstruct the Indo-European language from which Sanscrit and most European languages evolved, even though Indo-European left no written record. Saussure maintained that such studies, interesting though they may be, do not really tell us how language communicates at any given moment. The fact that the word *girl*, for example, actually evolved from the Middle English word for a young person of either sex does not mean that I am confused about someone's gender when I call her a girl today. To insist that older meanings somehow hang around is sometimes called the *genetic fallacy*, the idea that the origins of something tell us all we really need to know about it, even when it has changed so drastically as to become completely different. (The popular notion of the ritual origins of theatre are a good example of this. Theatre is *not* a ritual, even if it evolved from one, and it is foolish to try to pretend that it still is.)

Saussure's model of communication, then, was ahistorical. (His term was *synchronic*, in contrast to what he called the *diachronic* approaches that had traced the historical development of languages.) What happens, he said, when one person talks to another is that the speaker has a *concept*, which he translates into a *sound-image*. The latter is not just a sound or set of sounds, a purely physical phenomenon, "but the psychological imprint of the sound, the impression it makes on our senses."[5] The listener receives the sound-image (or *signifier*) and translates it back into a concept (the *signified*), which, if all goes well, is the same one the speaker had in mind. The listener's understanding is not piecemeal, one word at a time, based on the history of each word. Nor does understanding have anything to do with the sound of the word per se; the relationship between sound and meaning, Saussure insisted, is purely arbitrary. (To say that the word *chair* sounds like a chair, as one of my students once maintained, is an illusion caused by our long familiarity with the word and its meaning. It certainly does not sound like a chair to someone who never learned English!) The sound of a word and how it is formed by the organs of speech are very important in the historical analysis of the development of language, but have nothing to do with meaning. Instead, both speaker and listener achieve understanding by relating the sound-image to their language as a whole system. A particular utterance (*parole*) makes no sense without the linguistic system (*langue*) behind it, even though that system is not explicit at the time of the utterance.

Suppose, for example, I were to say, "I journeyed to school this morning via a motorized conveyance." A foreigner with only a smattering of English might, by picking his way through my sentence with a dictionary, get a general idea of what I was saying, but he would miss the actual essence of it, which is its pretentious tone. Since you understand English *as a system*, however, you are aware of the other ways I might have described my trip—neutral ways like "I drove" or "I came by car," slangy ways like "by jalopy." You place my utterance in relation to these unspoken alternatives, and recognize what I said as being pompous.

In fact, speaker and listener are not usually conscious of there being a system behind their actual spoken words. Nonetheless, it clearly must be there. Immediate and direct as spoken English may seem to us, for example, it is just a lot of gibberish to someone who does not know the language, just as his speech may sound like gibberish to us. Further evidence happens when someone makes a mistake: If, as I am delivering a lecture, I were to say, "I doesn't like pineapple," you would immediately notice the blunder. Even though you were not aware of it, you were *unconsciously monitoring my grammar* at every moment I was speaking. This notion of a background system, essential for communication yet rarely made explicit, is an important one for semiotics as well as linguistics. It means that communication is never as direct as it seems.

Valuable though Saussure's insights may be, they are too limited when we try to apply them to forms of communication other than language. The *linguistic sign*, as he called the relationship between sound-image and concept, may be arbitrary, but other kinds of signs are not. The sign on the door of a women's rest room depicting a stick figure wearing a skirt is not arbitrary; it is related to the fact that women traditionally wear skirts. Similarly, Laurence Olivier standing on stage representing Hamlet was not being arbitrary; he was a real young man representing a fictional young man.

Even Saussure's basic assumption about one person communicating a concept to another can run into trouble. Suppose I wake up one morning, gaze out the window, notice that the streets are wet, and infer that it rained the previous night. Here the wet pavement—not a sound-image but a visual one—is the signifier, and the concept of rain is the signified. The relationship between the two, however, is far from arbitrary; rain is wet, and so is the pavement. Furthermore, although I can be seen as the equivalent of the listener in Saussure's model of speech, who is the equivalent of the speaker? Even if we decide that it was the clouds that were "speaking" to me by dropping rain, *the clouds had no concept* that they wanted to transmit. I made the meaning of the experience happen, based on my similar past experiences. Nonetheless, just as with speech, I am not conscious of checking what I see against a remembered background; the meaning of rain just seems to be "out there."

To a semiotician, then, meaning does not have to be originally conceived in order to be transmitted. Meaning can be found, rather than just decoded, and with works of art, meanings tend to be found in the same way that I found the meaning of rain in the wet streets. That is, the artist is not sending us a message; instead, he is creating a work of art, which we then explore for meanings based not only on what he consciously had in mind, but on any number of wide-ranging cultural and personal systems of thought. We are rarely conscious of these systems, however, so that the meanings just seem to be there, making us feel that the artist must have somehow put them there. He put down the paint or the words or the musical notes, so he must have "meant" something by them. In fact, he may have meant nothing by them; or meant something different from what we now understand from them; or meant the same thing that we now understand but discovered that meaning himself only during the process of creation, or even afterward.

In the kind of speech communication that Saussure was describing, then, either the listener receives the same concept that the speaker intended, or else something has gone wrong—he encoded the concept wrongly (not saying what he should have), it got garbled in transmission, or the listener decoded it inaccurately. In artistic communication, however, the receiver may end up with a completely different concept from that of the sender (who may not even have had one), but it need not be because of error, but rather because of the very nature of the artistic process. This is clear enough with the visual arts; it does not seem strange that a sculptor or a painter was not trying to "tell" us something with his work of art. With a poem or a novel or a play, however, the fact that the author uses words makes us think about ordinary discourse, where words (or "sound-images") transmit intended meanings. Nevertheless, the author of a literary work is using language in a different way from that envisioned by Saussure, much more like the way a painter uses paint or a composer musical notes than the way a lecturer delivers a speech or a newspaper reporter writes an article. To sum up the differences, in artistic communication:

1. There is usually no fixed vocabulary. When you divide the artwork into constituent elements (and it is not always even possible to do so), like notes in a musical composition, you cannot go through the elements, one at a time, to determine what the artwork means. There is no possible "dictionary" for an art form. A work of art conveys meaning only as a whole; break it up, and it becomes meaningless. (You can use a dictionary to understand the words of a poem or a play, but you have not yet understood the poem or play *as a work of art*.)

2. The relationship between signifier and signified need not be arbitrary. When a poet uses rhyme or alliteration, for example, the sound of his words is part of the poem's effect.

3. Instead of a single system of signification, or "langue," there may be many, overlapping ones.

4. The concept received may have nothing to do with anything the artist originally had in mind.

All of the above qualities have significance for our understanding of acting. First, it is important in teaching actors not to go down the kind of garden path that lured Delsarte. (No one in the theatre uses his method anymore, but there are popular psychology books, like Julius Fast's *Body Language*, that sometimes find their way into our classrooms as elaborate bodily "dictionaries.") Of course, certain gestures—shaking the head, waving the hand, winking an eye, a hitchhiker putting out his thumb—do have relatively fixed meanings. The actor, however, should *not* just think about his positions and gestures in such a limited way, but instead be aware that his body is communicating all the time he is on stage in subtle ways that are hard to systematize. New branches of semiotics called *proxemics* (how we communicate by positioning ourselves in space) and *kinesics* (how we communicate by movements) have turned out to be unbelievably vast. Even things like the distance we put between ourselves, or the rate at which two people talking are simultaneously blinking their eyes, turn out to convey significance. It is possible, for example, to go into a lecture hall where there are people whom you have never met before and tell, just by the seats they have selected and how they are sitting on them, who knows whom and how intimately. There is an unwritten rule that strangers will sit as far apart from each other as possible (just think how you would feel if, while you were sitting in an almost empty theatre, a stranger came up and chose a seat right next to you); that casual acquaintances will keep a seat or two between them; and that friends will sit together. We did not learn these rules through conscious study, the way we learned language; there is no dictionary or grammar book for them. In fact, we are usually not even aware that such rules exist, yet they guide our lives in countless ways.

Realism, the presumably styleless form of acting, is supposed to disavow all convention on stage, though realists would probably acknowledge obvious signals like an upraised middle finger. Kinesics and proxemics, however, show that we are communicating in highly conventionalized ways even in real life. It is only because these ways cannot be systematized the way language can that we do not recognize them as being conventionalized. The body, even when not making overt, conscious gestures, is resonating meanings. The cultural anthropologist Edward T. Hall has cited studies showing that human rhythms of movement (which we begin to learn in our mother's womb, moving in synchronization with her movements) vary considerably from one group to another. These can lead to serious misunderstandings. The brisk, staccato rhythms of New Yorkers are notorious for making them seem brusque and callous to out-of-towners, even when the New Yorkers are trying to be friendly. Conversely, the legato rhythms of a southerner can make him seem slow and stupid to a New Yorker, even when the southerner is actually smarter than he is. Hall has described rhythms like this as part of our "informal" cultural patterns. "What sets the informal apart," he writes, "is that, unlike any other form of communication, there are *no senders* and *no receivers* and *no readily identifiable messages*. Everything is in the process itself, which releases the appropriate responses in others."[6]

Realism in acting, then, is not conventionless. Instead, it is a style of acting that tends to employ the conventions of everyday life, and to avoid those that are unique to the stage. Thus, an actor in a realistic role will not wear a mask, nor speak in verse, nor elevate his voice in a bombastic manner, nor strike heroic poses. He will avoid articles of costume that are stereotypical, like the black hat of the villain in cowboy movies. Nevertheless, he will position himself, move, and speak in ways that are in accord with the cultural codes of everyday life. In other words, his imitation of life is not *direct*; it is filtered through conventions of which he is only subliminally aware. The actor is not a camera, recording mindlessly whatever is in front of him, but rather an unconscious analyzer and synthesizer.

Consider, for example, something as simple as an actor sitting in a chair. We might think that there is nothing conventional about an action that is so ordinary and obvious. Surely the actor is merely imitating what he does in everyday life without any kind of selection, shaping, or commenting. But the point is that, even in real life, sitting in a chair is already a highly conventionalized act. Europeans, and to a certain extent the Chinese, developed the only "off the floor" cultures in the world. In most cultures, even today, when someone wants to sit down, he uses what seems obvious—the ground or the floor. Sitting in a chair seems awkward, unnatural, and downright uncomfortable, just as sitting on the floor or ground seems awkward and unnatural to us. When a person from another culture sees a Western actor in a movie sitting in a chair, the event seems odd, foreign, distant—in a word, *stylized.*

Note, again, that the seated actor has no idea that he is sending a message of strangeness. If he was trying to convey anything, it was probably naturalness, neutrality. But an important point in semiotics is that there is no such thing as neutral activity for human beings. The human mind abhors a vacuum; we are constantly making, and taking, meanings from everything we experience. We mix arbitrary and nonarbitrary systems of signification, barely conscious that there is any difference between the two, taking meanings from both kinds. The subtle aspect about the process is that most of the time it does not feel as though we are doing so. Meanings are "out there," rather than coming from us. Thus, the cultural fact that a woman has long hair and a man short hair seems as obvious as the fact that a woman has breasts and a man does not, although the former contrast is an arbitrary convention, while the latter is based on biology.

Often we are only aware that a cultural code exists when one gets broken. I was once in a restaurant that seemed like a pleasant, well-run establishment. We waited a few moments for a hostess to appear. She greeted us, took us to a table, and then, before we could sit down, asked us if we wanted to order drinks. We were shocked. It seemed incredibly hasty and rude of her not to let us sit down first, though in every other way she had been cordial. If anything, her behavior might have been intended to show efficiency and an eagerness to please. Now I doubt if there is any book of etiquette or written set of rules for hostesses and waitresses that says that customers must be seated before being asked to order. It is simply a custom that we have developed, unknowingly. No one would ever know it existed unless someone failed to observe it somehow.

Another way of becoming aware of the existence of codes is to observe how things are done in a different culture. I spent several months in China, for example, where many things are eaten that Americans would not think of as food at all—monkeys, lizards, rats. Snakes are gourmet items; there is even a restaurant in Canton where you pick out your live snake from a basket, just as we would pick out live lobsters from a tank. Most Americans, although they would admit that snake meat is perfectly nourishing, find the idea of eating it loathsome. It is not that there is any law against it; nor does Miss Manners list it as improper. Snake meat just seems *inherently* disgusting. That this is actually an arbitrary code of our culture only becomes apparent when we observe other groups consuming snakes with gusto.

The realistic actor, then, is operating under a huge complex of overlapping codes drawn from our culture, just as he is in everyday life. He is, if you will, drawing on the *semiotics* of everyday life, rather than drawing on life directly, which is in fact impossible for human beings. Thus, the kinds of things he takes from life will depend entirely on his unconscious preconceptions about life. It may feel as though he is only imitating what is "out there," but he is also imitating what is "in here," in his own mind. This is not to say that he is hallucinating instead of observing, but only that what he chooses to observe, and what he makes of it, will depend on his cultural and theatrical conditioning.

Take, for example, the notion, which is very important in the realistic theatre, that characters should be motivated and well-rounded. The realistic actor feels that any action his character performs on stage should be explainable somehow, in terms of that character's background. Willy Loman is motivated by his passionate, unquestioning commitment to the American Dream. Hickey is motivated by his guilt for his sexual philandering and an unfulfilled need to be punished for it. Brick Pollitt's aversion to his beautiful wife is motivated by his unconscious homosexual love for his dead friend Skipper. Well-roundedness means that these

224

motivations are not entirely conscious, resulting in multifaceted characterizations that mix good and bad. If asked why he thought about characterization in this way, the actor, and the playwright too, would probably say that it was because people are like that in real life—complex and deep rather than stereotypical and shallow. The influence of modern psychology would be apparent, even though the actor may never have actually studied it; the assumptions that psychology makes about human beings have been absorbed into our culture to the point where they are held automatically and unconsciously. They just seem to be "out there," qualities that human beings have, rather than being our cultural way of thinking about people.

At other times, and in other cultures, people have thought about human beings very differently. The Elizabethans, as I noted in Chapter 10, did not have a motivational psychology. Their psychology, based on a theory of humors, fluids in the body that imparted standard characteristics of health and temperament to an individual, made them perfectly comfortable with what we would call stereotyped characters. As far as the Elizabethans were concerned, human beings were stereotyped, so why shouldn't characters in a play be stereotyped too? Nor did the Elizabethans have as highly developed a sense of the mind-body polarity as we do. The idea that every person has a secret self, including an unconscious mind that is a secret even to the person himself, would have seemed strange to them. In most Elizabethan plays, characters are what they seem, with their motivations simple and obvious— greed, lust, ambition, etc. When an Elizabethan character has a secret self, it is usually the result of conscious dissembling, rather than "depth."

Of course, Shakespeare was a great playwright who transcended his era. We cannot limit him in our thinking to the kind of plays that an Elizabethan hack would have written. Some of his characters do indeed seem modern in their psychology, at least some of the time. Hamlet is not a stereotypical character (though his "melancholy" can be diagnosed in terms of the humors theory); Othello's motives seem complex; even a comic character like Malvolio seems to have depth. Some of Shakespeare's contemporary playwrights also anticipated modern psychology at times. But this is not to say that all the characters of the period were complexly motivated. The secondary characters almost never are. Modern American actors have particular trouble with one like Malcolm, in *Macbeth*, who describes himself as follows:

> I am yet
> Unknown to woman, never was forsworn,
> Scarcely have coveted what was mine own,
> At no time broke my faith, would not betray
> The devil to his fellow, and delight
> No less in truth than life. (IV.iii.125–30)

The actor cannot help thinking that anyone who would catalog his own virtues like this should not be taken seriously. Surely Malcolm must be a liar, or, more likely, a neurotic. In fact, he is not even supposed to be boasting. His presentation of himself must be taken at face value; it is simply Shakespeare's way of presenting Malcolm as a righteous character, in contrast to "black Macbeth," whom he will replace as King of Scotland. Any hint by the actor in performance that Malcolm is not just what he says he is will throw the ending of the play totally out of balance. Instead of restoring order, Malcolm's taking the throne will simply foreshadow more disorder, a bit of cynicism that a modern actor or director might find appealing, but which is not what happens in Shakespeare's play.

Iago is another character who is notorious for presenting a problem to the modern actor. Coleridge actually called him "motiveless." Iago himself does give several reasons for his treatment of Othello—he was passed over for promotion, he loves Desdemona too, he suspects that Othello has seduced Emilia, Iago's wife—but these seem rationalizations, which only add to our feeling that there are unconscious depths to the man of which we know but little.

In the 1930s, Laurence Olivier, playing Iago to Ralph Richardson's Othello, decided that Iago's motivation was actually a homosexual passion for the Moor; Iago was thus jealous of Desdemona, so he conceived a plot to destroy her and her husband. In one rehearsal, Olivier even went over and kissed Richardson on the mouth, which disconcerted Richardson not a little. This was an attempt to turn the play into a modern psychological one. In Olivier's filming of *Hamlet*, he decided that the problem of the motive for Hamlet's delaying could be explained by an Oedipus Complex. At one point in the film, Olivier even gets into bed with the actress playing his mother. Such outlandish approaches to these characters—which Olivier later recognized as distortions—serve only to remove the mystery from them. Shakespeare is like a modern playwright in giving an impression of depth to Iago or Hamlet, but unlike one in not providing an explanation, which certainly makes *Hamlet* or *Othello* a lot more fascinating than, say, *Tea and Sympathy*. In other words, the mystery is *part of the play*; it is not something to be explained in performance, but instead something to be *included* in performance.

Olivier, then, was projecting onto a historical play the attitudes he had learned from reading, seeing, and performing in modern psychological plays. He was also influenced, of course, by modern psychological novels and films, as well as by popular works on psychology like those of Ernest Jones. Psychological drama seemed normal, natural—surely all good plays must be psychological, no matter when or where they were written. It is exactly the same as thinking that all people, at all times and in all places, must find snake meat disgusting. It's just the way things are. In fact, things are not always that way, and just as many cultures find snakes or dogs or rats perfectly good to eat, and others would look on our prized food, beefsteak, with loathing, so too do other cultures have different ideas from ours on what constitutes a human being, and how one should be depicted on stage.

Michel Saint-Denis, in his important book, *Theatre: The Rediscovery of Style*, insisted that "style is not something superficial or merely external." It is integral to the artist's meaning. Although the notion of style suggests historical periods, Saint-Denis maintained that this was a secondary, derivative meaning. All periods have a style; even "an actor who takes part in a realistic play of today can show style in his acting."[7] Saint-Denis did not use semiotic terms, but it is clear from his writing that he is referring to the cultural codes by which people in a given time and place live. We can look at a photograph of people in the 1940s, for example, and instantly recognize the period from the style of clothing they wear. The people themselves, however, had little sense that they were living in a "period." Our style of living today seems similarly neutral, but in future years people will look back on it with the same kind of nostalgia with which look back on previous periods today.

The theatrical conventions of a different time or place may appear quaint and artificial from our perspective, though they were anything but that for their performers and audiences. In understanding the theatrical conventions of the past, it is necessary to try to get *inside the minds* of those individuals, to see acting as they saw it, rather than as we see it. We should not be like Bertolt Brecht, who looked at a Chinese actress steering a nonexistent boat with a paddle that barely reached to her knees, and concluded that "the artist's object is to appear strange and even surprising to the audience."[8] The actress seemed strange and surprising *to Brecht*, because he was not familiar with the conventions, but she would have seemed unremarkable to a Chinese audience long accustomed to them. Nor did the actress think of her performance as being antirealistic, because she had no realistic tradition to compare it to. She acted with a totally imaginary boat and an impracticably short paddle because that was the way she was used to acting. It did not occur to her to do it any other way—and why should it? Her efforts were aimed at doing it well on its own, traditional terms, rather than hypothesizing how a Western actress might do it.

The most damaging approach of all is to think of a style as being realism plus "artificialities." The style *did not seem artificial* in its own time. Language here provides a good analogy. If you want to learn to speak a foreign language well, you must learn to think of it the way a native speaker does. French is not English made funny. It is not artificial to put a pronoun before the verb instead of after; to a Frenchman, our way of putting it after seems artificial. If the only way you can say something in French is first to think of it in English and then translate it, your French will forever be stilted and halting. Similarly, if you think that wearing a mask, or speaking blank verse, or carrying a walking stick and wearing a monocle, are artificial, you will forever do them awkwardly on stage. You are "translating," rather than speaking like a native. The question to ask is, what did these actions mean to the original actors performing them, within the theatrical and other cultural codes of their day? What did they *feel like*?

The ancient Greek actor, for example, did not think of his mask as an artificiality. It goes without saying that people then, as now, did not wear such masks in real life, but that does not mean that the actor said to himself, "I sure wish I could act naturally, but unfortunately I have to wear this big mask because of the large size of the theatre." Mask-making was an art in itself;[9] the actor based his characterization on the mask and drew inspiration from it. Not only did actors play more than one part in the same play by wearing different masks (which might include such extremes as women, old men, and gods), but different actors would, at different times during the same performance, play the *same* part. The mask was not just a means for getting the role across, it was the role itself! The actor would no more have wanted to do without it than a modern American actress, playing Blanche in *A Streetcar Named Desire*, would want to put one on.

Nor did ancient Greek audiences sit there wanting to shout, "Take it off! Take off that mask and show us some real, honest acting!" Masks were the norm. Their mere existence would not have "heightened" or "exaggerated" reality, as it does for us today, in a theatre that does not include masks as one of its standard devices.

229

Ancient audiences would thus have been interested in how good the masks were, and how well the actors were using them, but would have reacted to their use per se as something unremarkable. Acting *without* a mask, if an actor were imaginative enough even to think of such an unusual thing, would have seemed bizarre, daring, or "stylized."

Saint-Denis's distinction between style and stylized, then, has nothing to do with how close to or far from life something is on stage, how real or artificial it is. Instead, it has to do with how something is presented and, more important, how it is received. *Style* is unavoidable; there is always style (though it may be the wrong style for the particular play), because human beings cannot perceive anything without relating it to some cultural code, and style is merely the collection of theatrical and other cultural codes operating at a given performance. Something is *stylized* when it calls attention to one or more of those codes. Ordinarily, the codes are in the background; the Greek audience did not consciously think about masks as being conventionalized, just as a modern actor does not think about sitting in a chair as being conventionalized. Similarly, we do not consciously think about grammar when we listen to somebody speak, though we could not understand him without knowing grammar. *Stylization* occurs when the codes become conscious, moving from the background of our awareness to the foreground. Masks were thus not stylized for the Greeks, but they are for us, simply because they are so unusual on our stage. If an actor walks on stage wearing one, we immediately think, "Good heavens, he's wearing a mask. I wonder why?" The Greek audience, of course, would have had no such thoughts.

Style, then, is never artificial; even though it is based on artifice, it always *seems* natural, neutral. Stylization, on the other hand, always seems artificial by definition. Stylization is thus not always present on stage, to say the least, and is not always desirable when it occurs, though sometimes it can be exploited for artistic effect. The many rebellions against realism that have occurred in the past

230

hundred years usually have employed stylization in this sense, boldly flouting convention in order to jar the audience. The avant-garde productions of Richard Schechner, for example, which constantly acknowledged the presence of the audience and even at times drew them into the action, were calling to the audience's attention the convention of the "fourth wall," the pretense that they were watching something of which they had no part. But the fourth wall was itself a convention that was stylized when it was introduced in the nineteenth century. Even the practice of dimming the lights in the auditorium only began around a hundred years ago, and it certainly seemed odd at first to the audiences unaccustomed to it.

In sum, realism in acting is *not basic*. It seems basic to us simply because it is our style, in the same way that the English language seems basic to us because it is our language. It is the easiest style for most (but not all) American actors today to learn, but only because it is the style they have most often seen and heard about. The kinds of questions that a realistic actor asks, such as "How would I say this line to my girlfriend?", come obviously to his mind only because he has heard or seen or read of that kind of approach to acting countless times. We should remember, however, that actors of a hundred years ago had great difficulty in learning realism; it took two generations of realistic acting for it to become entrenched. Older actors found it hard if not impossible to learn something that seemed so flat, muted, and untheatrical. No one had ever complained about their being "stagy" before. Audiences had been paying good money to see them perform in the traditional ways. Why ask nit-picky questions about how they lifted a teacup or scratched their heads when they were at home?

Thus, not only is realism on stage not conventionless, its conventions (or *codes*, as semioticians like to say) are complex and numerous. Some of them I have already identified, like the convention, rooted in Cartesian dualism, that a character must be psychologically deep and have many different facets. There is also the convention of scientific causality; events on stage must not be fortuitous, but rather logically interconnected. We will no longer accept the idea of God, or gods, or fate, or luck controlling things behind the scenes, but instead insist that things only be controlled by what is happening *in* the scenes. We expect a characterization, despite its multiple facets, to be logically consistent. Thus, we do not mind the fact that Lady Macbeth seems like a demon in the beginning of the play and like a frightened, guilty little girl in the sleepwalking scene, but we *do* mind the fact that Shakespeare has not bothered to provide any connecting scenes to get her from point A to point B, nor even any exposition to explain how her drastic conversion came about.

In addition, some of the conventions of realism are actually negative; traditional elements like footlights, heroic declamation, or two-dimensional flats are not only not there, but *conspicuously* not there. When an actor tries to impress us by how "natural" he is acting, he does so as much by what he leaves out—fine poses, a lofty voice, stereotypical behavior—as by what he puts in. Early realistic directors like Stanislavski directed much of their effort at *removing* traditional conventions, but they left, as it were, a trace. In other words, the absence of a convention can itself *be* a convention.

Other realistic conventions are simply drawn from the conventions by which we live; an actor eating a meal onstage will use a knife and fork, just as he would at home or in a restaurant. Such real-life conventions are so familiar to us that they do not seem to be conventions, but they certainly are. Eating with a fork can seem a pretty awkward and silly business to someone from another culture who has never experienced it.

Finally, there may also be other conventions of realism that we simply are not aware of, because many cultural conventions, like the one about not taking orders in a restaurant before the customers are seated, only become apparent to us when they are broken. All in all, the realistic actor is like a player in a game with many intricate rules, most of which are not written down but simply taken for granted.

It is important, then, in shifting to a different style of play, that the actor not simply drag along the old rules of realism in the naive belief that they have universal application. To speak blank verse, for instance, in a flat, rhythmless, understated manner, in hopes that the audience will admire your naturalness, is as ridiculous as trying to play, say, Harold Pinter's dialogue as inflated bombast. Nor will it help to learn speech and movement in a mechanical, uncreative way while still going about preparing roles in Shakespeare or other nonrealistic drama by introspective emotional techniques. Speech and movement are not veneers to be laid on top of a role; they are integral to it, especially in oratorical drama like Shakespeare's. As Bernard Shaw once said, you cannot play Shakespeare between the lines or behind the lines, but only *on* the lines.

All this is not to denigrate realism itself, nor realistic acting. In fact, if we view realism semiotically as one style among many, we will recognize that, while it is not inherently better than any other style, neither is it any worse. While realism remains the dominant theatrical style in our theatre today, there are many who would belittle it. Echoing the many rebels against realism over the past hundred years, they exalt style in the sense of stylized, and denounce realism for being flat, dull, untheatrical, old-fashioned, or even (as with Bertolt Brecht) somehow politically repressive. This only takes the prevalent view of realism as conventionless and "basic" and turns it on its head, now seeing its supposed lack of convention as a drawback rather than a benefit. Instead, realism is actually a style of great artistic potential, both in playwriting and acting, as its many masters have shown us. American theatre and film have a great tradition of realistic acting, which is not just limited to the work of the Group Theatre or the Actors Studio, but to such widely differing actors as Gary Cooper, Bette Davis, Henry Fonda, Humphrey Bogart, Katharine Hepburn, Marlon Brando, Meryl Streep, and Dustin Hoffman. To characterize their work as bland and featureless is ridiculous. They and many others like them are perfect examples of what Saint-Denis meant when he said it was possible to have style—a mastery of the conventions of their art form—even in contemporary realistic material.

FIFTEEN

A HUMANISTIC ACTOR TRAINING, CENTERED ON PLAY PRODUCTION

In the past three decades, there has been an explosion of new programs in American colleges and universities for the training of actors. Thirty years ago, only a handful of departments offered the Bachelor of Fine Arts (BFA) or Master of Fine Arts (MFA) in acting; now there are several hundred that offer one or the other or both. In addition, the traditional Bachelor of Arts programs in theatre now include many more practical courses in acting than they used to.

Theatre in universities is nothing new. In the Middle Ages, schools and universities regularly produced plays, usually in Latin, as a method of instruction. The ability to speak Latin was important for any educated man, and plays, whether taken from antiquity or written for the occasion, were a means of learning how. They were also means of learning how to speak and move well in general. This tradition continued in the Renaissance. Students of English literature are aware of the importance of the "University Wits" as

Elizabethan playwrights. (Shakespeare was not one of these wits, but he was strongly influenced by them.) Less well known is the fact that Elizabethan universities experimented in new styles of staging; the first use of perspective scenery in England may have been at Oxford, early in the seventeenth century. In Shakespeare's day, then, most educated people would have had experience in theatrical production, and it would sometimes have been experience of a very high order.

A similar tradition of drama in education existed on the Continent. The Jesuits, in particular, used drama extensively in their schools in Germany, Austria, Poland, France, Italy, Spain, and eventually even in the Philippines. The antitheatrical prejudice seems to be relaxed when the acting is nonprofessional and education-oriented. In France, two of Racine's plays were actually commissioned for a girls' school at St. Cyr.[1]

In American colleges and universities, theatre programs came late. The first degree-granting program in theatre was instituted by Thomas Wood Stevens at the Carnegie Institute of Technology in 1914. Other programs soon followed, so that by 1940, theatre education was an accepted part of most American universities.[2] In most instances, however, theatre programs focused on dramatic literature and theatre history, and, of course, on the production of plays. The purpose of play production was not primarily to teach students how to act, but rather to introduce them to dramatic literature from all periods, and to serve as a cultural resource for the academic community. The latter function had special importance, since most American institutions of higher learning were located in rural areas, far from professional theatres.

In the 1960s, American universities themselves expanded spectacularly. New institutions were founded, and old ones greatly enlarged. Theatre departments were part of the general expansion. It was a crucial moment in the history of American theatre. Many people were dissatisfied with the traditional, humanistic approach of American theatre departments on the one hand, and with the narrow, self-centered approach of professional schools like the Actors Studio on the other. The model of the new theatre departments, or the enlarged old ones, was to be the theatre conservatories of continental Europe. Acting students would receive extensive training in speech, movement, improvisation, dance, fencing, and singing, along with classes in acting.

The results were odd. Acting classes tended to stress the traditional, introspective approach of the Actors Studio, which had never been popular in colleges and universities previously. The classes in speech, movement, and so on, were taught separately from "acting," with little attempt at integration. In addition, play production changed. Work in acting classes consisted mostly of monologues and scenes; in some departments, students were not even *allowed* to act in plays until they had taken classes for several years. When plays were actually performed, the repertory, which had previously been drawn from the whole history of Western drama, tended to focus on contemporary American realism. Choosing appropriate roles for students, rather than providing broad experience, became the primary criterion in play selection. Being a cultural resource for the local academic community was of declining importance; many of the new departments were in urban areas, while modern transportation made rural colleges and universities less remote and self-contained. An "appropriate" role usually meant a character of the same age, sex, nationality, and time period as those of the student himself.

The drastic change in American theatre departments from a liberal arts orientation to a "professional" one, which happened in less than a generation, was notable for its lack of central coordination. There was little mechanism for and even less interest in setting standards, accrediting faculty, or limiting growth. The professional society, the American Educational Theatre Association (AETA),[3] was a weak, disparate organization that eventually went bankrupt through mismanagement. The National Association of Schools of Theatre (NAST) only began to set standards after the "professionalization" of theatre departments had already taken place. It too is a feeble organization, whose criteria tend to fit the lowest common denominator—when they are enforced, which they rarely are. The result has been an explosive growth in the numbers of students majoring in acting in colleges and universities. Every year, thousands of students graduate, of whom only a few dozen will ever have successful careers as professional actors. Their training has been haphazard, yet highly specialized—long lists of credits in acting, speech, movement, and so on prepare the students for little else besides acting, a profession that offers almost no opportunities. Aside from occasional hand-wringing by administrators, no one seems to recognize this cruel paradox—which is, of course, typical behavior for an entrenched bureaucracy. Means to an end become ends in themselves. The real reason we now train students to become actors is to provide teaching jobs for out-of-work actors. It is like those pyramid schemes or chain letters. Those who get in early can do well, but it is mathematically obvious that the scam cannot continue forever.

The original justification for the change in the orientation of theatre departments, of course, was to improve the quality of American acting, a worthy goal. But what was wrong with American acting at the time? Primarily, the problem was seen as an inability to perform the classics. The model of the European theatre conservatory, which trained actors in a wide variety of styles, was invoked precisely to enlarge the abilities of our actors. No one denied that Americans could be superb in contemporary, psychological realism. The Actors Studio itself had turned out many actors who were stunning in their ability to play Williams, Miller, Inge. They also were wonderful in film, primarily a realistic form. But the same actors were obviously incapable of playing Shakespeare, Molière, or Shaw, not to mention Brecht, O'Casey, or Pinter.

Less obvious, but no less a problem, was the fact that the prevailing realistic approach to acting, which stressed playing the self, gave little preparation for character acting. The kind of dazzling self-transformation that European actors (including Stanislavski himself) were capable of was rarely seen on our stage or in our films, and rarely valued when it did occur. The startling thing, then, is that the very purposes for which college and university theatre departments had changed—to expand American actors beyond realism—has been largely forgotten. The stress is still on realistic acting, plus the acquisition of some technical skills, which even the Actors Studio has added, too. American acting is no better—in fact, not much different—than it was a generation ago. Our best actors (who often are *not* university trained) are more likely now to do character acting, but they have the same old problems with the classics. Dustin Hoffman was no better as Shylock than Marlon Brando had been as Marc Antony. (If anything, he was *worse*.) The numerous young stars who have played in Joseph Papp's "Shakespeare Marathon" at the New York Shakespeare Festival have demonstrated only their total lack of experience or even comprehension of Shakespeare's plays.

If there is another academic discipline that our theatre departments have come to resemble, it is the education departments. Both education and theatre departments have taken traditionally humanistic disciplines and turned them into mechanistic ones. Both show the same bureaucratic tendency to change means into ends. Both proliferate sterile methodological courses (my favorite is "Costume Techniques and Wardrobe Practices," required of all acting majors in the large theatre department where I recently taught), which squeeze out the liberal arts courses. Both place a narrow emphasis on the self rather than on subject matter, or in the case of acting, on the play. Both turn out students who cannot do what they are supposed to do—teach or act. The only difference is that students in education departments end up with actual jobs as teachers, while acting students in theatre departments end up as waiters and word-processor operators.

What, then, can be done about the deplorable state we are now in? It is not likely that theatre departments will reform themselves overnight, nor that they will decrease the numbers of students they enroll. Cutting back on students would mean cutting back on teachers too, and who would want to do himself out of a job? An organization like NAST would offer some hope if it could set rigorous standards, but the fact that standards must be approved by the constituent theatre schools runs into the same problem.[4] No theatre school will approve guidelines that would put itself out of business.

The only chance for improvement, then, is if a few schools, on an individual basis, will reform themselves. There are already signs that this has begun to happen. Our better theatre departments are at least no longer locked into the prevailing realistic ideology. Some even try, without apology, to teach students how to speak verse. Mask work, dialects, and comic technique are occasionally taught. There has also been a significant infusion of British actors and acting teachers into our universities, who bring their traditional, straightforward, healthy approach to classical acting and character work.

Encouraged by these signs, I offer the following proposals for any school that wants to consider them. They are rooted in the beliefs, promulgated throughout this book, that an actor is a creative artist; that fundamental to his art form is the ability to create characters, in the imaginary world of a play; that the fundamental acting experience is the feeling of being someone else; and that the actor is always operating under semiotic codes (though they are often subliminal and unrecognized) which must be mastered for any particular role and play.

1. The education of an actor, even in professional BFA or MFA programs, must be broadly humanistic.

2. Speech and movement need to be integrated into the teaching of acting rather than being taught in isolation. "Academic" courses

in dramatic literature and theatre history also need to be coordinated with studio acting classes and with public performances.

3. The education of an actor should be centered on performing in *plays*—as many as possible, in as many different styles as possible, starting as early as possible.

4. Character acting should be encouraged wherever possible from the very beginning of an actor's study.

A humanistic education for actors recognizes that theatre is an art form, whose purpose is to enlighten, to question, to liberate. A narrow emphasis on "practicality," in which an actor is taught a grab bag of disconnected skills, assumes that theatre is a business, an industry, in which the actor must find a niche. This is true only when acting is applied in fields peripheral to theatre—movies, television shows and commercials, modeling, nightclub performing—and not consistently true even there. The entertainment industry is so disorganized in this country as to be chaotic; there is certainly no orderly procedure for developing a career, as there is in, say, engineering, medicine, or teaching. Even in a mercenary, unartistic medium like TV commercials, success is based on general savvy and drive rather than any particular acting skill. An actor aspiring to do commercials might take classes in certain areas like speech, but it is ridiculous to think of designing an overall program of study for him.

When acting is viewed in blunt, practical terms, then, there is no such thing as a "course of study" that makes any sense. In fact, the most practical thing to tell an actor seeking marketability is to give up, since his chances of commercial success, regardless of talent or training, are minuscule. If he persists in his pursuit, the next most practical piece of advice he can receive is not to spend a lot of time in acting classes, but to get out and hustle instead. The only truly logical approach to teaching acting, especially in a university setting, is not to treat it as "training," for some highly problematic "career," but instead to teach it for its own sake, as an art. We do this with other art forms without embarrassment. A person can study music without intending to become a professional musician, or painting without intending to become a professional artist. It is assumed that these are worthwhile activities in themselves, that they are a valuable means of teaching a person about his world, his culture, and himself. A few people who study music or art will go on to have professional careers, but most will not, and the education for these arts will not be oriented toward a narrow careerism.

Studying acting for its own sake implies a respect for it as an art form. Just as a person studying a musical instrument also studies the history and theory of music, or a person studying how to draw or paint also studies the history and theory of art, so too must the actor study the history and theory of theatre. The actor should read extensively in the history of acting, and of theatre generally, and beyond that, study other approaches to history as well, since theatre never floats in a vacuum but has always been the product of its time. He should know the literature of theatre, and literature generally, and know something of its literary criticism, literary theory, and aesthetics. There is no point in studying only *how* to act if you do not know what acting *is*, in the broadest sense. There is no point in preparing students only for the theatre as it exists, since it now exists in America only in a degraded state. We should instead teach how it got to be the way it is—and how it might be improved.

Besides, there are significant, practical, "how-to" consequences for actors in studying history, literature, and theory. If we assume again that the fundamental experience of acting is to escape the limitations of yourself, to become somebody else in a temporary, controlled situation, the very aim of the humanities is to achieve the same thing in a more analytical manner. The reason that the humanities are also called the "liberal arts" is that they are *liberating*. With the liberal arts, we study other cultures—both those of the past and those of foreign cultures today—with the goal of understanding other people and, conversely, gaining perspective on ourselves. Traditionally, liberal study was centered on foreign languages, both ancient and modern. A foreign language was a route into another culture, another mind-set. The goal of studying, say, Latin, although it was not usually described that way, was to learn to think like an ancient Roman. This had no immediate practical advantage, since there were few ancient Romans still walking around, but it took the student out of the limitations of his own place and time, teaching him how things might be viewed differently, which, in turn, gave him perspective on his own language and culture. Foreign language study, which is slowly returning to American colleges and universities as a requirement for graduation, is thus highly valuable for actors. In a sense, it *is* acting, though the process is gradual and unspectacular, in contrast with the sudden, intuitive changes that can occur to an actor in rehearsal.

When we study literature, history, and foreign languages, then, we gain a sense of what it is like to live in a different milieu, which is exactly what the actor must learn, especially in dealing with the classics. It is impossible to act Shakespeare well, for example, without knowing what it was like to live as an Elizabethan, or to act in Ibsen without understanding the mind-set of a late-nineteenth-century European. As I noted in the previous chapter, every culture operates within a vast set of semiotic codes that the actor must try to understand. Otherwise, his acting in plays of that culture will always seem stilted and external. If, for example, an actor in a Shakespeare play is told that the verse does not matter (an amazingly common attitude among American directors), he is not approaching the play from the perspective of an Elizabethan, for whom verse mattered a great deal. If an actor believes that democracy is the only possible form of sensible government, he will have a great deal of trouble acting in a play like *Richard II*, where the problems of kingship are intimately explored. To the modern actor, the Divine Right of Kings, if he has heard about it at all, will seem merely quaint and stupid, but *Richard II* explores its implications, including its contradictions, from a viewpoint of passionate concern. The actor must suspend his disbelief, and enter into that passion, or his performance will be hollow.

In place of the popular view of the actor as an isolated self, an atom floating in a vacuum, we need to see the actor as having a cultural self. Acting does not consist of merely drawing on direct, personal sensations, but of drawing upon cultural codes that shape those sensations and give them coherence. This ought to be obvious in the case of historical or foreign plays, but it is even true with contemporary American realism. Lanford Wilson's plays, for example, deal with our deteriorating common values. The actor playing in one of Wilson's plays needs to understand this, and the source of such understanding will come as much from reading American literature, sociology, and history as it will from examining his own personal life. I have stressed in this book the importance of the *role* and the *play* as sources of inspiration for the actor. To understand these, in turn, requires competency in the language in which they are written, meaning not just the English language per se, but all the customs, traditions, habits, and mores that shape a particular play. And just as you do not really understand your own language until you have learned another, you cannot master your own culture until you have studied other cultures—i.e., have studied the humanities. In the long run, studying Sophocles, Shakespeare, and Molière, along with their cultures, helps you in playing Lanford Wilson, David Mamet, and Wendy Wasserstein, not because they are all the same, but precisely because they are *different*.

The problem of treating an acting student like an isolated individual is aggravated by our habit of teaching speech and movement in classes isolated from those called "Acting," which are usually devoted to improvisation and scene work. Treating speech and movement separately from acting is the result of Cartesian dualism, a view of the actor that inhibits using speech or movement in a creative way as a source of inspiration. It is probably too much to expect to find teachers who are fully adept at teaching all aspects of acting (I certainly am not myself), but much more could be done in terms of team teaching, so that all his teachers could help a student work on a role. As a large number of important theorists have stressed, a move, a way of standing, a gesture, a tone of voice, a dialect, are more than just external refinement; they are often the emotional key to a scene or even to an entire role. Thus, speech and movement teachers, if they are any good, are actually teaching *acting*. They use a different nomenclature from someone stressing, say, affective memory or objectives, but the purpose is the same, to stimulate a good performance. Sports, as usual, provide a good analogy: A football team or a baseball team will have many coaches, most of whom specialize in different aspects of the sport. They will of course work with athletes in isolation part of the time, but their efforts are carefully coordinated by the head coach. Each is seen as teaching a central *aspect* of the game rather than a peripheral refinement. Nor do coaches just teach their specialties and go home. They all attend the scrimmages and games, directly relating their specialties to the athletes' performances. If such coordination is possible in sports (where, after all, the *players* specialize much more than actors do), it certainly should be possible in teaching acting.

The teaching of dramatic literature and theatre history should also be integrated with the teaching of acting. A major problem with the old, liberal-arts-oriented drama departments, unrecognized at the time, was that there was little or no coordination between what was taught in the classroom and what was performed on the stage. Many of the same plays were likely to show up in performance as were to be found on the literature or history syllabuses, but the fact was rarely acknowledged. The play in performance ought to have been a major resource for those teaching the academic courses, but it was rare for teachers even to acknowledge its existence. Students were more likely to hear about John Philip Kemble and Sarah Siddons performing in *Macbeth* than about their classmates Johnny Jones and Sally Smith playing the same roles in the college production. The shift from liberal arts to professionally-oriented theatre departments did nothing to change this fragmentation in the students' education, in fact aggravating it by teaching performance classes in the same manner, isolated from the productions.

Over twenty years ago, Victor Mitchell at the University of Calgary in Canada set up a drama department specifically oriented toward an integrated education. Each year, students were required to take seminars in literature and history, *focusing on the plays in performance*. Thus, if there was a student production of *Waiting for Godot*, students would study postwar European culture, reading novels and philosophical works like those of the existentialists, seeing films, learning about theatrical conditions, reading other plays by Beckett, and reading other works from the Theatre of the Absurd. Over a four-year period, all the major historical genres of western theatre (including nonliterary forms like Commedia dell'Arte) would be covered.

The system drew mixed reactions; the professors either loved it or hated it. Performance teachers felt that it took up too much of students' time, and pressured for more courses in speech and movement. Teachers of the seminars found that they took far more preparation than a traditional survey course. It was also hard to find people to direct all the various genres; directors tended, as in other theatre departments, to gravitate toward contemporary realism. The time could have not been less propitious for such a system, which was going directly against the trend toward fragmentation and "professionalism." Nevertheless, Mitchell's system continued. Students undoubtedly received the best undergraduate drama education in North America. Very few became professional actors (as in all undergraduate theatre departments, no matter how professional their pretensions), but all learned significant things about their theatre, their culture, and themselves.

Modifications of Mitchell's approach, which was perhaps overly ambitious, are possible. I have developed a course called *Dramaturgy*, in which students work as dramaturgs, or literary advisors, to the director of a major production. The course is given in the fall, but oriented toward a play to be done in the spring, so that the director can be helped with his planning. For a spring production of *Othello* at Florida State University, for example, students first read and discussed about a dozen of Shakespeare's plays and heard lectures on Elizabethan culture and theatre history. They then did a range of projects, from production histories of *Othello* in various periods, to a critical bibliography, to the preparation of a text for performance. It is best, of course, to have a director who is interested in using dramaturgs; in this case, the director, Dean Gil Lazier of the School of Theatre, was quite enthusiastic, visited the class, and made considerable use of the students' materials. But even if the director is uninterested, students benefit from doing the projects as a classroom exercise; their experience of the final production (whether it is done well or badly) is greatly enriched. They see connections between their scholarship and performance, and see theatre as something more than glamour and stardom, as something linked with our deepest ideas and feelings.

Rather than starting with the productions from the theatrical season, another approach to integrating theatre education is to have a theatrical production arise from an academic course. In a class called *Encounters*, originally conceived by Stuart Baker of Florida State University, students study the works of a great playwright both in the classroom and on the stage. When I taught the course on Ibsen, for example, students read and discussed his plays and heard lectures on them, but also did a production of Ibsen's *Little Eyolf*, cast entirely with class members. Anyone who has ever been in a play realizes how much more you learn about it by doing it than by experiencing it in a classroom; memorizing your part in it, rehearsing it over and over, and performing it for an audience are a kind of intimate confrontation that cannot be duplicated any other way. (I have published many scholarly articles based on my insights that came from acting in or directing plays.) The Encounters course tries to formalize that experience. It has the pleasant side effect of gaining course credit for putting on a play, which was never possible in the old, liberal-arts-oriented theatre departments and rarely possible in the new, practical-oriented ones, despite the enormous effort by both faculty and students in play production.

There is no reason why a course like Encounters cannot be the central part of any actor training program. It is certainly harder to direct students in a play than merely have them do monologues and scenes, but since the acting teachers are usually directing the same students in plays anyway (for which the students now receive no course credit and the director receives no released time from teaching), the net result can actually mean *less* work for everyone. It may also be difficult to find acting teachers who can also lecture and lead serious discussions on dramatic literature and theatre history. The solution is, again, team teaching, plus better education for acting teachers.

In any event, the importance of making *plays* the center of actor training cannot be overstressed. Michel Saint-Denis, the best acting teacher who ever worked in North America (where he set up the acting programs at the National Theatre School in Canada and at the Juilliard School in New York City), insisted that students do *only* plays, rather than monologues or scenes.[5] Doing entire plays provides a discipline that is totally lacking in scene work. The experience of working with others, the sense of creating a work of art, and the special challenge that comes from performing with an audience are essential to learning to act.

The resistance to putting acting students into plays arises from a false model of actor training. Broadly, there are two ways of learning subjects: incrementally or cyclically. A classic example of incremental learning occurs in mathematics. Starting with definitions and axioms, the student proves basic theorems, which are used to prove more advanced theorems, which are used to prove still more advanced ones, for as far as the student can go. This stepwise procedure is typical of all the sciences, and since the sciences are currently the most prestigious subjects taught in our educational institutions, incremental teaching and learning are seen as somehow more rigorous and important than cyclical learning or teaching. Since the arts are very low in educational prestige, and theatre probably the lowest in prestige among the arts, the people who set up actor training programs in the sixties tried to boost the status of their departments by insisting that acting should be taught incrementally, like the sciences or engineering. Just as you would not let a student get his hands on a cyclotron until he has studied a lot of physics, so these austere, rigorous teachers of theatre were not going to let a student get near a stage until he had several years of studying acting in a classroom.

This was a dubious choice. Certainly, it has no historical basis; actors throughout history learned acting from being in plays rather than from being in classrooms. No one thought it necessary for a Richard Burbage or a David Garrick to "hone his skills" or "perfect his instrument" before he could go near the stage. This is because acting is generally *not* learned incrementally. The actor does not advance by adding skills on top of other skills, but by improving and refining the same basic skills, over and over. There are only a few things that need to be learned in acting, but they must each be learned a thousand times. Relaxing, relating, pursuing objectives, getting the feel of a character, are things that all actors must work on, whether they are children putting on *Puss in Boots* in kindergarten or professionals putting on *Hamlet* for the Royal Shakespeare Company.

Teaching acting incrementally comes down to first teaching speech, movement, improvisation, and interpretation (first in monologues and then in scenes), before allowing the student to act in a play for an audience. There is nothing wrong with studying speech, movement, and improvisation, but they are *not a basis* for acting in plays; they should be studied concurrently with it. Monologues and scenes should not be done at all (see Michel Saint-Denis), except when taken from a play the student is actually performing. An actor does not "progress" from monologues to scenes to plays. Monologues, in particular, are insidious; removing the other actors, and the play as a whole, does not make performing easier, but *harder*. Your fellow actors, plus your costume, props, set, and lighting, plus (most important) the overall action of the play are *not things added to a monologue to complicate it*; they are there to *support* the monologue and make it simpler. Actors who are trained excessively through monologues become stiff and inhibited when they finally get to plays; not only do they not know simple things like not covering another actor or moving on his line, but their habit of always looking inward makes it difficult for them to draw imaginative or emotional sustenance from their fellow actors and their surroundings. Because they relate badly, the other actors and the director find them hard to work with; their performances will be fitful, full of emotion one minute and dead the next. Ultimately, they do not participate in telling the story of the play, which is the responsibility not only of the actors but of all the theatre artists.

The play in performance is the obvious means for integrating the work of the various teachers of acting. Team teaching need not mean everyone always working in the same classroom if all teachers use the play as the focus of their work. It is important to recognize that *work done in a classroom is not acting*; it is only practice for acting, which is something that happens in a play. The work of a speech or movement teacher should be directly related to what the actors are doing in performance at any given time. Furthermore, speech and movement teachers should have a say in what plays are chosen and how they are cast; they should also attend rehearsals and confer regularly with the director, as well as with the actors in their classes.

It is not necessary for plays chosen for teaching purposes to be fully mounted. In the Encounters course, for example, they are given low-budget, minimalist staging in a "black box" theatre. It is essential, however, that the plays be done for an audience (whether paying or not), rather than just for classmates and teachers. As I maintained in Chapter 5, the presence of the audience verifies the performance; it certainly makes the subjective experience of the actor vastly different from that of merely doing class work. Any

250

approach to actor training that ignores the actor's subjectivity is doomed to failure.

The plays chosen for performance should represent the widest possible range of drama, from many different periods and countries. Furthermore, contemporary American plays should not be limited to those of white, middle-class playwrights. Some of the best playwriting today is by black, Hispanic, or Asian-American authors. Studying their plays provides a window on the rich, complex worlds of their minority groups. It would also be valuable to include non-Western drama. I have seen Chinese professionals alternate Peking Opera with modern realism, playing both superbly; if they can do both, why can't we?

The drift toward contemporary American realism, and the related drift toward casting students only in roles resembling their real-life selves, must be resisted. As I mentioned in Chapter 7, it is not always necessary in character acting that the character differ radically from the actor's everyday self. The feeling of being in a different milieu, in a magical world of the stage, is enough for many actors. But as I recall from my own memories, there is nothing more stifling to an acting student than to have to play only himself, in a scene or a monologue from a contemporary American realistic play, without stage lighting or a costume or even a delineated stage, in some dingy classroom. To see that kind of experience as a basis for moving on to perform in plays is ridiculous.

Some actors do need to change radically in order to be liberated in performance, however. For such actors, mask work, dialects, animal studies, experiments with makeup, and working with period costumes and properties, are essential right from the beginning. The idea that you must learn to play yourself before you can play a character, like the idea that you must learn to act in realism before you can do style, is not only erroneous, it is potentially destructive. I recall a very talented young actress who, early in her training, gave a bold, startling performance as a neurotic murderess; her tempo was rapid, machinegunlike, driven, yet clear and compelling. As in all

251

good acting, her performance had the quality of being *possessed*. (Needless to say, this was in a play rather than in a class.) Later, after a few years of being taught "honesty" and "truth," she could no longer perform the simplest roles. She was so self-conscious and faltering that she was embarrassing to watch—and she had come to hate acting.

This actress needed to play a strong, bold character in order to be released. Why should that be wrong? Why should actors who play closer to their everyday selves be seen as somehow morally superior? Again, if we are talking about practicality, is it not *results* that count?

Acting teachers should be on the alert for students such as she. All acting students should do mask work, dialects, etc., early on. For those who do not respond to such a strong character approach, there is nothing to be lost, while for those who do, there is everything to gain. In the same vein, the plays chosen for instructional purposes should, as noted, be from the widest possible repertory, and actors should be cast in all kinds of roles, including archetypal heroes and heroines, stock villains, psychopaths, rustics, buffoons, fops, old men and women, little children, animals, ghosts, and supernatural creatures. Even cross-gender and interracial casting should be explored. Of course, every actor has limitations, so that some of these experiments will fail, but if there is no experimenting while an actor is learning in school, when will there be after that? Besides, it is arrogant for an acting teacher or director to presume that he knows a student's range just by looking at him.[6] Let the student try different things, and be prepared for surprises. Actor training is a *heuristic* activity, which means that although you know the methods by which to proceed, you do not know what the outcome will be until you achieve it. It is like climbing a mountain in a fog; you know that you must try to keep moving upward, but you do not know what the peak looks like until you get there.

Michel Saint-Denis, in his training programs, stressed transformation—"into circus types, into animals, even into the world of dreams." Mask work included masks representing "the four ages of man: the adolescent, the adult, mature middle-age, and old-age."[7] Students learned about Greek, Chinese, and Japanese theatres, plus Commedia dell'Arte and Music Hall comedy, and "were allowed the use of half-masks, noses, padding, disguises of all kinds, simple scenery and props that were stimulating to act with."[8] Unfortunately, Saint-Denis died shortly after establishing the program at Juilliard, so that he had little opportunity to publicize his approach for other American acting programs, which have felt little of his influence. It is time to recognize his achievement, with its solid aesthetic and psychological underpinnings, and adapt his methods elsewhere. Some of our best younger actors have gone through the Juilliard acting school (e.g., Robin Williams, William Hurt, Christopher Reeve, all superb character actors).

Saint-Denis also included a great deal of liberal arts study as part of an actor's training:

> This included ... seminars and workshops of three main styles—classical tragedy, classical comedy, and realism in all its aspects; reading of plays of all styles; ... lectures to provide an imaginative background to practical work on period texts, history of drama throughout the world, history of arts and customs as they are related to the great dramatic periods; study of the world's great novels ... ; study of period style in connection with the technical courses—exhibition of documents, wearing of costumes, handling of period properties (for example, swords, fans, snuff boxes), movement and dance related to the manners of the period (for example, curtseys, bows, etc.); and music of the period.... Makeup, the study of the world's great paintings, and visits to museums, were a part of this curriculum.[9]

This extensive list includes far more of the humanities than was included in the traditional, liberal-arts-oriented theatre departments, or even of nontheatre liberal arts majors of today! Yet it was done in addition to the classes in improvisation, speech, and movement, and in addition to putting on plays. It is also worth noting that such "academic" work was done *right from the beginning*, rather than added on later as a kind of polish.

Saint-Denis's humanistic approach would have seemed only natural to him, given his European background. American training programs inaugurated in the sixties and seventies were supposedly inspired by the model of the European conservatory, but only Saint-Denis's version recognized that such programs did *not* offer a narrow, career-oriented training, but a broad, humanistic one.

For example, Raymonde Temkine, in her book on Jerzy Grotowski, notes that in Grotowski's native Poland there are three Advanced Schools of Dramatic Art, which all have the standing of universities. Actors are taught over a four-year period. No formal diploma is given, but students must show that they have the general knowledge equivalent to that of the holder of a baccalaureate. Students are examined twice a year in the history of art, literature, and two modern languages. Students are also immediately assigned to a theatre, where they perform small roles.[10] As with Saint-Denis's programs, the total work load is of course tremendous. But is that not also true of valid professional programs in other fields, like medicine or law or engineering? Theatre is a great art form, found in all cultures, and having a 2400-year history in our own. Acting cannot be mastered quickly and easily.

In sum, what we need is *a humanistic actor training, centered on play production*. Such an approach will recover the best qualities of traditional, liberal-arts-oriented theatre departments, and will add much of the practical study of the newer, professionally-oriented ones, while providing an overall coordination that both kinds of department lacked. Students will not graduate from a humanistic, play-centered program with certifiable skills or a guarantee of a job, any more than they can now. Instead, however, they will be *educated* actors, able to explore theatre in the fullest sense. Theatre will change them, and they will change our theatre.

APPENDIX

A Midsummer Night's Dream

Act 1, Scene 2

Enter QUINCE, *the Carpenter, and* SNUG, *the Joiner, and* BOTTOM, *the Weaver, and* FLUTE, *the Bellows-Mender, and* SNOUT, *the Tinker, and* STARVELING, *the Tailor.*

Quin. Is all our company here?

Bot. You were best to call them generally, man by man, according to the scrip.

Quin. Here is the scroll of every man's name which is thought fit, through all Athens, to play in our inter-   5
lude before the Duke and the Duchess on his wed-
ding-day at night.

Bot. First, good Peter Quince, say what the play treats on, then read the names of the actors, and so grow to a point.   10

Quin. Marry, our play is "The most lamentable comedy and most cruel death of Pyramus and Thisby."

Bot. A very good piece of work, I assure you, and a
    merry. Now, good Peter Quince, call forth your
    actors by the scroll. Masters, spread yourselves.   15
Quin. Answer as I call you. Nick Bottom the weaver.
Bot. Ready. Name what part I am for, and proceed.
Quin. You, Nick Bottom, are set down for Pyramus.
Bot. What is Pyramus? a lover, or a tyrant?
Quin. A lover that kills himself, most gallant, for love.   20
Bot. That will ask some tears in the true performing of it.
    If I do it, let the audience look to their eyes. I will
    move storms; I will condole in some measure. To the
    rest. Yet my chief humor is for a tyrant. I could
    play Ercles rarely, or a part to tear a cat in, to make   25
    all split.

> "The raging rocks
> And shivering shocks
> Shall break the locks
>   Of prison gates,   30
> And Phibbus' car
> Shall shine from far
> And make and mar
>   The foolish fates."

This was lofty. Now name the rest of the players.   35
This is Ercles' vein, a tyrant's vein. A lover is more
condoling.
Quin. Francis Flute the bellows-mender.
Flu. Here, Peter Quince.
Quin. Flute, you must take Thisby on you.   40
Flu. What is Thisby? a wand'ring knight?
Quin. It is the lady that Pyramus must love.
Flu. Nay, faith, let me not play a woman. I have a beard
    coming.
Quin. That's all one. You shall play it in a mask, and you   45
    may speak as small as you will.

Bot. An I may hide my face, let me play Thisby too.
I'll speak in a monstrous little voice:—"Thisne,
Thisne!" "Ah, Pyramus, my lover dear, thy Thisby
dear, and lady dear!" 50

Quin. No, no, you must play Pyramus; and Flute, you
Thisby.

Bot. Well, proceed.

Quin. Robin Starveling the tailor.

Star. Here, Peter Quince. 55

Quin. Robin Starveling, you must play Thisby's mother.
Tom Snout the tinker.

Snout. Here, Peter Quince.

Quin. You, Pyramus' father; myself, Thisby's father;
Snug, the joiner, you the lion's part. And I hope here 60
is a play fitted.

Snug. Have you the lion's part written? Pray you, if it
be, give it me, for I am slow of study.

Quin. You may do it extempore, for it is nothing but
roaring. 65

Bot. Let me play the lion too. I will roar that I will do
any man's heart good to hear me. I will roar that I
will make the Duke say, "Let him roar again; let
him roar again."

Quin. An you should do it too terribly, you would fright 70
the Duchess and the ladies, that they would shriek:
and that were enough to hang us all.

All. That would hang us, every mother's son.

Bot. I grant you, friends, if you should fright the ladies
out of their wits, they would have no more discre- 75
tion but to hang us; but I will aggravate my voice
so that I will roar you as gently as any sucking
dove; I will roar you an 'twere any nightingale.

Quin. You can play no part but Pyramus; for Pyramus
is a sweet-faced man, a proper man as one shall see 80

in a summer's day, a most lovely gentleman-like
man: therefore you must needs play Pyramus.

Bot. Well, I will undertake it. What beard were I best to
play it in?

Quin. Why, what you will.   85

Bot. I will discharge it in either your straw-colour beard,
your orange-tawny beard, your purple-in-grain
beard, or your French-crown colour beard, your
perfect yellow.

Quin. Some of your French crowns have no hair at all,   90
and then you will play bare-faced. But masters,
here are your parts; and I am to entreat you, re-
quest you, and desire you to con them by tomorrow
night; and meet me in the palace wood, a mile without the town, by moonlight. There will we rehearse,   95
for if we meet in the city, we shall be dogged with
company, and our devices known. In the meantime
I will draw a bill of properties, such as our play
wants. I pray you fail me not.

Bot. We will meet, and there we may rehearse most ob-   100
scenely and courageously. Take pains, be perfect:
adieu!

Quin. At the Duke's Oak we meet.

Bot. Enough: hold, or cut bowstrings.   *Exeunt.*

NOTES

CHAPTER ONE

1. This is not entirely fair, since the worst excesses associated with "the Method" (making students disclose intimate secrets from their personal lives, forcing them to strip naked, having sex with them) were and are committed by others. Strasberg's own approach was more complex and sophisticated than is popularly believed, as I shall attempt to explain later. Nevertheless, he certainly set the Method in motion. The peculiar weaknesses of American actor training can all be traced back to Strasberg, which is why I have used the adjective "Strasbergian" frequently in this book.

2. A century ago, for example, Augustin Daly took his New York theatre company, starring Ada Rehan and John Drew, to England, where they triumphantly performed Shakespeare in London and Stratford. The idea of, say, Joseph Papp's New York Shakespeare Festival doing the same thing today is inconceivable.

CHAPTER TWO

1. Jonas Barish, *The Antitheatrical Prejudice* (Berkeley: University of California, 1981), pp. 22–23.

2. Sigmund Freud, *Civilization and Its Discontents* (1930), trans. Joan Riviere (Garden City, N.Y.: Doubleday, n.d.), pp. 4–5.

3. Ibid., p. 5.

4. Ibid., p. 6.

5. Ibid., p. 11.

6. Erik Erikson, *Childhood and Society*, 2nd ed. (New York: W. W. Norton, 1963).

7. David Cole, *The Theatrical Event* (Middletown, CT: Wesleyan University, 1975), p. 7.

8. Lee Strasberg, *A Dream of Passion* (New York: New American Library, 1987), p. 16.

9. David Garfield, *The Actors Studio: A Player's Place* (New York: Macmillan, 1980), p. 285.

CHAPTER THREE

1. Philip Weissman, *Creativity in the Theater: A Psychoanalytic Study* (New York: Basic Books, 1965), p. 11.

2. R. D. Laing, *The Self and Others* (New York: Random House, 1969), p. 30.

3. Jacques Lacan, *The Seminar of Jacques Lacan, Book I*, ed. Jacques-Alain Miller, trans. John Forrester (Cambridge: Cambridge University Press, 1988), p. 193.

4. *The Village Voice*, 22 October 1979 and 3 December 1979.

5. Sigmund Freud, "Observations on 'Wild' Psychoanalysis," in *Collected Papers II*, trans. Joan Riviere (New York: Basic Books, 1959), p. 299.

6. Ibid., pp. 301–302.

7. Constantin Stanislavski, *An Actor Prepares*, trans. Elizabeth Reynolds Hapgood (New York: Theatre Arts, 1948), p. 147.

CHAPTER FOUR

1. Toby Cole and Helen Krich Chinoy, eds., *Actors on Acting* (New York: Crown, 1970), p. 14.
2. Ibid., p. 23.
3. "The Prime Minister of Mirth," *Time* 116.5 (August 4, 1980), p. 49.
4. Freud, *Collected Papers vol. 2*, p. 299.
5. Freud, *Civilization*, p. 5.
6. Quoted in Shoshana Felman, *Jacques Lacan and the Adventure of Insight* (Cambridge, MA: Harvard, 1987), p. 164.
7. Peter Handke, *Kaspar*, trans. Michael Roloff (London: Eyre Methuen, 1972), p. 16.
8. Ibid., p. 87.
9. Cole, p. 37.
10. "The Prime Minister of Mirth," p. 49.

CHAPTER FIVE

1. William Wordsworth, "Preface," *Lyrical Ballads*, ed. R. L. Brett and A. R. Jones (London: Methuen, 1963), p. 260.
2. Ibid., p. 240.
3. Antonin Artaud, "No More Masterpieces," in *The Theatre and Its Double*, trans. Mary Caroline Richards (New York: Grove, 1958), p. 75.
4. Charles de Tolnay, *Michelangelo: Sculptor, Painter, Architect*, trans. Gaynor Woodhouse (Princeton, NJ: Princeton, 1975), pp. 13–14.
5. Only after many years did I realize, for example, that the English Doctor in Act IV, scene 3 who had seemed to be there only to deliver an irrelevant panegyric to Edward the Confessor, was actually foreshadowing the Scottish Doctor in Act V, who cannot cure Lady Macbeth nor Scotland itself. The health of Edward's England contrasts with the corruption of Macbeth's Scotland.

6. Mikel Dufrenne, *The Phenomenology of Aesthetic Experience* (Evanston, IL: Northwestern, p. 30.
7. Ibid., p. 35.
8. Arthur Miller, *Timebends: A Life* (New York: Grove, 1987), pp. 187–88.
9. Susanne K. Langer, *Feeling and Form* (New York: Scribner's, 1953), p. 212.
10. Susanne K. Langer, *Philosophy in a New Key* (Cambridge, MA: Harvard, 1957), p. 216.

CHAPTER SIX
1. Uta Hagen, *Respect for Acting* (New York: Macmillan, 1973), p. 36.
2. Ibid., p. 39.
3. Stanislavski, pp. 9–10.
4. Stephen Aaron, *Stage Fright: Its Role in Acting* (Chicago: University of Chicago, 1986).
5. Stanislavski, p. 274. The unfortunate term subconscious, which psychoanalysis specifically rejects as a synonym for unconscious, is the result of the Hapgood translation of Stanislavski's texts. These translations have been criticized on many grounds; see Sharon Marie Carnicke, *"An Actor Prepares/Rabota aktera nad soboì, Chast' I*: A Comparison of the English with the Russian Stanislavsky," *Theatre Journal* 36.4 (December 1984), pp. 481–94. Even the translation of the title as *An Actor Prepares* turns out to be misleading.
6. Ibid., p. 14.
7. Ibid.
8. Ibid., p. 44.
9. Ibid., p. 38.
10. Ibid., p. 50.
11. Ibid., p. 14.

12. Shelley Russell-Parks, "Perception and the Actor's Process: A Phenomenological Analysis of the Creative Act" (Ph.D. dissertation, Florida State University, 1989), p. 18.

13. Ibid., p. 90.

14. Quoted ibid., p. 136.

15. Alan W. Watts, *Psychoanalysis East and West* (New York: New American Library, 1963), p. 93.

16. Cole, pp. 14–15.

17. Artaud, p. 25.

18. Peter Brook, *The Empty Space* (Harmondsworth, England: Penguin, 1972), p. 11.

19. Stanislavski, pp. 90–104.

20. Ibid., p. 77.

21. Viola Spolin, *Improvisation for the Theatre* (Evanston, IL: Northwestern, 1963), p. 388.

22. Stanislavski, p. 81.

CHAPTER SEVEN

1. Freud lists techniques like "condensation" and "representation through the opposite" in addition to "displacement," but the last term seems to sum them all up. *Displacement* is the psychological equivalent of the literary term *trope*, the use of a word or words in a sense other than their proper or literal one.

2. Charles Rycroft, *The Innocence of Dreams* (Oxford: Oxford, 1957), pp. 156–57.

3. Ibid., p. 158.

4. Jean Benedetti, *Stanislavski: A Biography* (New York: Routledge, 1990), p. 28.

5. Ibid., p. 40.

6. Robert Brustein, "Further Thoughts on Olivier," *The New Republic* 201.5 (October 9, 1989), p. 25.

7. John Gielgud, "Creating My Roles," in Cole and Chinoy, p. 398.

8. Henry Fonda and Howard Teichman, *Fonda: My Life* (New York: Signet, 1982), p. 15.

9. Neal Gabler, "Redford Talks," *New York* 23.48 (December 10, 1990), p. 36.

10. Simon Callow, *Charles Laughton: A Difficult Actor* (London: Methuen, 1988), p. 26.

11. Hagen, p. 210.

12. Michael Chekhov, *To the Actor: On the Technique of Acting* (New York: Harper & Row, 1953), p. 31.

13. Ibid., p. 34.

14. Ibid., p. 65.

15. Constantin Stanislavski, *Creating a Role*, trans. Elizabeth Reynolds Hapgood (New York: Theatre Arts Books, 1961), p. 217.

16. Ibid., p. 208.

17. Bertolt Brecht, "Some of the Things That Can Be Learnt from Stanislavsky," in *Brecht on Theatre: The Development of an Aesthetic*, ed. and trans. John Willett (New York: Hill & Wang, 1964), p. 236.

18. This is not to say that Stanislavski's own skills at text analysis were well developed. His literary tastes and interpretations were notoriously erratic; furthermore, at times in discussing the Method of Physical Action he seems to imply that the actor does not need the text at all. But his respect for the play, at least in performance, in all its details, is unquestionable.

19. I have dealt extensively with the problem of analyzing playtexts for production in my book, *Script into Performance: A Structuralist View of Play Production* (New York: Paragon House, 1987).

CHAPTER EIGHT

1. Denis Diderot, *The Paradox of Acting* (sic), trans. Walter Herries Pollock (New York: Hill and Wang, 1957), p. 14. (Published

in a single volume with William Archer, *Masks or Faces?*; see note 13.)

2. This was Pierre Rémond de Sainte-Albine's *Le Comédien*, published in 1747. (Cole and Chinoy, p. 161.)

3. Diderot, p. 19.

4. Joseph R. Roach, *The Player's Passion: Studies in the Science of Acting* (Newark, Delaware: University of Delaware, 1985), *passim*.

5. Diderot, p. 40.

6. Gilbert Ryle, *The Concept of Mind* (New York: Barnes and Noble, 1949), p. 19.

7. Ibid., pp. 15–16.

8. Terry Landau, *About Faces* (New York: Doubleday Anchor, 1989), p. 114.

9. Cole and Chinoy, p. 193.

10. Ibid., p. 199.

11. Ibid., p. 357.

12. Ibid., p. 554.

13. William Archer, *Masks or Faces?* (New York: Hill and Wang, 1957), p. 82. (Published in a single volume with Denis Diderot, *The Paradox of Acting*.)

14. Cole and Chinoy, pp. 14–15.

15. Archer, p. 122.

16. Ibid., p. 188.

17. Ibid.

18. Constantin Stanislavski, *Building a Character*, trans. Elizabeth Reynolds Hapgood (New York: Theatre Arts, 1949), p. 19.

19. Strasberg, p. 36.

20. Garfield, p. 173.

21. Ryle, p. 16.

22. Ibid, p. 25, *et passim*.

CHAPTER NINE

1. George Henry Lewes, *On Actors and the Art of Acting* (New York: Grove, [1875]), p. 96.

2. Susanne K. Langer, *Feeling*, p. 176.

3. Langer, *Philosophy*, p. 216.

4. Aristotle, *Aristotle's Poetics*, trans. Leon Golden (Tallahassee: Florida State University, 1981), p. 7.

5. Stanislavski, *Creating*, p. 219.

6. Bobby Jones said that if he had to think consciously about three things in his golf swing, he could never win; if he thought about two, he might finish in the top ten; if he thought about only one, he had a chance to win; if he didn't have to think about any, no golfer on earth could beat him.

7. Strasberg, pp. 22–23.

8. Carl Georg Lange and William James, *The Emotions* (reprints of various articles 1884–93), ed. Knight Dunlap (Baltimore: Williams & Wilkins, 1922), pp. 12–13.

9. Ibid.

10. Ibid., pp. 11–12.

11. Leon Festinger and James M. Carlsmith, "Cognitive Consequences of Forced Compliance," in *Role Playing, Reward, and Attitude Change*, ed. Alan C. Elms (New York: Van Nostrand Reinhold, 1969), pp. 18–32.

CHAPTER TEN

1. Aristotle, p. 51.

2. Oscar Brockett, *History of the Theatre*, 5th ed. (Boston: Allyn and Bacon, 1987), p. 348.

3. Frederick J. Marker, "An Actor Prepares: The Prenaturalistic Alternative," *Essays in Theatre* 1.2 (May 1983), p. 121.

4. J. William Hebel, Hoyt H. Hudson, Francis R. Johnson, A. Wigfall Green (eds)., *Prose of the English Renaissance* (New York: Appleton-Century-Crofts, 1952), p. 657.

5. Roach, p. 65.

6. Cole and Chinoy, pp. 118–19.

7. Roach, pp. 86–87.

8. Roach, p. 58.

9. The unity of *time* meant that the action should be continuous, or at worst not exceed twenty-four hours; the unity of *place* meant that the locale should not change, or at worst stay within a single city; the unity of *action* meant that there should be a single plot, rather than multiple ones. Shakespeare's plays, like those of most of his contemporaries, were notorious for ignoring all three unities.

10. Cole and Chinoy, p. 96.

11. Ibid.

12. Ibid., p. 327.

13. Martin Banham, *The Cambridge Guide to World Theatre* (Cambridge: Cambridge University Press, 1988), p. 892.

14. Cole and Chinoy, p. 328.

15. Ibid., p. 347.

16. Ibid., p. 351.

17. August Strindberg, *Six Plays of Strindberg*, trans. Elizabeth Sprigge (Garden City, NY: Doubleday, 1955), p. 63. My women students have sometimes expressed surprise that Strindberg associates Miss Julie's "monthly indisposition" with sexual desire. Menstruation was erroneously believed at the time to be the equivalent of the estrus of a female animal. Since physicians and scientists were almost all males, there was no one to correct the error.

18. Ibid., p. 69.

19. Ibid., p. 70.

CHAPTER ELEVEN

1. Carnicke, p. 484.

2. Right and left will always be from the point of view of the actor, unless otherwise stated.

3. This term has unfortunate connotations of T-Groups, encounter sessions, and other mawkish inanities of our time. A synonym, used in the Hapgood translations of Stanislavski, is

"communion," which has equally unfortunate religious connotations. Whichever word is used, one should remember that the concept has a strict technical meaning, as hereinafter explained, with nothing sentimental or mystical about it.

4. Francis Fergusson, "*The Poetics* and the Modern Reader," introductory essay to *Aristotle's Poetics*, trans. S. H. Butcher (New York: Hill & Wang, 1961), p. 9.

5. Francis Fergusson, *The Idea of a Theatre* (Garden City, NY: Doubleday, 1953), p. 117.

6. Francis Fergusson, "The Notion of 'Action,'" *TDR* 9.1 (Fall 1964). p. 86.

CHAPTER TWELVE

1. In 1934 he visited Moscow, where he did see a production of the MAT, but he avoided seeing Stanislavski! (Garfield, p. 32.)

2. Strasberg, p. 160.

3. Ibid., p. 161.

4. Ibid., pp. 89–90.

5. Lee Strasberg, *Strasberg at the Actors Studio: Tape-Recorded Sessions*, ed. Robert H. Hethmon (New York: Viking Press, 1968).

6. Strasberg, p. 112.

7. Lee Strasberg, "Working with Live Material" (interview), *Tulane Drama Review* 9.1 (Fall 1964), pp. 131–32.

8. Ibid., pp. 132–33.

9. Strasberg insisted that this was not to be something you *should* not do in public, only something you ordinarily *did* not do there. Only extremists, like Paul Mann, turned the exercise into something vile. The real trouble with the Private Moment is not its indecorum, but that it once again stresses personal life rather than drama. It also tends to contradict Strasberg's own insistence on remembered rather than real emotion.

10. Stanislavski, *An Actor Prepares*, pp. 154–81. The adjective *affective* comes from Ribot. Emotion memory is affective memory

involving emotions; affective memory is thus the broader concept, including such things as pure sense memory. Strasberg often uses the terms *affective memory* and *emotion memory* synonymously. The term *affective memory* is not found per se in Hapgood's translations of Stanislavski.

11. Ibid., p. 163.
12. Ibid., p. 166.
13. Ibid., pp. 179–80.
14. Benedetti, p. 180. Emphasis mine.
15. It is interesting to note that although the French word *affective* denotes moving or impressing emotionally, as its cognate does in English, it can also carry a connotation of being frequent or habitual. Stanislavski knew French; if he read Ribot in the original (according to Strasberg, Ribot's works were translated into Russian in the 1890s), he may well have understood the term *psychologie affective* in that sense.
16. Cole and Chinoy, pp. 516–17.
17. Richard Boleslavsky, *Acting: The First Six Lessons* (New York: Theatre Arts Books, 1933).
18. Strasberg, *A Dream of Passion*, between 140 and 141. Needless to say, Mrs. Strasberg is shown performing *alone*, remembering her emotions but not doing part of a play.

CHAPTER THIRTEEN
1. I am indebted to Dr. Donald Stowell, a Craig scholar, for this information.
2. Quoted in Marvin Carlson, *Theories of the Theatre* (Ithaca, NY: Cornell, 1984), p. 290.
3. Edward Gordon Craig, "The Actor and the Ueber-Marionette," in *On the Art of the Theatre* (Chicago: Brown's Bookstore, 1911), pp. 54–94.
4. Ibid., quoted in Cole and Chinoy, p. 381.
5. Ibid., p. 379.

6. Ibid., p. 379.

7. Ibid., p. 383–84.

8. The term is obviously an adaptation of Nietzsche's *Uebermensch*, or superman. The actor is to become a *super* puppet, and hence, superhuman.

9. Ibid., p. 377.

10. Igor Ilinsky, "Biomechanics," in Cole and Chinoy, pp. 504–505. Ilinsky was Meyerhold's favorite and most gifted performer.

11. Cole and Chinoy, p. 502. The word *plastic*, which often showed up in writing about acting in Meyerhold's day, here has its original meaning of pliable and adaptable.

12. Ilinsky, in Cole and Chinoy, p. 504.

13. Ibid., p. 505.

14. Brockett, p. 616.

15. Cole and Chinoy, p. 509.

16. *Creating a Role*, p. 213.

17. Ibid., p. 220.

18. Ibid., p. 224.

19. Ibid., p. 245.

20. Ibid., p. 228. Emphasis original.

21. See above, pp. 92-93. Stanislavski probably did not know of Chekhov's theories, which were written after he had left Russia.

22. Fergusson, "The Notion," p. 86.

23. Brecht, p. 26.

24. Ibid.

25. Viktor Shklovsky, "Art as Technique," in *Russian Formalist Criticism: Four Essays*, trans. and ed., Lee T. Lemon and Marion J. Reis (Lincoln, NB: University of Nebraska, 1965), p. 12.

26. The prefix *ver* carries the implication of making or causing. Thus, *Verfremdungseffekt* might better be translated as "estrangement effect." Translators have generally avoided this, because there is already a German noun meaning estrangement, *Entfremdung*. Nevertheless, alienation carries a possible connotation of stimulating

indifference or hostility, which Brecht did not intend, and which has dire consequences if applied to theatrical production. Brecht did *not* want to annoy, harass, or bore his audiences!

27. Martin Esslin, *Brecht: The Man and His Work* (Garden City, NY: Doubleday, 1961), p. 131.

28. Brecht, p. 42.

29. Ibid., pp. 200–201. Emphasis original. Willett has used the archaic English word *gest* to translate *Gestus*, a poor choice since the reader still does not know what it means. I have restored the original German word here and elsewhere; this at least signals the reader that it is a foreign term with a specialized meaning.

30. Artaud, p. 20.

31. Ibid., p. 24.

32. Ibid., p. 30.

33. Ibid., p. 77.

34. Ibid., p. 89.

35. Ibid., p. 46.

36. Ibid., p. 78.

37. Ibid., p. 96.

38. Ibid., p. 133.

CHAPTER FOURTEEN

1. Jerry L. Crawford and Joan Snyder, *Acting in Person and in Style* (Dubuque, IA: Brown, 1976), p. xv. Crawford and Snyder do go on to insist, however, that style does not mean stylized, and that realism is itself a style.

2. Quoted in Cole and Chinoy, p. 188.

3. Ibid., pp. 189–90.

4. Ibid., p. 187.

5. Ferdinand de Saussure, "Nature of the Linguistic Sign," in *The Structuralists from Marx to Lévi-Strauss*, ed. Richard and Fernande De George (Garden City, NY: Doubleday, 1972), p. 70.

6. Edward T. Hall, *The Dance of Life: The Other Dimension of Time* (Garden City, NY: Doubleday, 1984), p. 195.

7. Michel Saint-Denis, *Theatre: The Rediscovery of Style* (New York: Theatre Arts, 1960), p. 61.

8. Brecht, p. 92.

9. The standardized smiling and scowling masks that are often used today as emblems of comedy and tragedy have nothing to do with the actual masks used by the Greeks and, later, the Romans. Theatrical mask-makers were artists, and their masks were varied, detailed, and expressive. The Roman author Pollux, writing in the second century AD, catalogued hundreds of widely differing Greek theatrical masks.

CHAPTER FIFTEEN

1. Banham (ed.), *The Cambridge Guide*, p. 1030.

2. Brockett, p. 627.

3. The name was changed in the 1970s to the American Theatre Association (ATA). Dropping the word *educational* was symptomatic of the anti-intellectualism that had triumphed.

4. A few years ago, I put forth a modest proposal at a NAST meeting that, in order to become accredited, a school of acting would have to provide statistics to prospective students on both the numbers and percentages of graduates actually making their living as professional actors. This was rejected as impractical, though Actors Equity regularly manages to provide such information on its members, and theatre schools of course boast about their (few) famous graduates. NAST guidelines already show an ominous tendency to focus on means rather than, as I was proposing, on results.

5. Saint-Denis, p. 93.

6. It is common to speak of roles outside the student's supposed range as a "stretch" for the student. The terminology assumes, again, that playing his everyday personality is normal, while extremes of character are difficult. For many actors, however, the opposite is true; strong characterizations are not a stretch, but the norm of acting. Peter Sellers found the bland role of Chance the

gardener in the movie *Being There* the most difficult role of his life. Because Chance seemed so close to Sellers's own personality, it was a stretch for him.

7. Saint-Denis, p. 103.

8. Ibid., pp. 104–105.

9. Ibid., p. 100.

10. Raymonde Temkine, *Grotowski*, trans. Alex Szogyi (New York: Avon, 1972), pp. 17–18. The fact that there are only three theatre schools in Poland, with a population of about thirty-eight million, means that selecting and training students is far more rigorous than is possible here. Based on the same ratio, there should be only about nineteen theatre programs in the entire United States.

ANNOTATED BIBLIOGRAPHY OF ACTING TEXTBOOKS

This listing is intended to assist acting teachers and students in choosing textbooks. It was compiled with the assistance of Cheryl Nuzzo. The number of books in print on acting is vast; this bibliography is far from comprehensive, but includes most of the works you are likely to come across. I have mainly tried to include books that purport to tell you, in some way or other, how to learn to act, but have also added a few historical or theoretical works that have important practical implications. I have omitted books on the practicalities of show business; purely technical books on voice, movement, fight choreography, etc.; and privately published or vanity press books, which are usually bought only by the authors' own students. Textbooks originally published before 1970 are similarly omitted, unless still in print.

Adler, Stella. *The Technique of Acting.* New York: Bantam, 1988.

Hardly more than an outline, this short book nonetheless sums up Adler's teaching methods as she learned them from Stanislavski himself in 1934, stressing relaxation, imagination, character, and action. The chapter on "Working on the Text" is disappointing, dealing only with monologues, in a superficial manner.

Banham, Martin, ed. *The Cambridge Guide to World Theatre.* New York: Cambridge, 1988.

Excellent reference work, with entries written by major scholars. Superior to the Oxford Companion to the Theatre.

Barker, Clive. *Theatre Games: A New Approach to Drama Training.* London: Methuen, 1977.

One of many books to use games as a basis for teaching acting. Rather wordy, with surprisingly few specifics; not as good as the Spolin or Johnstone texts (see below).

Barkworth, Peter. *About Acting.* London: Secker; North Pomfret, VT: David, 1980.

A chatty book, with very short chapters, by a British actor and former teacher at RADA. Occasional bits of good advice.

Barr, Tony. *Acting for the Camera.* New York: Harper, 1986.

Very basic but valid text, with good advice about acting generally as well as about acting for the camera.

Barton, John. *Playing Shakespeare.* London: Methuen, 1984.

An excellent primer on speaking Shakespeare's verse, by a leading British director. Based on a television series, it is best read as a companion to the videotapes, which include readings by many of Britain's finest contemporary actors.

Bates, Brian. *The Way of the Actor: A New Path to Personal Knowledge and Power.* London: Century; Boston: Shambhala, 1986.

    A lot of sparks, but no fire. Bates is refreshing in his stress on possession, transformation, and mystery, but he is incapable of sustaining an argument for more than a few sentences. Instead of genuine analysis or insight, there are incessant references to and quotations from famous actors.

Benedetti, Robert. *The Actor at Work.* Englewood Cliffs, NJ: Prentice-Hall, 1986.

    Benedetti is a fine acting teacher, but overly eclectic. There is much that is good in this book; read it slowly and carefully, and do not expect a unifying theoretical framework.

————. *Seeming, Being, and Becoming: Acting in Our Century.* New York: Drama Book, 1976.

    A rhapsody on acting, with many citations and diagrams, which I can make little sense of. Benedetti at his worst.

Boleslavsky, Richard. *Acting: The First Six Lessons.* New York: Theatre Arts, 1949.

    Originally published as a series of articles in 1933, this includes the affective memory that Strasberg was to make so famous, but only as one part of a total training program.

Brockett, Oscar. *History of the Theatre.* 5th ed. Boston: Allyn and Bacon, 1987.

    Thorough, clear, accurate, and well-illustrated, this text outclasses all rivals, and is a necessity for the library of any serious theatre person.

Brown, Richard P., ed. *Actor Training 1.* New York: Drama Book Specialists, 1972.

    Since this consists of essays by four different individuals (Richard

Schechner, Robert Benedetti, William Jaeger, and Kurt Cerf), none of whom is very focused in his writing style, the book is haphazard, but some themes emerge: A rejection of realism; use of the theories of Stanislavski himself rather than those of the American Method; a stress on the connections between the physical and the emotional (i.e., a rejection of Cartesian dualism, though that term is not used). Although the editor disclaims the book as a text, there is a lot of good, practical advice in it, plus interesting acting exercises in Schechner's essay, "Aspects of Training at the Performance Group."

Bruder, Melissa, et al., *A Practical Handbook for the Actor*. New York: Vintage, 1986.

A short but effective essay by six authors(!) on how to use Stanislavski's Method of Physical Action.

Caine, Michael. *Acting in Film*. The Applause Acting Series. New York: Applause, 1989.

A series of witty, cogent observations on screen acting, about which far too little has been written. The section on "The Take" is especially good, with a lot of little-known, practical information.

Callow, Simon. *Being an Actor*. New York: St. Martin's, 1986; New York: Grove, 1988.

A brilliant work, part autobiography and part analysis, by a fine British actor. The discussion of the problem of finding the character is especially interesting. Callow is a rare example of an actor who writes well; his biography of Charles Laughton is also superb.

Cameron, Ron. *Acting Skills for Life*. Toronto: Simon & Pierre, 1989.

A hodgepodge that tries to cover everything from body exercises to Transactional Analysis to inner monologue to stage fighting to Shakespeare. No overview nor depth of understanding.

Carlson, Marvin. *Theories of the Theatre*. Ithaca, NY: Cornell, 1984.
Provides wide-ranging, well-written summaries of Western dramatic theory from the ancient Greeks to the present, including structuralist and poststructuralist approaches. The index is not always thorough enough for a reference work, however; search with care.

Chaikin, Joseph. *The Presence of the Actor*. New York: Atheneum, 1977.
A rambling, eclectic book, part autobiography and part acting text, by the founder of the Open Theatre. Strongly anti-Method, it stresses the group nature of acting and the social rather than individualistic purposes of theatre.

Chekhov, Michael. *To the Actor*. New York: Barnes-Harper, 1985.
Stresses images and psychological gesture. I have discussed these in Chapter 7.

———. *Lessons for the Professional Actor*. Transcribed and arranged by Deirdre Hurst du Prey. New York: Performing Arts Journal, 1985.
Notes transcribed by Chekhov's assistant from classes he taught in the early 1940s. A stimulating elaboration of the ideas in *To the Actor*.

Cohen, Robert. *Acting in Shakespeare*. Mountain View, CA: Mayfield, 1991.
Overly ambitious in its attempt to provide a comprehensive approach to acting Shakespeare in a mere 230 pages, the book nonetheless exhibits a good understanding of Shakespeare's drama and, as in Cohen's other books (see below), of the art of acting. It would be better if, as with Barton's *Playing Shakespeare*, there were some video or audio material to go with it.

_____. *Acting One: Foundation Lessons.* Mountain View, CA: Mayfield, 1984.

Comprehensive, practical text with a solid Stanislavskian base. Twenty-four lessons with exercises, stressing relaxation, relating, and objectives, plus rehearsal techniques, voice, speech, and body work.

_____. *Acting Power.* Mountain View, CA: Mayfield, 1978.

Another good text. Interesting and valuable distinction between motivation and objective, which clears up a major point of confusion for American Method actors.

Cole, David. *The Theatrical Event.* Middletown, CT: Wesleyan, 1975.

The phenomenology of acting from an anthropological viewpoint. Discussed in Chapters 2 and 6.

Cole, Toby. *A Handbook of the Stanislavski Method.* New York: Crown, 1955.

Despite the title, this is actually a collection of essays by Stanislavski and some of his Russian contemporaries on acting and directing. Though interesting and sometimes useful, it is in no sense a handbook.

_____, and Helen K. Chinoy, eds. *Actors on Acting.* Rev. ed. New York: Macmillan, 1970.

An anthology of writings that should be on every actor's bookshelf. Far more than just *actors* on acting, it includes passages by everyone of significance in Europe and America who ever wrote on the subject before 1970.

Craig, David. *On Performing: A Handbook for Actors, Dancers, Singers on the Musical Stage.* New York: McGraw, 1987.

A hodgepodge, consisting of rambling advice on how to audition, followed by lengthy interviews with nine famous directors of musicals.

Crawford, Jerry, and Joan Snyder. *Acting: In Person and in Style.* Dubuque, IA: Brown, 1983.

Extremely dualistic, as the title implies. The actor is warned not to work on style until "advancing in development." The book cites a wide range of theorists, including Stanislavski, Brecht, Artaud, and Saint-Denis (who would not have approved of the delay in learning style), but applies them in a diffuse, unsystematic manner. The exercises are sketchy, particularly in the style section, partly because it is impossible to present all the elements of a historical style in a few pages.

Delgado, Ramon. *Acting with Both Sides of Your Brain: Perspectives on the Creative Process.* New York: Holt, 1986.

Interesting attempt at an integrated approach. The writing is so compressed, however, that it reads like an outline; anyone who has not actually studied with Delgado will find it hard to follow.

Dmytryk, Edward, and Jean Porter Dmytryk. *On Screen Acting.* Boston: Focal, 1984.

Short, sketchy, and poorly written.

Dukore, Bernard. *Dramatic Theory and Criticism: Greeks to Grotowski.* New York: Holt, Rinehart and Winston, 1974.

Excerpts from all the major and many lesser theorists of Western drama up to the 1960s. The selections and editorial commentary are first-rate, but the book needs updating.

Easty, Edward Dwight. *On Method Acting.* New York: Ivy, 1989.

A forthright, uncritical handbook of the Strasberg Method, "as practiced at the Actors Studio." Clearer and better organized than most Method texts, including Strasberg's.

Fast, Julius, *Body Language.* New York: M. Evans, 1970.

Popularization of kinesics and proxemics. Some good insights into how humans in our culture position themselves and move, but oversimplified and sometimes lurid.

Felnagle, Richard H. *Beginning Acting: The Illusion of Natural Behavior*. Englewood Cliffs, NJ: Prentice-Hall, 1987.
Another text that tries to go back to Stanislavski's writings. Felnagle stresses units, objectives, given circumstances, relationships. Quite a lot of theorizing; few exercises; limited to realistic acting.

Franklin, Miriam. *Rehearsal: The Principles and Practice of Acting*. 5th ed. Englewood Cliffs, NJ: Prentice-Hall, 1972.
Intelligent, straightforward, older text that went through many editions. Shows the influence of the American Method, but also has chapters on the James-Lange theory, voice and speech, characterization, crowds, etc.

Goldman, Michael. *The Actor's Freedom: Toward a Theory of Drama*. New York: Viking, 1975.
An early attempt to deal with acting phenomenologically, this stresses the mystery and power of acting. The arguments are sketchily elaborated and often hard to follow, however.

Gordon, Mel. *The Stanislavsky Technique: Russia, A Workbook for Actors*. New York: Applause, 1987.
Both a history and a textbook, this work traces the work of Stanislavski and his followers (Sulerzhitsky, Vakhtangov, and Michael Chekhov) in Russia in the first half of the twentieth century, including the actual exercises they used in teaching students. An invaluable supplement to Stanislavski's own books (see below), whose exercises are more often hypothetical than actual.

Green, Michael. *The Art of Coarse Acting*. New York: Limelight, 1988.

A hilarious spoof, this book also contains a surprising amount of good, practical advice about acting.

Guthrie, Tyrone. *Tyrone Guthrie on Acting*. London: Studio Vista; New York: Viking, 1971.

Guthrie was not considered an actor's director, but his observations are valuable in helping you to see acting from a director's viewpoint.

Hagen, Uta, with Haskel Frankel. *Respect for Acting*. New York: Macmillan, 1973.

In an early chapter on identity, Hagen compares herself to an apple; her conscious image of herself is only a wedge of it, while her true self is the entire apple. After this encouraging start, however, she focuses mainly on the wedge, developing a method called substitution, by which the actor recalls incidents from his personal life that are analogous to those of the character being portrayed. This is simply a cruder version of the Boleslavsky/Strasberg technique of affective memory. It is doubtful that Hagen, a fine actress herself, actually uses the substitution method as extensively as she claims.

Hagen, Uta. *A Challenge for the Actor*. New York: Scribners, 1991.

An expanded version of the ideas in her *Respect for Acting* (see above). *Substitution* is now called *transference*. Again, she plays both sides of the fence: In everyday life "you change yourself a hundred times a day," but "in all forms of spontaneous role-playing, your own being is always at the center of it."

Hayman, Ronald. *Techniques of Acting*. Englewood Cliffs, NJ: Prentice-Hall, 1969.

A shallow and meandering book, with a lot of name-dropping, by a prolific British theatre writer. Despite the practical-sounding title, it contains no exercises and few specific techniques.

Harrop, John, and Sabin Epstein. *Acting with Style.* Englewood Cliffs, NJ: Prentice-Hall, 1982.

The best textbook yet on acting with style, which it defines as "the realism of a particular time as communicated through the theatrical conventions of that time." This does not quite hit the mark (see my arguments in Chapter 14), but is far better than seeing style as realism overlaid with artifice. In general, the theoretical material is well conceived and cogently written, while the specific exercises are imaginative and potent. The goal is always to impel the student mentally and physically into a particular period or genre, rather than to relate everything to himself.

Hindman, James, Larry Kirkman, and Elizabeth Monk. *TV Acting: A Manual for Camera Performance.* New York: Hastings, n.d.

Concise and practical. The best part of the book, and by far the longest, deals with technical matters; the advice on how to act is erratic, stressing relaxation and objectives, but also inner monologues and elaborate character biographies that are of dubious value.

Hull, S. Lorraine. *Strasberg's Method: As Taught by Lorrie Hull.* Woodbridge, CT: Ox Bow, 1985.

Stanislavski begat Boleslavsky and Ouspenskaya, who begat Strasberg, who begat Ms. Hull. The further you get from the source, the worse off you are.

Johnstone, Keith. *Impro: Improvisation and the Theatre.* London and Boston: Faber and Faber, 1979.

Written with disarming modesty and straightforwardness, this book is nonetheless imaginative and compelling. It makes a good complement to Spolin's *Improvisation for the Theater* (see below), with fewer exercises, but a much better theoretical framework. Especially good on the notions of status, narrative, and masks.

Joseph, Bertram. *Acting Shakespeare*. New York: Theatre Arts, 1969.

The misleading title has led many acting students to infer that this is an acting text, when in fact it is a historical study of Elizabethan acting and its relation to rhetoric.

Kahan, Stanley. *Introduction to Acting*. 2nd ed. Boston: Allyn and Bacon, 1985.

Straightforward but unimaginative, without a single original idea in it. The theoretical material is locked into the traditional dualities—emotional versus technical acting, character versus personality, representational versus presentational. The best part of this book is the low-level practical information that other texts often leave out, like the difference between stage left and stage right, or how to make a cross; there is similar helpful technical information about television and radio acting.

Kuritz, Paul. *Playing: An Introduction to Acting*. Englewood Cliffs, NJ: Prentice-Hall, 1982.

Trite high school text.

Lewis, Robert. *Advice to the Players*. New York: Harper, 1980.

————. *Method—or Madness?* New York: French, 1958.

Lewis was a Group Theatre member who came to disagree with Strasberg's excessive use of affective memory. Nevertheless, Lewis's own approach, as presented in these two texts, does not seem terribly different from Strasberg's.

Marowitz, Charles. *The Act of Being*. London: Seeker, 1978.

Rambling, often vague observations by a noted avant-garde director.

McGaw, Charles J. *Acting Is Believing: A Basic Method.* 5th ed., edited by Gary Blake. New York: Holt, 1986.

The unfortunate title suggests a hallucinatory approach to acting, but it becomes clear that for McGaw, believing actually means imagining. A well-written textbook, based on Stanislavski's writings rather than on the American Method. Stresses relaxation, relating, objectives ("purpose"), characterization, and the play; includes affective memory, but warns that it must be adapted to the lines and actions of the character. Good exercises.

Meisner, Sanford, and Longwell, Dennis. *Sanford Meisner on Acting.* New York: Vintage-Random, 1987.

Mostly transcriptions of Meisner's classes. Meisner is a distinguished acting teacher whose pupils have included some of America's best actors. Because of the lack of editing, however, or perhaps because Meisner's teaching prowess only comes across in person, this book is lifeless and confusing .

Mekler, Eva. *The New Generation of Acting Teachers.* New York: Viking Penguin, 1987.

Interviews with twenty-two contemporary American acting teachers. Not a textbook per se, but valuable for anyone thinking of studying with one of these individuals, who vary widely in their approaches.

Miles-Brown, John. *Acting: A Drama Studio Source Book.* 1985. London: P. Owen; Chester Springs, PA: Dufour, 1985.

Terse little text by a British acting teacher. Good exercises, similar to those of Spolin and Johnstone.

Moore, Sonia. *The Stanislavsky System: The Professional Training of an Actor.* 2nd rev. ed. New York: Penguin, 1984.

A short, sketchy summary of *An Actor Prepares.*

_____. *Stanislavski Revealed: The Actor's Guide to Spontaneity on Stage*. New York: Applause, 1991.

A revised and expanded edition of her *Training an Actor* (New York: Viking, 1968), this consists of transcripts of tapes of Ms. Moore teaching acting classes. Better than her other, more well-known book (see above); often very insightful.

Morris, Eric. *Acting from the Ultimate Consciousness*. New York: Perigee-Putnam, 1988.

_____. *Being and Doing*. New York: Perigee-Putnam, 1981.

_____. *Irreverent Acting*. New York: Perigee-Putnam, 1985.

_____, and Joan Hotchkis. *No Acting Please*. New York: Perigee-Putnam, 1979.

Morris's books are New Age versions of the American Method, stressing introspection, personal development, and sensitivity training. The title *No Acting Please* sums up his approach all too well.

Ogden, Dunbar, and Shireen Strooker. *Actor Training and Audience Response*. Fresno, CA: Oak House, 1984.

Subtitled "An Evaluation of Performance Techniques Taught at Berkeley by Shireen Strooker from the Amsterdam Werkteater," the book is extremely sketchy, consisting mostly of letters, questionnaires, and quotations, with very little summation or analysis.

Olivier, Laurence. *On Acting*. New York, Simon & Schuster, 1987.

Disappointing work by the greatest English actor of the twentieth century. His autobiography, *Confessions of an Actor*, reveals more about the intimate details of his personal life than this book does about his acting.

Richardson, Don. *Acting Without Agony: An Alternative to the Method.* Boston: Allyn and Bacon, 1988.

An attack on the Method, this book is chatty and underdeveloped, providing no actual techniques or exercises to speak of.

Snyder, Joan, and Michael P. Drumsta, *Dynamics of Acting.* Lincolnwood, IL: National Textbook, 1989.

Basic high-school text, with echoes of Stanislavski and other theorists, plus advice like reminding actors to hang up their costumes. Brief descriptions of historical styles, types of theatres, the kinds of people who work backstage, etc.

Spolin, Viola. *Improvisation for the Theater: A Handbook of Teaching and Directing Techniques.* Rev. ed. Evanston, IL: Northwestern, 1983.

A wonderful collection of exercises based on children's games that any acting teacher ought to make use of. The book is a grab-bag, however; there is little or no overall theory, so that it is often unclear how the exercises are supposed to lead to better acting in plays or films.

Stanislavski, Constantin. *An Actor Prepares.* New York: Theatre Arts, 1948; New York: Routledge, 1989.
_____. *Building a Character.* New York: Routledge, 1989.
_____. *Creating a Role.* Edited by Hermione I. Popper. Translated by Elizabeth R. Hapgood. New York: Theatre Arts, 1961; New York: Routledge, 1989.

Despite the notoriously bad translations, every actor should read these, which remain the best source we have of Stanislavski's ideas translated into English. Explore them again and again, remembering that all three were meant to be part of a single work that Stanislavski insisted be read as a whole. The exercises do not work well when you attempt to duplicate them in class. On the other hand, the books cannot really be understood unless you constantly relate them to your own acting experiences.

Stiver, Harry E. Jr., and Stanley Kahan. *Play and Scene Preparation: A Workbook for Actors and Directors.* Boston: Allyn and Bacon, 1984.
   Incredibly pedantic. The actor is supposed to fill out endless worksheets, answering questions like "How does the mood of the play affect the type of movement to be used?"

Strasberg, Lee. *A Dream of Passion: The Development of the Method.* Boston: Little, Brown, 1987; New York: NAL, 1988.
   Discussed extensively in Chapters 5 and 11.

Suzuki, Tadashi. *The Way of Acting.* Translated by J. Thomas Rimer. New York: Theatre Communications Group, 1986.
   Writings of a major Japanese actor and director. After an interesting initial section on sitting and walking (the latter very important in Japanese Noh Theatre), with some actual exercises, the book peters out in random memoirs. The chapter on his production of *Clytemnestra*, adapted from Greek tragedies, consists almost entirely of the playscript.

Yakim, Mori, and Muriel Broadman. *Creating a Character: A Physical Approach to Acting.* New York: Backstage-Watson, 1990.
   Unusual in that it treats movement in creative, artistic terms.

INDEX

Hill, Aaron, 141, 146, 147
Hitchcock, Alfred, 99, 100
Hitler, Adolf, 38
Hoffman, Dustin, 24, 66, 149, 233, 239
Howe, Tine, 26
Hudson, Rock, 22
Humors, 139, 140, 225, 226
Hungan, 75
Hurt, William, 253

Ibsen, Henrik, 25, 26, 35, 57, 109, 160, 174, 243, 247. *See also* individual play titles.
Icons, Russian, 57
Identity, 15-22, 27, 28, 30-32, 40
Ilinsky, Igor, 270n
Image, 89-94
Indicating, 128-30
Inge, William, 238
Inner monologue, 89, 113
Inspector General, The, 95, 97, 194, 196
Intimate Theatre, The, 147
Irving, Henry, 106-108, 143
Isolation, 76-78, 81

Jackson, Glenda, 59
Jacobi, Derek, 73
Jacobson, Edith, 27
James, William, 126, 127, 187
James-Lange Theory, 126, 127, 129, 130, 193, 195
Japanese theatre, 56, 57, 91, 155
Jazz, 49
Jefferson, Joseph, 107
Jesuit schools, 236
Jesus, 176

About the Author

Richard Hornby, theatre critic for *The Hudson Review*, is Chair of the Theatre Department, University of California at Riverside. He is author of *Script into Performance: A Structuralist View of Play Production*; *Pattern in Ibsen's Middle Plays*; and *Drama, Metadrama and Perception*, plus many articles on various aspects of theatre. A professional actor for thirty years, Hornby has performed with such notable colleagues as Jane Alexander and Faye Dunaway.